# VICTORIAN INTERIOR DECORATION

# Victorian Interior Decoration

## American Interiors
## 1830–1900

——————— BY ———————

## *GAIL CASKEY WINKLER*

*AND*

## *ROGER W. MOSS*

HENRY HOLT AND COMPANY    NEW YORK

Copyright © 1986 by LCA Associates
All rights reserved, including the right to reproduce
this book or portions thereof in any form.
Published by Henry Holt and Company, Inc.,
115 West 18th Street, New York, New York 10011.
Published in Canada by Fitzhenry & Whiteside Limited,
195 Allstate Parkway, Markham, Ontario L3R 4T8.

Library of Congress Cataloging-in-Publication Data
Winkler, Gail Caskey.
Victorian interior decoration.
Bibliography: p.
Includes index.
1. Interior decoration—United States—History—
19th century. 2. Decoration and ornament—United
States—Victorian style. I. Moss, Roger W., 1940–.
II. Title.
NK2003.5.W56   1986        747.213        86-4675
ISBN 0-8050-0078-X

Henry Holt books are available at special discounts
for bulk purchases for sales promotions, premiums,
fund raising, or educational use. Special editions
or book excerpts can also be created to specification.

For details, contact:

Special Sales Director
Henry Holt and Company, Inc.
115 West 18th Street
New York, New York 10011

Designed by Susan Hood
Printed in the United States of America
3   5   7   9   10   8   6   4

ISBN 0-8050-0078-X

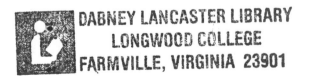

# CONTENTS

*Plates 1 through 24 follow p. 132.*

# ACKNOWLEDGMENTS

It might be imagined that a book based largely on primary sources from the last century could be written without incurring debts to colleagues and friends. Happily that is not the case, and while the many curators, librarians, and homeowners who helped us cannot be blamed for the deficiencies in what follows, they certainly deserve a healthy measure of credit for the book's positive features. Throughout the text we have acknowledged the help of curators and photographers, and even a brief glance at the notes and bibliography will show our debt to the growing number of scholars who are turning their attention to the nineteenth century. We hope they will find these references adequate recognition of their work.

There are, however, several persons we would like to mention here for special thanks: Donald Bergmann, St. Louis, Mo.; Kathleen Catalano, Longfellow National Historic Site, Cambridge, Mass.; Margie Chrisney, Phoenix, Ariz.; Nancy Richards Clark, Princeton, N.J.; John O. Curtis, Old Sturbridge Village, Sturbridge, Mass.; Sharon Darling, The Chicago Historical Society, Chicago, Ill.; Christine and Gerald Doell, Cortland, N.Y.; Samuel J. Dornsife, Williamsport, Pa.; Jared I. Edwards, Hartford, Conn.; Kenneth Finkel, Library Company of Philadelphia, Philadelphia, Pa.; Renee Friedman, Sleepy Hollow Restorations, Inc., Tarrytown, N.Y.; John L. Frisbee III, Lyndhurst, Tarrytown, N.Y.; James W. Garrison, Phoenix, Ariz.; Ruth Hagy, Chester County Historical Society, West Chester, Pa.; Amy Hardin, Historical Society of Pennsylvania, Philadelphia, Pa.; Arlene Horvath, Chester County Historical Society, West Chester, Pa.; Mrs. Patrick Harrington, Landmark Society of Western New York, Rochester, N.Y.; Curtis B. Johnson, State of Vermont, Montpelier, Vt.; Wynn Lee, Mark Twain Memorial, Hartford, Conn.; Calder Loth, Commonwealth of Virginia, Richmond, Va.; Michaela McCausland, Historic Speedwell, Morristown, N.J.; Maureen McKasy-Donlin, Minnesota Historical Society, St. Paul, Minn.; Janet A. Mannix, James Whitcomb Riley Memorial Association, Indianapolis, Ind.; Nancy Martin, The Rosson House, Phoenix, Ariz.; James K. Mellow, Old Sturbridge Village, Sturbridge, Mass.; Pat O'Donnell, Goldie Paley Design Center, Philadelphia, Pa.; Peter Parker, Historical Society of Pennsylvania, Philadelphia, Pa.; Ford Peatross, Library of Congress, Washington, D.C.; Ellie Reichlin, Society for the Preservation of New England Antiquities, Boston, Mass.; Rodris Roth, Smithsonian Institution, Washington, D.C.; Don W. Ryden, Phoenix, Ariz.; Frank H. Sommer, H. F. duPont Winterthur Museum, Winterthur, Del.; Nancy Strathearn, Morris County Park Commission, Morristown, N.J.; George Talbot, Wisconsin State Historical Society, Madison, Wis.; Neville Thompson, H. F. duPont Winterthur Museum, Winterthur, Del.; Beth Twiss-Garrity, Maxwell Mansion, Philadelphia, Pa.; Theron R. Ware, Campbell House Museum, St. Louis, Mo.; Jeanne Watson, Acorn Hall, Morristown, N.J.; Kenneth M. Wilson, Henry Ford Museum, Dearborn, Mich.; Roland H. Woodward, Chester County Historical Society, West Chester, Pa.; Andrea Urbas, Phoenix, Ariz.; and Philip Zea, Historic Deerfield, Deerfield, Mass. We are particularly grateful to Channa Taub, our editor at Henry Holt and Company, for her unfailing good humor and persistent pursuit of logical thought and readable prose.

Since most of the research and the bulk of the illustrations came from the collections of The Athenaeum of Philadelphia, we are particularly indebted to Sandra L. Tatman, Keith A. Kamm, and Jean Lenville, who showed infinite patience and good humor as this project competed with hundreds of others over the past three years. Finally, we want to thank our patient photographer, Lou Meehan, who is responsible for all the illustrations taken from sources in the collection of The Athenaeum of Philadelphia.

# PREFACE

We've been asked the same question hundreds of times: "Can you recommend a single book that summarizes Victorian interior decoration?" From Cooperstown to San Antonio, from Tampa to Flint, we've been asked that question by old-house owners, architects, developers, museum curators, and collectors of nineteenth-century decorative arts. All felt frustrated because, as one recently wrote, "There are dozens of books that tell us how to live in or furnish old houses today, but none that helps us to understand the interior design history of our houses—how they got the way they are. None of us needs another book on furniture! What we need is a book that explains what kinds of wall and window treatments the original builder and subsequent owners might have employed, what color schemes were popular, what floor coverings were used, what sort of draperies and shutters covered windows." This book answers all those questions.

It must be said straightaway that there is no such thing as a *Victorian style* of interior decoration—any more than there can be said to be a single twentieth-century style. Even assigning stylistic labels derived from architecture or furniture history—say, Gothic or Rococo Revival—may be misleading because such terms suggest an improbable uniformity in most domestic interiors. It is rarely possible to force the decoration of a house into a single style uncontaminated by those that came before or after. This is particularly true of late-nineteenth-century decoration, when American domestic interiors were affected by overlapping and competing styles, each claiming to reform what came before. To escape this impenetrable thicket, many historians have lumped a large segment of the nineteenth century into something called the "eclectic decades," which is simply an admission that compartmentalizing by style breaks down in the face of Victorian diversity.

Yet it is impossible to ignore the shorthand of style. Not only did Victorian critics, architects, and designers use such terminology—albeit with uncertain or conflicting meaning—but every old-house owner derives understandable satisfaction from being able to say, "My house is *Gothic Revival*," or "Ours is a late *Queen Anne*," or "We have an *Italianate* villa." Unfortunately, most nineteenth-century American houses were not professionally designed and decorated; therein lies the root of another common lament, "Our house doesn't fit any of the illustrations in guidebooks to furniture or architectural styles."

So how is this book to be useful if we don't follow such conventional divisions? As you'll see, most American houses erected or redecorated between 1830 and 1900 may be grouped roughly into one of four broad design philosophies that changed less rapidly than the decorative arts placed against them. Each of these may encompass several conventional architectural or furniture styles. Consequently, we have divided this book into four chronological periods. Chapter 1 covers the early Victorian years from 1830 to 1850 when Gothic, Elizabethan, and Rococo styles began to replace the late Neoclassical Grecian style. Chapter 2 examines the midcentury design sources and the full development of the Rococo and Renaissance Revival styles between 1850 and 1870. Chapter 3 considers the reformist reaction of the late Victorian Aesthetic Movement from 1870 to 1890, and Chapter 4 describes the seemingly conflicting design influences at work during the 1890s in the Craftsman and Colonial Revival styles.

In each chapter we look closely at the way walls, ceilings, woodwork, floors, and windows were treated in that period—keeping in mind that there rarely are sharp edges dividing interiors of one "style" from another, and that the dates may have to be adjusted for geographical location or the availability of transportation at the time a particular house was built. Lest you've begun to worry that we expect every old-house owner to create a little museum by decorating strictly in the fashion of the time the house was built, let us put your mind at rest. We do believe that the following chapters will help you "read" your house and better understand, for example, why it has soft pine floors that were originally carpeted wall to wall, or handsome parquet ones that cry out for Orientals. Or why modern traverse rods and pinch-pleated curtains do not seem right for the windows of your nineteenth-century house. If, once you understand how your house was intended to be decorated by its original designer or owner, you should wish to duplicate some of the same effects, perhaps using modern materials, the information in this book can help you achieve that goal.

To help you understand Victorian interior decoration, we have allowed nineteenth-century architects and critics to speak for themselves throughout this book, offering up their advice to today's homeowners just as they did a century ago. The guidelines you will be reading are drawn from sources that the original owners of your house may well have consulted. After all, yesterday's and today's owners share many of the same concerns, as can be seen in the title of a book by the nineteenth-century critic Clarence Cook—*What Shall We Do With Our Walls?*

# VICTORIAN
# INTERIOR
# DECORATION

# 1

# THE 1830 TO 1850 PERIOD

From a late-twentieth-century perspective, the America of the 1830s seems simple and unsophisticated. Andrew Jackson, the seventh President of the United States, was serving his first term in 1830. At the time of his election, 13 million Americans lived in twenty-four states, more than 90 percent of them in rural areas. Over the next two decades the population would double, urban residents would increase to 15 percent of the population, and seven states would enter the Union (Arkansas, Michigan, Wisconsin, Iowa, Texas, Florida, and California).[1]

The transportation network expanded to accommodate the growing nation. Between 1830 and 1850 canals and rivers provided the most efficient forms of transport for both passengers and cargo. The Erie Canal, completed in 1825 at a cost of $9 million, proved to be an excellent investment and spawned new "Western" cities such as Chicago and Milwaukee. It launched a boom in canal digging that linked lakes and rivers to form a unified shipping network reaching into the heart of the continent. Shipping costs fell dramatically and the cities along the system prospered as ports, transshipment points for goods, and manufacturing centers. By 1840, manufactured goods could be moved between New York and Cleveland, Cincinnati, or Louisville in a week; to New Orleans, St. Louis, or Detroit in two; and to Chicago or Milwaukee in three. Urban residents clustered along major trade routes might thereby acquire the comforts and fashions denied many other more isolated Americans.[2]

Wealth, as well as location, determined how a house might be furnished. For instance, in 1841 William Gibbons, a wealthy Southern planter, could afford to pay $119.11 for a cask of the best grade of whale oil to light the Argand burner lamps of his summer residence in Madison, New Jersey, near New York City; but many Americans could not afford such luxuries.[3] As

*The stair hall of the Vail House, Historic Speedwell. (Historic Speedwell, Morristown, New Jersey; photograph by Louis Meehan)*

whales became scarce and their oil increasingly expensive, middle-class Americans began to substitute lard oil, which they burned in solar lamps. Still less fortunate Americans had to rely on candles, simple lamps that burned animal fats, and fireplaces to cast light into their rooms.

Few houses contained water systems or plumbing. In 1849, the Philadelphia architect John Notman provided a complete water system for the Charles L. Pearson house in Trenton, New Jersey, using a lead-lined cistern in the attic. But outside of homes for the wealthy, plumbing was practically nonexistent. Traveling along the lower Mississippi in 1857, Frederick Law Olmsted, the landscape architect who designed Central Park, described his hotel room (which he was forced to share with a stranger) thus: "One washbowl, and a towel which had already been used, was expected to answer for both of us, and would have done so, but that I carried a private towel in my saddle-bags." As for plumbing, he added, this "requirement of a civilized household was wanting, and its only substitute unavailable with decency."[4]

For families that did not live near urban centers or navigable water, mail service was limited and delivery of shipments of household goods was extremely difficult. In 1830, America contained only seventy-three miles of railroad track. Although that figure increased dramatically—by more than 12,000 percent during the next twenty years—the result was little more than nine thousand miles of track throughout the country. By 1845, the U.S. Post Office Department included some track in its 143,940 miles of "post roads" but most mail still moved by coach or horse and wagon. The roads were unpaved and seasonably impassable, making service irregular. For instance, in 1850 the mails traveled between St. Louis and Salt Lake City only once every thirty days. Outside of cities, no mail delivery existed and rural residents collected their mail whenever they traveled to the closest post office. Furthermore, postage was relatively expensive. In 1845, a half-ounce letter cost five cents to send a distance under three hundred miles, and ten cents over that distance. It is small wonder that some correspondents filled a sheet of paper with writing that first went horizontally and then vertically, sometimes in different-colored inks to make reading less difficult.[5]

Yet mail and bulk goods moved more easily than small packages. In the Colonial and Federal periods, packages had not been considered part of the mails, although post riders often carried them for a fee or as a favor. This gap in service was filled by "express companies," the first being Harnden's Express, begun on February 13, 1839, when William F. Harnden personally carried materials entrusted to him, traveling by train, boat, and ferry to Buffalo. The early routes were quite limited. Harnden's carried packages between Boston–Albany–New York City and a few Southern ports. Western Express, owned by Henry Wells, William G. Fargo, and Daniel Dunning, shipped from Buffalo to Detroit and from there by stage, steamer, and wagon to reach Chicago, Cincinnati, and St. Louis in 1845. Slow by current standards, express companies promoted themselves as dependable ways to ship goods and valuables. They also made it easier for buyers to purchase and receive special goods not available in their region.[6] Through such developments, regional differences in household furnishing and decoration would ultimately be broken down and a national market would be formed.

The widely dispersed American population began to be linked in other ways as well. The beginning of modern telecommunication occurred in 1837 when Samuel F. B. Morse managed to send the first telegraphic message ten miles. He formally dedicated the first telegraph line between Baltimore and Washington on May 24, 1844. By 1848, all states east of the Mississippi River (except Florida) were part of the first primitive network.

Newspapers also bound the population together; virtually every town, no matter how small or new, had its own paper. Many big-city daily papers and small-town weeklies begun in the nineteenth century have continued uninterrupted publication to the present time. In addition to spawning hundreds of newspapers, the nineteenth century witnessed the creation of a new phenomenon: magazines for women. One of the first and certainly most successful in nineteenth-century America was begun in Philadelphia in July 1830, by twenty-six-year-old Louis Antoine Godey. By 1850, Godey could count 62,500 subscribers to his magazine, *Godey's Lady's Book*. The monthly issues attracted tens of thousands of middle-class American readers who gleaned a definition of what it meant to be a "lady," and not a little information on how to decorate and furnish a tasteful house.

Books provided another useful source of information. The works of British critics circulated in America and influenced American critics as well as American households. For example, when John Claudius Loudon, a Scottish authority on horticulture and architectural design, published *An Encyclopedia of Cottage, Farm, and Villa Architecture and Furniture* (1833), five thousand notices were circulated in the United States. Andrew Jackson Downing, the great American critic, was profoundly influenced by Loudon. Downing even traveled to Britain to meet Loudon, and Downing's work owes much to Loudon. Louis A. Godey, publisher of the *Lady's Book*, must have owned a copy of Loudon's work, for he frequently reprinted information from it during the 1840s, and thus, like Downing, spread Loudon's influence. Individual homeowners in America also purchased Loudon's works: William Gibbons, the Southern planter mentioned earlier, acquired a copy in 1836 while building his summer residence (at a cost of $98,000) in Madison, New Jersey. Another British text wildly popular in America was Thomas Webster and Mrs. Parkes's *An Encyclopedia of Domestic Economy* (1844); this compendium of household furnishing and management was reprinted in the United States in 1845 and nearly every year thereafter for over a decade.[7]

These tentative starts in communication during the early decades of the nineteenth century would ultimately produce a well-defined image of "home" acceptable throughout America. And the improving transportation system would slowly move westward the new furnishings decorating Eastern homes to supply the growing market of homesteads widely scattered along the frontier.

# WALLS AND CEILINGS

The selection of parlor wall finishes, usually a homeowner's first interior-decorating decision, is today too often resolved by a coat of fresh, clean white paint. This choice says more about twentieth-century taste than actual nineteenth-century practice. White paint was but one of a wide range of alternative wall finishes used throughout the Victorian period. Listen to Andrew Jackson Downing, America's first great architectural critic, who wrote in 1850, "Since we look upon bare white walls, in the principal apartments of a country house, as, in point of taste, a complete nullity, destructive of all tone, and harsh and glaring in effect, we would, in all cases, either paint the walls in oil, color them in distemper, or cover them

*Two Gothic interiors.* Right: Mr. and Mrs. Charles Henry A. Carter, *probably by Nicholas Biddle Kittel (c. 1848), contains several interesting details, such as the wall-to-wall carpeting, the height at which the pictures are hung, and the mixture of Grecian and Gothic furniture. The window curtains copy a design in John Claudius Loudon,* An Encyclopedia of Cottage, Farm, and Villa Architecture and Furniture. *(Museum of the City of New York)* Opposite: *The drawing room at Kenwood, the country seat of J. Rathbone, Esq., near Albany, New York, as illustrated in Andrew Jackson Downing,* The Architecture of Country Houses. *There is no border on the wall-to-wall carpeting, and the hearth rug is a different pattern. The room is Gothic and the furniture Elizabethan. (The Athenaeum of Philadelphia)*

with paper."[8] Thus, Americans decorating their rooms in the first half of the nineteenth century had several alternatives to white paint.

Early-nineteenth-century critics suggested that the intended use of a space determined the color choice for paint or paper. Entry an stair halls were "sober," drawing rooms "gay," and libraries "grave," for instance. The angle of the sun also mattered; rooms facing north or east should have warm colors, those facing south or west cooler ones.[9] "Warm colors" are those that range from yellow-green through yellow, gold, orange, and red; "cool colors" are blue-greens through blue, violet, and purple. Grays may be either cool or warm depending upon their composition: yellow-grays are warm and blue-grays are cool.

For entry and stair halls, critics suggested cool or sober tones, such as gray, stone color, or drab, since the hallway color should not contrast with those of the rooms opening onto it. The color gray was achieved by mixing charcoal (known as "blue black") and white. Naturally, the more black pigment added, the darker the value, or shade. One critic offered two formulas for stone: "light stone" was composed of Prussian blue, spruce yellow, and umber mixed with white; while "dark stone" was yellow ocher and lampblack mixed with white. "Drab" was raw umber mixed with white, resulting in a dull yellowish brown. Gray, stone, and drab could each serve as a base for

*Two Grecian interiors.* Top: Jane Rebecca Griffith, *by Oliver T. Eddy (c.
1840). This view shows half of a double
parlor finished in the Grecian style. The
pattern covering the entire floor might
be carpeting or a painted floorcloth. (The
Maryland Historical Society)* Right: *A
parlor in the country house finished in
the Grecian style, as illustrated in
Downing,* The Architecture of Country Houses. *The window appears to have
interior shutters and the floor wall-
to-wall carpeting without borders. The
pictures are hung in relation to the architectural features of the room. (The
Athenaeum of Philadelphia)*

marbleizing the walls or woodwork, a technique known to most housepainters in the nineteenth century, although rarely practiced by painters today. Another treatment for hallway walls was to score the plaster while it was still wet to resemble blocks of cut stone (ashlar), then marbleize the wall or paint it one of the above shades, and stripe the scoring in a darker color. Ashlar-patterned wallpapers were also popular for hallways since any damage to the paper could easily be repaired by gluing on a new "block."

Parlors and drawing rooms were to be gay and elegant. Downing recommended light colors to maintain a brilliant effect in the low levels of evening illumination. He disapproved of transplanting to country cottages the Neoclassical fashion of white and gilt finishes that he claimed could be found in the parlors of some city houses. Instead he recommended walls painted "ashes of rose" (grayish pink), pearl gray, or pale apple green, with woodwork and moldings in darker shades of the same hue for contrast. Paintings of interiors from the period suggest that green was particularly popular; and Thomas Webster and Mrs. Parkes mentioned sea green, pea green, and olive green as three of the most commonly used colors.[10] (See Plate 1.)

Critics disagreed on dining-room colors; John Claudius Loudon preferred somber or grave hues, while Downing recommended strong, warm, rich colors and greater contrasts. Downing felt that strong colors and contrasts could be used to better effect in the dining room than in any other room in the house.[11]

Libraries continued to be portrayed as places of retreat and quiet contemplation. Their colors, the critics agreed, should be subdued, grave, hues such as fawn (a yellowish-brown color mixed from white, charcoal, India red, and yellow ocher).

Bedrooms, the critics felt, should be "chaste" or "cheerful spaces," with light-colored walls. The best bedrooms were to be papered rather than painted. *The Workwoman's Guide* (1838), written anonymously by "a Lady," included a precise list of colors appropriate for bedrooms. "Blue is pretty," she wrote, "but rather cold; yellow gives great cheerfulness, as also pink, but the latter is apt to fade soon and is perhaps a little too shewy. Crimson, claret, stone-colour, buff [tan], and light green all look well; a darker green is very refreshing to the eye, and therefore suitable for very light sunny rooms."[12]

## PAINTS

*Painting walls or ceilings in oil* in the nineteenth century required a "hard-finished" or "stuccoed" wall, built up of three coats of plaster, with the final coat plaster of Paris, creating a perfectly smooth surface. New walls had to dry, or "season," for a year before being painted in oils; otherwise they would absorb the oil as they dried, giving an unsatisfactory, mottled finish. When the walls were ready, the painter applied an average of *five coats* of paint, each composed of white lead, pigments, and oil. The final coat was often thinned with turpentine to reduce the gloss.

Unlike oils, *distemper paint*, an opaque watercolor paint made from tempera, could be applied immediately to any newly plastered wall or ceiling—there was no need to wait for the surface to cure—and could also be applied to walls and ceilings finished more cheaply in lime and sand. The American name for distemper paint was calcimine (or "kalsomine"). Distemper—calcimine—is closely related to "whitewash," a finish based on whiting (finely ground chalk) and a solution of water, salt, and lime. The term "whitewash" should not be taken literally, since coloring agents could be added to the mixture.

Distemper paints and whitewash had several advantages over oil-based paints: Because they were water-based, they were far less expensive. They could be applied immediately to new walls, and their drying time was rapid. They were relatively odorless. As they were fairly easy to work with, a skilled painter was not required to apply them. Critics also praised the flat or matte finish they produced. Because they could be applied immediately to new hard-finished walls, they were often used as a temporary first coat

## UNDERSTANDING COLOR

The terms "hue," "value," and "intensity" describe color. *Hue* refers to common names assigned to colors, such as blue, yellow, red. *Value* refers to the shade or tint of a particular color. A dark value (a shade) indicates how much black has been added to the pure color, or chroma, and a light value (a tint) indicates how much white has been added. A dark value is described as a shade of a color; a light value is described as a tint. Pink, thus, is a tint of red, while dark red is a shade of it. *Intensity* refers to the purity of a color; a dusty rose is less intense than a pure pink because it has been grayed and then lightened.

Each chapter of this book describes the colors and color schemes popular during a particular period. Not only did fashions in colors change over time,

but color combinations appropriate for one period may not be appropriate for another. For example, russet, citrine, and peacock blue, all used during the 1880s, would not have been found in rooms of the 1830s.

Enormous changes in color technology over the decades of the Victorian era affected the choice of colors. Initially, most colors were obtained from one or more natural pigments or dyes such as ocher or indigo. By the 1850s, however, aniline dyes made from coal tar, a byproduct of the gaslighting industry, were discovered. The first aniline dye was mauve, accidentally found by William Henry Perkin (1838–1907) while he was searching for artificial quinine. Artificial dyes permitted a greater range of colors and a smaller margin of error, although in homes of the well-to-do until the oil-based paints could be applied.

Distemper and whitewash were also applied to walls finished more cheaply in lime and sand. While nineteenth-century authorities recommended up to five coats for previously unfinished walls, actual practice averaged only two.

The major drawback to distemper and whitewash was their lack of durability and washability compared to oil-based paints. This was especially true of whitewash, which contains no sizing, or glue, to render it insoluble after drying. Critics recommended removing whitewash or distemper with a solution of vinegar and water before repainting or papering a wall—which may indicate just how little durability and washability distemper and whitewash had.[13] This practice may also account for the loss of so much early color evidence.

## Paint Colors

Before the development in the 1870s of commercially successful ready-mixed paints, homeowners relied upon their own mixing skills or those of the local painter. The colors chosen by a householder varied according to personal taste, regional preferences, and the cost or availability of certain

---

many faded from sunlight and cleaning. Consequently, the windows of little-used formal rooms were often kept closed and covered during the nineteenth century.

Changes in artificial lighting over the century also affected the choice of colors. The kind of lighting used in the house had to be taken into consideration when selecting colors, since quality and quantity of light alter the appearance of colors. Generally, dim light dulls colors, as in the old adage, "When all candles be out, all cats be gray." Oil lamps usually emitted less light than gas fixtures. In addition, some light sources reflect certain parts of the color spectrum more than others, causing some hues to stand out and others to disappear. (Contemporary lighting creates similar effects; colors appear different under cool-white fluorescent lights, which heighten blue and green, compared to standard incandescent lights, which heighten red and yellow.) As homeowners began to entertain more in the evening, nineteenth-century critics gave consideration to the new lighting sources when recommending colors, fabrics, and wallpapers. Thus Neoclassical interiors of the early nineteenth century relied on vivid colors, of nearly pure chroma or greatest intensity, obtained from natural pigments and dyes. These colors appeared muted at night since light sources were a few oil lamps or candles. In contrast, the classical revival at the end of the nineteenth century employed the same *hues*, but greatly altered their *values* toward pastel tints. These pale hues were easily distinguished at night by gas or electric light.

pigments. Microscopic examination of surviving surfaces as well as guides published in Britain and America suggest the same color palette was used in both countries during the first half of the nineteenth century. Critics in both countries listed the same color names and supplied similar mixing formulas.

Downing, Loudon, and Webster and Parkes all listed colors. Unfortunately, most color names do not describe the colors precisely. These critics indicated the pigments used to make the colors, but they did not give exact formulas. Other writers tried for greater accuracy. Werner's *Nomenclature of Colours* (Edinburgh, 1814) included color samples, assigned each a name, and provided a description: "ash gray," for instance, was identified as being like the "breast of a long tailed Hen Titmouse." Somewhat less arcane is a small book written by Hezekiah Reynolds of Connecticut entitled *Directions for House and Ship Painting* (1812), which gave formulas for mixing specific colors.[14] However, following Reynolds's formulas may not result in colors

## A WORD ABOUT PAINTS

All paints are composed of three parts: *pigment, vehicle* or *binder,* and *thinner.* Nineteenth-century oil paints used linseed oil as a vehicle and turpentine or mineral spirits as thinner; the pigments, however, have changed greatly since that time. During the nineteenth and early twentieth centuries, paint pigments were composed of white or red lead bases, with colors added to tint them. Since lead may no longer be used by American paint manufacturers, other materials, including titanium dioxide, zinc oxide, and titanium calcium, have replaced it.

Latex paints are a product of the twentieth century. The thinner used in latex is water and the vehicle is acrylic resin. Latex paints dry much darker than they appear in the can. If you are tinting latex at home to achieve a specific color, be certain to do a sample to check the color—this is easy to do since latex generally dries in a few minutes. Latex paints are today's replacements for nineteenth-century distemper and calcimines. Use a brush with synthetic fibers, such as polyester, when applying latex because the water that is used as thinner will ruin a natural bristle brush.

Latex and oil paints come in various levels of gloss ranging from shiny to flat. The finish depends on the percentage of vehicle (either oil or acrylic resin) in relation to thinner—a ratio expressed as the Pigment Volume Concentration, or PVC. The amount of pigment remains constant; only the ratio changes as more thinner is introduced. In the glossiest paints, the amount of vehicle is very great; the vehicle surrounds the pigment and creates a smooth, highly reflective surface when the paint is dry. Flat paints, on the other hand, contain far less vehicle and more thinner. The thinner evaporates as the paint dries, leaving a finish in which the pigments, not floated in oil, present a rough surface when viewed under a microscope. This nonreflective surface gives a flat or "matte" finish. To reduce the gloss of oil paint, nineteenth-century painters simply added more turpentine to the final coat.

identical to those used in the nineteenth century, because the pigments available today are far purer than those of 150 years ago. Since impurities in pigments created variations in colors in the past, owners of old houses need only *attempt* to approximate the early-nineteenth-century schemes. Individuals responsible for museum-quality restorations, however, must resort to the microanalysis of surviving paint layers to ensure authenticity.

## WALLPAPERS

By the 1840s, critics preferred paper as a treatment for walls. Webster considered paper the most common way to treat walls, while Downing confessed "a strong partiality for the use of paper-hangings for covering the walls of all cottages."[15] Before the 1840s only wealthier homes had papers; certainly the average "cottage" did not. The wider use of wallpaper resulted from advances in technology.

Before the 1840s, all paper had to be made by hand from cotton, linen, and, occasionally, woolen rags that had been reduced to a pulp suspended in water. Then the papermaker dipped a wooden frame with a wire-screen bottom into the vat, scooped up some pulp, and shook the frame to spread the pulp evenly across the screen. After the thin layer of pulp was drained, it was removed from the frame, pressed between felts, dried, and bundled into reams. Thus each sheet of paper was a separate manufacture and hardly larger than twenty-two inches by thirty-two inches—the size frame that the papermaker could hold.

These sheets were glued together to form long strips. Then workers known as paper stainers decorated the strips with distemper paint, using three techniques. First, the entire strip might be stained to form the background color or "ground." Second, the design could be printed using carved wooden blocks, a separate block for each color. Third, some hand painting might be added to achieve delicate lines not possible with wooden blocks. Consequently, the cheapest papers had a simple pattern in one color on an unstained ground, while costly papers utilized all three techniques and many colors. Since early paper stainers used water-soluble distemper paints, even the most expensive wallpapers required great care in hanging and cleaning.

The pigments used on wallpapers were limited in number and derived from mineral, animal, or vegetable sources. Andrew Ure's *A Dictionary of Arts, Manufactures, and Mines* (London, 1839) includes a list of nine colors used by paper stainers: white lead; yellows from vegetable extracts, yellow ocher, or chrome yellow from chrome ore; reds from Brazil wood; blues from Prussian blue or blue verditer; greens from copper arsenite, green verditer, or a mixture of yellow and blue; violets from logwood and alum, or a mixture of blue and red; brown from umber; black from Frankfurt black;

*The production of rag paper was time-consuming and laborious. These illustrations from the March 1854 issue of Godey's Lady's Book depict the steps involved. Top: This woman cuts the rags, preparing them for the vat. Bottom: One man uses a frame to scoop up some pulp from the vat, while the second places a newly made sheet of paper between felts in preparation for pressing them. (The Athenaeum of Philadelphia)*

308. FRONT OF PRINTING BLOCK.

309. PRINTING PRESS.

310. BACK OF WOODEN BLOCK FOR PRINTING.

*Printing wallpaper using wooden blocks and applying the pattern by hand, as illustrated in Charles Tomlinson,* Illustrations of Trades *(London, 1860). (The Smithsonian Institution)*

and grays from a mix of Prussian blue and Spanish white.[16]

In 1799, Nicholas Louis Robert invented for the English manufacturing firm of Sealy and Henry Fourdrinier a papermaking machine that bore the firm's name. The "Fourdrinier" machine formed a *continuous roll* of paper that could be cut to any length. America imported the first Fourdrinier machine in 1827. A second advance occurred in 1841, when the English firm Potters of Darwin, Lancashire, perfected a steam-powered machine that printed wallpapers using cylinders with raised patterns. The textile printing industry had used brass cylinders with etched designs since the early years of the nineteenth century. Attempts by the wallpaper industry to use similar etched rollers instead of wooden blocks met with failure because the surfaces could not hold the thinner colors used in wallpaper printing. Instead, a new sort of roller was devised using raised brass outlines stuffed with felt to hold the color; each roller printed one color onto the paper. The early machines could print 420 rolls an *hour* of a two-color paper, as compared to three hundred rolls a *day* that a good workman could print by hand. American manufacturers adopted these advances and harnessed them to steam power, rapidly transforming the wallpaper-manufacturing craft into a major industry. Downing encouraged his readers in 1850, "Paper-hangings offer so easy, economical, and agreeable a means of decorating or finishing the walls of an apartment, that we strongly recommend them for use in the majority of country houses of moderate cost."[17]

Writers on interior decoration in the 1840s specifically recommended the use of wallpapers in the better rooms of the house, especially the parlor and the best bedroom. Wallpapers were applied following French taste, papering from the baseboard to the cornice using one paper and applying borders for ornamentation, a fashion popular in America until the fourth quarter of the nineteenth century. The dominant hue in the wallpaper determined the color of paint used on the ceiling and woodwork.

Loudon, Webster and Parkes, and Downing agreed on the proper designs for wallpapers. Their lists included architectural papers, landscape papers, papers with natural subjects like plants or animals, historical or "biographical" papers containing groups of figures or portraits, ashlar papers representing cut stone, and papers imitating woven fabrics such as damask. These critics all opposed what Downing described as "flashy and gaudy patterns" and "imitations of church windows, magnificent carved wood, pinnacles, etc." His words echoed A. W. N. Pugin (1812–1852), the English architect and designer quoted in Loudon's *An Encyclopedia of Cottage, Farm, and Villa Architecture and Furniture*: "I will commence with what are termed Gothic pattern papers, for hanging walls, where a wretched caricature of a pointed building is repeated from the skirting to the cornice in glorious confusion; door over pinnacle, and pinnacle over door. This is a great favorite with hotel and tavern keepers. Again, those papers which are shaded are defective in principle; for, as a paper is hung around a room, the ornament must frequently be shadowed from the light side." What critics condemn, the public may adore. Loudon and Downing notwithstanding, many nineteenth-century homeowners preferred the naturalistic designs, which were manufactured—and one assumes purchased—throughout the century.[18]

The critics favored architectural papers, called "fresco-papers" by Downing, which imitated panels, cornices, friezes, moldings, columns, and dadoes (decorative paneling on the lower portion of walls), creating architectural elements in a room where none existed. A Richmond, Virginia, merchant advertised architectural papers in 1831; seven yards of columns cost $1.16 and ten capitals and bases $2. Downing assured readers, "if the fresco-papers (which may now be had in New York, well designed, of chaste and suitable patterns for any style of architecture) are chosen, they will produce a tasteful, satisfactory, and agreeable effect, in almost any situation." However, if readers could not afford printed fresco papers, Downing urged them to create

*A wallpaper pattern of the type so disliked by Pugin and other critics during the second quarter of the nineteenth century. The fact that so many critics complained undoubtedly meant that such papers were extremely popular. This paper was reproduced for the parlor of the Ebenezer Maxwell Mansion. (The Ebenezer Maxwell Mansion, Inc., Germantown, Philadelphia, Pennsylvania)*

their own using "decorative paper." The technique, he explained, "consists in using a paper of one uniform color upon the walls, which, by means of stripes of other harmonious or contrasted colors thereon, cut in such forms as the design requires, will produce an effect equal to that which any Polychromatic artist can secure, and at one-fifth the cost." He added that he had just seen a room of eighteen by twenty-four feet done in such a manner by Howell and Company of Philadelphia, the total cost being $16. Just such a technique employing marbleized paper was used in the stair hall of Acorn Hall, the country home of the Crane family built in Morristown, New Jersey, in 1853. However, since the average annual wage for nonagricultural work-

*The restored stair hall at Acorn Hall, Morristown, New Jersey, built in 1853. It is finished in "fresco-paper" of the type favored by Andrew Jackson Downing. The reproduction paper is marbleized, as was the original. (The Morris County Historical Society, Morristown, New Jersey)*

ers at the time was $400, such papers were beyond the means of most Americans.[19]

Architectural papers often accompanied scenic papers, known in the nineteenth century as "views," "landscape papers," or as *paysages panoramiques*. Scenic papers first appeared in France in the last years of the eighteenth century and shortly thereafter in America. Louis A. Godey, publisher of the *Lady's Book*, was recommending their use as late as 1857. Today's reproduction scenic papers are so expensive that it is difficult for modern homeowners to believe that scenic papers were common in America and not restricted to grand houses along the Eastern seaboard. In fact, scenic papers were popular across the country. In *Retrospective of Western Travel* (1838), Harriet Martineau commented on the "old-fashioned" scenics she encountered in hotel parlors throughout the country; she was particularly taken with the grafitti that previous travelers had written, cartoon style, in the mouths of the figures portrayed in the views. Advertisements for scenic papers appeared as early as 1808 in New Orleans and by 1816 in Lexington, Kentucky. Records of Jean Zuber et Compagnie of Alsace-Lorraine listed shipments of scenics and other papers to ninety-nine American dealers and individuals between 1829 and 1834, after which the company funneled all its papers through a single New York distributor, Ernest Fiedler. Scenics were indeed widely distributed—a set was recently found in a modest home in California, where, during the nineteenth century, it had been pasted directly onto the interior wooden partitions.[20]

The price of scenics in the nineteenth century varied according to the number of rolls in a set and the number of colors used. Monochromatic scenics in grays or browns were less expensive than polychromatic sets, although for a slight increase in price monochromatic scenes could be printed with a blue sky, giving a more natural effect. Some idea of costs can be obtained from the 1819 account book of a Virginia importer who noted prices for sets of scenics ranging from $10 to $40. Assuming twenty rolls of paper per scenic, each roll of scenic wallpaper cost between fifty cents and $2. At the same time, single rolls of wallpaper cost between twenty-five cents and $5. In short, if one could afford to use wallpaper, one could afford a scenic.[21]

While the manufacturer of the first scenic paper is unknown, French firms such as Zuber (still in existence), Dufour, Jacquemart et Bernard, Délicourt, and Desfossé et Karth produced a great many of them during the first sixty years of the nineteenth century. The number of blocks needed to print the intricate panels of scenics constituted a major investment; once designed, the same scenic was printed for decades, sometimes with amusing adjustments to ensure continued popularity. Indians and sightseers in Zuber's "Views of North America" (1834–1836) became English and American

*Two versions of the same scenic paper produced by the firm of Jean Zuber. In 1834, the company produced "Views of North America," which it issued some years later as "War of Independence," substituting soldiers for sightseers and cannon smoke for the spray of Niagara Falls. (A. L. Diament & Company)*

soldiers when the paper was reprinted as "The War of Independence" some years later.[22]

Scenics generally sold in sets of twenty to thirty rolls; each roll—approximately twenty inches wide and eight to ten feet in length—contributed a different segment of the view. The upper portion of every scenic was "sky"—with or without clouds—which could be trimmed to fit the height of the room.[23] Typically, scenics hung above chair rails or above architectural papers. Column papers occasionally framed scenics, and it was not unusual to find a wallpaper border of swags placed at the top of them, even if the room had a cornice.

Statuary papers were also manufactured in France. During the first thirty or forty years of the nineteenth century these papers generally depicted half-sized gods and goddesses tinted to resemble bronze or marble statues. By midcentury, however, companies manufactured statuary papers of national heroes for the American market; in 1856–1857, the firm of Jules Desfossé produced a series entitled "Les Grands Hommes," which featured Washington, Franklin, Lafayette, and Jefferson. Almost immediately, Godey announced "those statues . . . may now be found ornamenting the houses of many of our subscribers. They are very popular." In addition to the four mentioned above, Godey notified readers they could also secure the more contemporary heroes Henry Clay and James Buchanan. Trompe l'oeil papers depicting pedestals and niches accompanied many of the statuary papers. Such papers were commonly hung in front halls so that middle-class homes might seem to possess statuary galleries.[24]

Ashlar papers depicting stone walls appeared most frequently in stair halls where damage was easily repaired by replacing a "block." Early-nineteenth-century ashlar papers contained simple stone patterns, often in gray; by the 1840s, however, more ornate designs appeared with fancifully cut "stones" and scrollwork in blues, greens, or reds filling the space between each block.[25]

Also popular, particularly for parlors and bedchambers, were papers printed in overall repeating patterns such as stripes or diapers (small diamond shapes with diagonal repeats), often containing simple geometric designs; fruits, flowers, and ribbons; or more intricate designs employing C-curves and S-curves. Among the most spectacular papers with an overall design were the "rainbow papers," also known as *ombré*, or *irisé*. The name referred to the subtle shading of colors throughout the pattern, forming a secondary pattern of light and dark on which the major pattern appeared superimposed. This technique was developed by Zuber et Compagnie about 1820. Most "rainbow papers" employed large motifs of abstracted flowers and scrolls. These papers were advertised in America by 1826.[26]

Loudon and Downing approved of flocked papers, sometimes called "velvet papers," particularly in patterns imitating woven fabrics such as damasks.

*Ashlar paper was recommended for entry halls throughout the first half of the nineteenth century. This paper and border were reproduced for The Hermitage, Andrew Jackson's home in Nashville, Tennessee. (A. L. Diament & Company)*

Early papers were flocked by printing a design in varnish over a stained ground; while the varnish remained wet, a lint of chopped wool was applied, resulting in a stiff flock quite unlike today's flocked papers. Furthermore, the paper was one color; additional colors were printed onto the dried flock. These techniques were also used to manufacture borders with flocked backgrounds and unflocked patterns, and wallpapers with designs printed on a smooth ground against a flocked background. Flocked papers were relatively costly in the nineteenth century and usually hung in the best rooms of the house, such as the parlor. For a variety of reasons, including wear and maintenance, critics did not recommend them for dining rooms, hallways, or bedrooms. Flocked borders, however, did appear in those areas.[27]

Borders were an integral part of any wall treatment during the 1830–1850 period. They appeared in rooms with or without cornices, and they covered minor mistakes made in trimming wallpapers during installation. By the 1840s, borders were fairly narrow (about three inches wide), often flocked, and usually in a darker shade than the paper on the wall. The most common border patterns were florals, trailing vines, or architectural details.

*An illustration of flock being applied to paper still wet from the printing table. The technique was employed throughout the nineteenth century; this engraving is from the November 26, 1881, issue of* Scientific American. *(The Athenaeum of Philadelphia)*

*Examples of wallpaper borders produced during the first half of the nineteenth century. The shading of the block modillions in the architectural border* (above) *make it appear very realistic. (Collections of Greenfield Village and the Henry Ford Museum, Dearborn, Michigan)*

Borders representing swags of fabric were also used and many of these continue to be available from modern manufacturers, although none are flocked. Because many borders were narrow, up to sixteen strips could be printed on a single width of wallpaper. Some borders were printed in sets of four, each with the light coming from a different focal point, so that an enterprising paperhanger could hang them to take into account the natural sources of light in the room.[28]

## COLOR PLACEMENT: WALLS, CEILINGS, WOODWORK

Color placement was as important as color choice; the painting of the ceiling, woodwork, and molding in a room contributed as much to the overall effect as did the color of the walls. Regardless of the overall color scheme selected, writers maintained that the ceiling, walls, and woodwork should be of *three separate values*. (See Plate 2 for a particularly complex arrangement of colors.) Most recommended that the ceiling be the lightest value in the room, the walls darker, and the woodwork lighter *or* darker than the walls, while the cornice should be painted a value different from those of the ceiling and walls. A light-colored ceiling gave the effect of height to a room. Although white was used on ceilings, critics preferred that a lighter tint of the wall color be used. Papers were rarely used on ceilings during this period.

By the 1830s and 1840s, the ornate plasterwork ceilings of earlier years had passed out of vogue; Webster and Parkes, writing in 1844, derided them as a waste of labor since "it is painful to look up at such a ceiling."[29] The growing numbers of the prosperous middle class adopted simpler designs in papier-mâché and wood, as well as plasterwork, to decorate the walls and ceilings of their homes. Webster and Parkes recommended center ceiling medallions of papier-mâché in parlors, from which hung the chandelier. Ceiling medallions for cottages of this period were usually no larger than two feet in diameter and based on a single flower, a circle of acanthus leaves echoing Neoclassical designs, or a molded, fairly plain disk.

All authors of the period recommended some sort of cornice to distinguish the ceiling from the walls. Loudon believed no room had a finished appearance without a cornice; the living rooms and principal bedrooms "of even the humblest cottages" should have them. He included a series of cornice profiles in Gothic, Grecian, and Roman designs to be executed in plaster or wood; even the most humble cottage parlor could afford a one-inch-diameter bead between walls and ceiling, which, if made of iron, would be an ideal picture rail. In *The Architecture of Country Houses* (1850), Downing illustrated two plaster cornices for use in parlors or "best rooms" of cottages, one suitable for Grecian or Italian houses, the other for Gothic.[30] To accentuate the cornice, critics suggested painting it a different value, preferably

*Center medallions illustrated in John Claudius Loudon,* An Encyclopedia of Cottage, Farm, and Villa Architecture and Furniture. *(The Athenaeum of Philadelphia)*

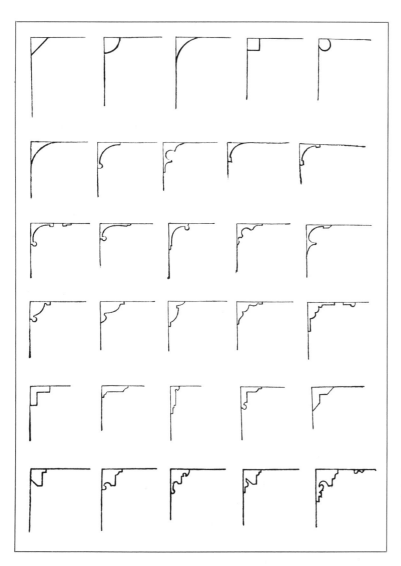

*A series of cornice profiles from Loudon, An Encyclopedia of Cottage, Farm, and Villa Architecture and Furniture. Most of these cornices would lend themselves to pencil striping, as Loudon recommended. (The Athenaeum of Philadelphia)*

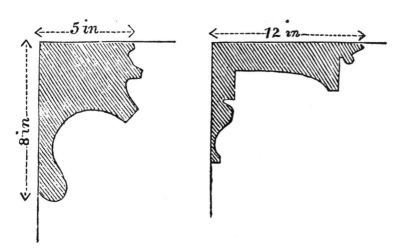

*Andrew Jackson Downing illustrated these cornice profiles in* The Architecture of Country Houses. *The one on the left is identified as suitable for "Grecian or Italian forms," while the one on the right is labeled "Gothic." (The Athenaeum of Philadelphia)*

darker, from the adjoining surfaces. Loudon proposed decorating cornices by painting simple lines using several values of the same color and instructed his readers that narrow lines of color gave the effect of distance, while broad lines reduced it. The simple profiles of Loudon's designs for cornices lent themselves to this "pencil striping." To properly accentuate the cornice, Loudon advised, the color selection must be subtle, comprising different values of the principal hue used throughout the room.[31] In rooms without cornices, a border of wallpaper achieved a similar effect.

The remaining woodwork was usually painted. Although Downing included a single recipe for a wood stain made from tobacco, he and other critics preferred paint; surviving examples suggest householders did too. Oil paint was used on woodwork because it was both washable and more durable than water-soluble distemper or whitewash. Writers considered white woodwork appropriate only when the walls of the room were also white. Where walls were painted a color, critics recommended some value of the color be used on the woodwork, in most cases a darker value because it hid soil. Downing also warned that light hues, made from white lead and linseed oil, changed color over time.[32]

Grained and marbleized finishes frequently appeared on doors and woodwork during the first half of the nineteenth century. These techniques confuse today's old-house owners because modern housepainters rarely receive the training in these skills that their nineteenth-century counterparts had. Decorative painting was not restricted to the wealthy. Homeowners who

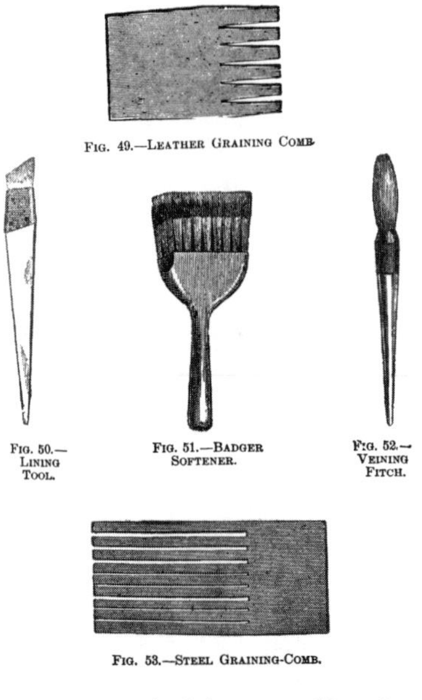

FIG. 49.—LEATHER GRAINING COMB.

FIG. 50.—LINING TOOL.

FIG. 51.—BADGER SOFTENER.

FIG. 52.—VEINING FITCH.

FIG. 53.—STEEL GRAINING-COMB.

*Graining tools of the type used by painters throughout the nineteenth century, as illustrated in Franklin B. Gardner, The Painter's Encyclopedia. (The Athenaeum of Philadelphia)*

## GRAINING AND MARBLEIZING

Graining and marbleizing are executed over a coat of oil paint applied directly to the woodwork. The color of the base paint is determined by the wood or marble being imitated. Ash, maple, birch, and oak, all popular graining choices in the nineteenth century, are light woods; hence yellowish-white bases are used. Walnut, another popular choice, requires an orangy base, while mahogany requires a reddish one. The graining coat, unlike the base coat, is quite thin and allows the base coat to show through as the lighter areas of the grain. A varnish coat is laid over the finished surface to protect it.

The relative thickness of these three coats causes confusion for many owners of old houses when they scrape small sections of woodwork. The discovery of a base coat of yellowish-white or orange may lead to the conclusion that the woodwork was simply painted that color originally. While this is possible, it is more probable that that is the color of the base coat used for graining. Since the glaze of the graining coat is quite thin, evidence of its presence under more recent layers of paint is often fugitive. Careful scraping and the use of magnification are required to reveal the graining. (An easier way is to remove any later moldings or partitions, which may expose the original surface treatment.)

Graining is most often found on doors,

could afford to paint in oil could afford graining or marbleizing—Downing characterized the cost difference as "very trifling." Consequently, graining appeared on doors, window sashes, and baseboards, the areas most exposed to soil. Fireplace surrounds and mantels made of wood, iron, or slate were also frequently grained or marbleized. A varnish coat protected the decorative finish, leaving it smooth and easy to dust and wash. Furthermore, graining imitated "better" woods, such as oak, mahogany, and walnut, that were more expensive than pine and more difficult to work. Critics unwittingly offered testimony to the skill of nineteenth-century grainers when they insisted that the results should only *imitate* the real thing, not be a dishonest facsimile.[33]

# FLOORS

Having wrestled with wall treatments, homeowners' next area of concern is usually the floors. Victorian homeowners had a wide range of alternatives, some predating the nineteenth century. Matting, floorcloths, and druggets, for example, all were available in the eighteenth century, while hand-loomed ingrain and Brussels carpets—available but rare in the eighteenth century—became widely popular in the nineteenth century as mechanization increased production and reduced costs.

---

and surviving nineteenth-century examples suggest that the use of grained doors with plainly painted frames was a common treatment. If evidence of graining is found, it should be restored, or the woodwork should at least be painted in a semigloss oil paint in a color as close to the original graining glaze as possible. However, graining is relatively easy to do and there is little justification for not regraining, if the original treatment cannot be saved by carefully removing the paint that covers it.

Before attempting graining, some of the following books should be studied: Jocasta Innes, *Paint Magic: The Complete Guide to Decorative Finishes* (New York:

Van Nostrand Reinhold, 1981); Isabel O'Neil, *The Art of the Painted Finish for Furniture & Decoration* (New York: William Morrow & Co., 1971; paperback, 1980); and Nat Weinstein, "The Art of Graining," *The Old-House Journal*, vol. VI (December 1978), pp. 133ff, and vol. VII (January 1979), pp. 5ff.

Graining glaze is not paint that can be purchased over the counter. It is mixed on the job and is usually a combination of boiled linseed oil, satin or velvet varnish, paint thinner, paint drier, and universal or oil color that varies depending on the wood or marble being imitated. All of these materials are readily available from paint stores.

*Marbleizing and graining were extremely popular finishes throughout the nineteenth century. Above: Lyndhurst, in Tarrytown, New York, was built by Alexander Jackson Davis in 1838 and substantially expanded in 1864–1865. The walls of the entry hall were marbleized and scored to resemble ashlar blocks. Right: The Athenaeum of Philadelphia was designed by John Notman and completed in 1847. The doors and pilasters of the Reading Room were originally grained and marbleized, finishes that were restored in 1975. (Lyndhurst/National Trust for Historic Preservation, and The Athenaeum of Philadelphia)*

The majority of American floors during the first half of the nineteenth century were bare softwood boards, often laid in random widths, and never stained and varnished as would be the hardwood floors of the last quarter of the nineteenth century. If the boards were not wholly overlaid by floor covering, cleaning them involved scrubbing with sand and a stiff brush, and sometimes bleaching with lye, an alkaline solution derived from common wood ashes.

Several questions arise for today's homeowner when selecting an historically appropriate floor covering: What products were available when the house was built? Could the original owners afford them? What products and styles did nineteenth-century writers recommend for various rooms in the house? And finally, which products at what cost are available today?

## PAINTED FLOORS

Painting the floorboards was a step above leaving them plain and one that homeowners could undertake themselves. For example, Mrs. Ruth Henshaw Bascom, the wife of a minister in Fitzwilliam, New Hampshire, painted her softwood floors in oils to simulate another type of floor covering. In 1830, she recorded in her diary: "29 June Tuesday—fair . . . I began to paint my parlor floor in imitation of a striped carpet     30 June Wednesday . . . I painted ¼ of my striped floor     3 July Saturday . . . I finished painting my floor, at 6 P.M. Striped with red, green, blue, yellow and purple—carpet like."[34]

Floor painting has long been considered a regional technique, confined primarily to New England and New York. However, the discovery of surviving examples in other parts of the country suggests that this treatment was more widespread. Painted softwood floors may lie undiscovered beneath newer hardwood flooring, and a great many painted floors doubtless were sanded away when polished floors and Oriental carpets came into vogue later in the nineteenth century. John Carwitham's *Various Kinds of Floor Decorations Represented in Plano and Perspective* (London, 1739) contained twenty-four illustrations of geometric patterns for floor painting. In the nineteenth century, Loudon suggested painting masonry floors to imitate marble, stone, or wood, and Webster and Parkes urged readers to paint the exposed boards around the edges of rugs. American sources also recommended painting floors. Rufus Porter, an itinerant painter, published *A Select Collection of Valuable and Curious Arts and Interesting Experiments* (1825), which included a section on making figured or floral stencils from cardboard for painting floors and floorcloths. Furthermore, a number of family portraits from the 1830s illustrate what appear to be floors painted to imitate carpeting. There is no reason to suspect this technique ended abruptly, since any housepainter and most householders could paint a floor. Downing ignored painted floors in *The Architecture of Country Houses* but he did suggest that "using narrow matched floor-planks, of good quality, and *staining* every other plank of a dark color, like black walnut," would produce "a very good effect."[35] The floor of the Vail House in Morristown, New Jersey, preserves a similar treatment *painted* in buff and fawn. (See Plate 3.)

## FLOORCLOTHS

It is a short step, although a costly one, from painted floors to painted floorcloths. Early records of the use of floorcloths in America include the personal property inventories taken after the deaths of William Burnet (1688–1729), governor of Massachusetts, and Robert "King" Carter of Virginia (1663–1732). George Washington, Thomas Jefferson, and John Adams owned floorcloths. Most of these floorcloths probably came from England; however, near the end of the eighteenth century, Americans also produced them. A painter in Charleston, South Carolina, in 1786 advertised that he painted floorcloths, and in 1793, Joseph Barrell of Pleasant Hill in Charlestown, Massachusetts, canceled a floorcloth ordered through his London agent, explaining he could obtain what he desired in America. Hezekiah Reynolds, the ship- and housepainter, also included directions for painting floorcloths in his book, *Directions for House and Ship Painting.*[36]

Reynolds suggested using seamed canvas as a base for paintings, although by the nineteenth century several English companies wove cloths twenty-four to twenty-seven feet wide and up to seventy feet in length for seamless floorcloths.[37] Cotton, linen (flax), and hemp fibers were used, with hemp preferred for its absorbency. Webster and Parkes described the factory production of floorcloths in 1844. First, cloth was stretched on a vertical frame able to accommodate pieces as large as 220 square yards. Both sides of the cloth were sized and then smoothed with pumice to remove the small fibers raised during the sizing process. Next, they explained, "four coats of stiff oil paint are laid on successively, on one side of the canvas, suffering each first to dry, and then three coats on the other side. After this paint is quite dry, the cloth is detached from the frame, in order to be printed in the manner of calico printing; for this purpose it is rolled up on a roller, and unrolled as required for the process. In giving the surface pattern, stencilling was formerly employed; but printing with blocks is now generally practised."[38] Outside of factories, however, hand painting and stenciling remained the most common methods.

Floorcloth, Webster and Parkes warned, "is better for being kept for some considerable time before it is used, the paint getting harder, and it, therefore, is charged for partly according to its age; new floor-cloth being cheaper than that which has been kept a year or two." Miss Eliza Leslie, author of *The Lady's House Book* (1854), concurred, "We have seen an English oil-cloth that, not having been put down till five years after it was imported, looked fresh and new, though it had been ten years in constant use on an entry floor. An oil-cloth that has been made within the year is scarcely worth buying, as the paint will be defaced in a very little time, it requiring a long while to season." Well-made floorcloths were relatively expensive, priced by the yard according to "the strength and goodness of the canvass, the number of coats of paint, the number of colours in the face, and the age of the cloth." As a simple rule of thumb, Webster and Parkes suggested a good floorcloth weighed 3½ to 4½ pounds a square yard.[39]

Some homeowners made their own floorcloths rather than hiring professional painters or purchasing factory-made items. Recounting his years in Southampton, Long Island, Lyman Beecher recalled that his bride, Roxana, introduced the first floorcloth in the area in 1800–1801. After having the cotton backing woven, she took the piece to the attic where she sized and then painted it in oils with bunches of flowers in the center and a border all around. Another writer remembered that in 1828 her mother had woven her own linen cloth which she then nailed to the side of the barn and painted. When finished, the writer added, the floorcloth "did not cover the south room entirely, but did almost and saved scrubbing." All nineteenth-century writers advised that floorcloths might be cleaned by wiping them with water, but must never be scrubbed with soap, which might remove the paint. Once dry, floorcloths might be brushed to a shine or, according to *Godey's Lady's Book*, polished with milk.[40]

For the most part, householders placed floorcloths in vestibules, hallways, and parlors, although Webster and Parkes supposed that a good, well-seasoned floorcloth might even last nine or ten years on a veranda exposed to the elements. Nineteenth-century sources mentioned a variety of patterns. For vestibules and hallways, they preferred designs imitating tiles of "different colored stones" or wooden floors. Hezekiah Reynolds's directions for imitating traditional diamond or square patterns—with or without "clouds"—produced floorcloths recommended for formal halls or parlors. Webster and Parkes preferred patterns copied from Persian or Turkish carpets. They urged readers to purchase designs with many colors and small patterns, for "when the pattern is large, defects are sooner perceived" except when marbleized, for then "defects may be repaired by a house painter." Writers rarely recommended floorcloths for stairs, probably because they were too slippery and wore rapidly against the edges of the treads.[41]

The Middlebury, Vermont, *National Standard* described on September 3, 1822, a substitute for floorcloths painted in oils as "a new carpeting substance . . . invented in Philadelphia. It consists of paper, highly varnished and painted after any pattern. It is called 'prepared varnished paper,' and when finished has the appearance of the best and most elegant oil cloth. A pattern for an ordinary room which would take $50 worth of oil cloth may be covered by this material for $12.50—and at the end of 5 years you can lay down a new pattern for the interest of the sum which the oil cloth cost. It is cool and very pleasant and will wear handsomely for five years at least."[42]

More than a decade later, Loudon supplied instructions for a similar substitute—gluing onto linen or cotton fabric plain colored papers, with printed wallpapers in the center, corners, and borders. When dried, two coats of sizing were applied over the paper, followed by one or two coats of boiled linseed oil, and a coat of varnish. Loudon assured his readers that these carpets could be rolled and moved just like floorcloths painted in oils.[43] There is, however, no way to estimate how many households might have used these ephemeral coverings.

## TILES

Paper carpets remind us that floorcloths painted in oil were expensive and required regular upkeep; as a result, writers began to recommend more durable materials. Loudon favored two types of tiles, which he identified as plain or figured quarries. Plain quarries were tiles about six inches square and available in red, blue, drab, black, or brownish-yellow. Figured quarries were tiles with patterns baked in. Loudon advised using only plain "quarries of different colours . . . set in mortar or cement, so as to appear like tessellated pavement" or in combination with "Wright's figured quarries" as borders and centers. By midcentury, plain or patterned English tiles were marketed in the United States as "encaustic tiles"—a name used in England today to describe only the patterned tiles; plain ones are termed "geometrics." Downing recommended patterned tiles, chiefly available in "browns, enriched with patterns and figures of fawn or blue." He assured readers that these tiles with inlay designs fused together during the firing process were "far more durable and characteristic, and, in the end, much more economical" than carpet or floorcloth in entries or halls.[44] Most surviving midcentury floors contain patterns formed of tiles in solid colors of buff, red, blue, brown, or black; only rarely were the more expensive patterned tiles employed. (See Plate 4.)

## MATTING

One of the most universally used floor coverings of the nineteenth century was matting, recommended for almost every room in the house. The term actually included many different types of floor coverings manufactured of at least eight different types of plant material, both foreign and domestic. Nineteenth-century writers often differentiated between "carpet matting" and "mats," the former generally laid wall to wall and the latter in front of doors as rugs. Webster and Parkes proposed two types of mats: coarse ones in the entrance hall to wipe dirt from shoes and finer ones at the foot of stairs and the thresholds of rooms to reduce carpet wear. Coarse mats were available in coconut fiber, straw, and corn husks, with coconut fibers being particularly adaptable. The fibers might be plaited into chains and formed into a mat with a zigzag design, or used to create a mat with a brushlike surface. Finer mats were made of sheepskin (dyed and trimmed into a rectangular shape), thick woolens (with fringes and perhaps fancy embroidery), or flat-woven grass mats from India or China. Lydia Maria Child suggested in *The American Frugal Housewife* (1835) that servants or children cut worn-out clothing into strips to braid and stitch into mats for use at the thresholds of rooms.[45]

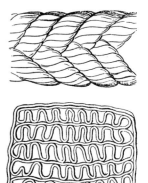

*Matting to place at exterior doors, illustrated in John Claudius Loudon,* An Encyclopedia of Cottage, Farm, and Villa Architecture and Furniture. *Loudon noted that the mat was made in Germany of tarred rope. Thomas Webster and Mrs. Parkes illustrated a similar design in* An Encyclopedia of Domestic Economy, *stating it was made of "cocoanut fiber." (The Athenaeum of Philadelphia)*

Carpet matting, as a floor covering for large areas, dates to the eighteenth century. The best matting came from India or China, hence the names "Indian Matting" or "Canton Matting" for products imported to America via England. George Washington ordered large quantities of Canton matting from a London agent for Mount Vernon in the 1760s. When America began direct trade with China in the 1780s, Washington purchased his matting through Robert Morris of Philadelphia.[46]

Carpet matting had various applications. Some nineteenth-century households undoubtedly used matting only in summer in place of or over woolen carpets. Others kept it in place year round as the only affordable floor covering—it cost between thirty-five and fifty cents a yard throughout the nineteenth century. Matting also was laid wall to wall under a better carpet or rug where it could serve two purposes: it could act as a pad, protecting the good carpet or rug from wear, and it could also cover softwood floors, providing a neat finish around the edge of the room if the rug was not laid wall to wall.[47]

Matting was appropriate for all these uses because it came in strips—generally no wider than thirty-six inches—that could be seamed together and bordered to create a rug easily moved from room to room, taken outside to be washed, or put away for the winter. *The Workwoman's Guide* recommended bindings of red or green leather or whatever color suited the furnishings of the room, while Loudon suggested black or colored ferreting (tape or binding).[48] However, when used wall to wall, particularly under a rug, one simply nailed the strips to the floor with the edges abutting.

Grass matting had its limitations. It never covered stairs, for instance. Miss Leslie explained, "It wears out very soon against the ledges of the steps, and is, besides, too slippery to be safe for those that go up and down, particularly if they have to carry articles that may be broken." Furthermore it soiled easily "from flyspots, and a multitude of vermin which harbor in such things, and from kitchen smoke, which is universal." Lydia Maria Child instructed her readers to "wash" matting with salt water to keep it light—or prevent vermin—and dry it thoroughly with a coarse towel to prevent it from rotting.[49]

## DRUGGET

Another floor covering used during the nineteenth century was drugget. The term—derived from the French word *drogue*, meaning a "cheap article" or rubbish—actually referred to an inexpensive, coarse cloth of wool or wool and flax woven in widths from one to four yards. Drugget had several uses; it could serve as a cover for better carpets, particularly in dining rooms, or as the sole floor covering, or occasionally *underneath* better rugs as protection and as camouflage for unattractive floorboards around the perimeter

*Notice the drugget under the dining table protecting what appears to be ingrain carpeting, in* Asking a Blessing, *by Alexander F. Fraser (c. 1830–1842). (Milwaukee Public Museum of Milwaukee County)*

of the room. So popular was drugget that the fabric name became synonymous with any covering used to protect a better carpet, including baize and heavy linen.[50] The term "drugget" will be used in the general sense henceforth, rather than as reference to the specific fabric.

*The Workwoman's Guide* recommended that a drugget be used daily to protect better carpeting, except when company was expected.[51] (Quite the reverse appears in Sargent's oft-reproduced painting *The Dinner Party* in which a drugget is clearly evident under the dining-room table around which a party of well-dressed and seemingly well-mannered men enjoy a meal.)

When drugget was used as the only floor covering in a room, *The Workwoman's Guide* suggested stitching lengths of brown or "marone" drugget together, abutting the selvages, and hemming with a herringbone stitch before stretching tightly into place. Single widths with decorative borders stitched along their length made excellent stair carpeting held in place by rods. Loudon preferred simple borders consisting of a band of black or dark-colored fabric around the perimeter, about two inches from the outer edges of the goods. Factories also manufactured druggets with fancy patterns. If these were beyond the means of the householder, Loudon proposed that "industrious housewives" make them of "remnants of cloth bought from the woollen-draper, or tailor, and cut into any kind of geometrical shapes, . . . sewed together, so as to form circles, stars, or any other regular figures that may be desired. . . ." He assured readers that "when arranged with taste," these snippets would "produce a very handsome and durable carpet, at a very trifling expense." As to the final design, he preferred symmetrical patterns with a border around the piece.[52]

Webster and Parkes, however, must be credited with the most novel suggestion for druggets. The most "economical mode" for householders, they suggested, "may be a border only of carpet round the room, and the middle part may be covered with a drugget, painted or not, which will look as if the latter covered the middle of a large carpet; and this has the advantage, particularly for bedrooms, that it is easily taken up to be shaken and dusted."[53]

## CARPETING

A. J. Downing declared in 1850, "the floors of the better cottages in this country—at least in the Northern States—are universally covered with carpet or matting."[54] Read closely, this passage admits that carpeting appeared in *some* American homes, though Downing neglected to identify the type of

## FLOOR COVERINGS

All of the floor-covering alternatives discussed in this chapter can be recreated today; the least costly approach is the plain or decoratively painted floor.

Although few companies manufacture floorcloths today, they can be made by the homeowner or commissioned from a local craftsman, just as they were in the nineteenth century. Directions for making floorcloths are available in *The Art of Decorative Stenciling*, by Adele Bishop and Cile Lord (New York: Penguin, 1978), and the process is explained in *Paint Magic* by Jocasta Innes (New York: Van Nostrand Reinhold, 1981). Commercial firms manufacturing floorcloths are listed in *The Old-House Journal Catalog: A Buyer's Guide*, issued annually by *The Old-House Journal*, Brooklyn, New York.

Encaustic tiles—such as those illustrated by Samuel Sloan in 1861 (see Plate 4)—are not manufactured in the United States at this time but are available from an English manufacturer who regards each order as "custom work" suitable for historic restorations; consequently the material is expensive and slow to be delivered. Existing tiles within the house should be carefully maintained. Loose tiles should be reset, and damaged pieces replaced with intact ones that might be found underneath large items of furniture, on closet floors, or beneath radiators.

Exterior doorway mats made of cocca matting ("coir") duplicate the sort recommended by Loudon and Webster and Parkes. Carpet mattings are not so easy to replicate, however. One alternative is Japanese *tatami*, which is woven entirely carpeting. There were a number of varieties at the time, but the first produced by machines—hence the least expensive and most available to middle-class households—were those without face pile known as "flat-woven" carpets. This category included list or rag carpeting, Venetian carpeting, and ingrain carpeting. All three share certain characteristics. All were woven rather than "tufted" or "punched" as many carpets are today. All used natural fibers such as wool, linen, cotton, hemp, or jute. All were woven on the narrow looms of the time, which produced strips of carpeting that were sewn together to create larger sizes. (*Broad* looms used today for tufted carpeting twelve feet wide were rarely used in the nineteenth century and then only for rag or list carpets.) Finally, all flat-woven carpets were reversible, which extended their wear.

Rag carpeting was usually thirty-six inches wide, with a warp composed of wool, cotton, or linen and a weft of evenly cut rags or strips of fabric. The term "list carpeting" referred to goods woven from "list," narrow strips of fabric or the selvages of cloth, which formed the weft threads. In both cases, the stripes formed by the weft could create either a regular repeat of colors or a random pattern. List and rag carpeting could be seamed to form a carpet or used in pieces for rugs or doormats. Homeowners sometimes wove rag carpets themselves in the early decades of the nineteenth century, and the fruit of their labors appeared in local fairs. *The New England Farmer*

---

of grass, and another is a product woven of grass with cotton warp; both provide smooth but somewhat fragile floor coverings that closely resemble nineteenth-century matting. Carpets of cocoa fiber or sisal are more durable, but their rough textures have neither the appearance nor the tactile qualities of nineteenth-century matting. Until recently there has been at least one flat-woven carpet made of jute that may replicate the nineteenth-century hemp carpets mentioned by Webster and Parker. These strips of jute carpet are useful on stairs, where they are held in place by rods, and can also be seamed to cover larger areas. These jute carpets resemble grass matting and might substitute for it in high-traffic areas.

Drugget is manufactured in the United Kingdom but not in the United States.

Modern householders desiring the look of a nineteenth-century drugget might use awning canvas, which could be embellished with designs as some nineteenth-century authors suggested. Solid colors, such as the brown and "marone" mentioned in *The Workwoman's Guide*, are historically correct as well as practical; they could also be bordered to further embellish them as some authors recommended. In addition to these nineteenth-century uses, modern householders might lay them over reproduction carpeting in halls, and house museums might use them to protect carpets located in traffic areas during bad weather. For museums, canvas druggets would be far more handsome—and authentic—than the plastic runners too often employed.

reported that the Essex Agricultural Show of October 1827 awarded "to Miss Rebecca Greenough, of Bradford, for 24 yards of handsome Rag Carpeting—made by hand, 4 yards wide, and without a seam, a gratuity of $3.00." Even with factory production of rag carpeting, handlooms—many of them "broad looms" up to fifteen feet wide and requiring two operators—remained in home use.[55] Homemade rugs were also made of thick woolen yarns colored a variety of hues by natural dyes. Carpeting made of rags and yarns remained in use on the floors of modest homes throughout the nineteenth century.

The Mrs. Bascom who painted her floor "carpet like" might have been imitating rag carpeting when she painted stripes on her parlor floor, or perhaps she was copying another type of striped carpet called "Venetian." Webster and Parkes informed their readers, "it is not known that what we call Venetian carpeting was ever made in Venice," but, whatever its origin, Venetian carpeting was available in New York City as early as 1799 in eighteen-, twenty-seven-, and thirty-two-inch widths. Unlike rag and yarn carpets, which took their colors from the weft threads and consequently were striped the *width* of the roll, Venetian carpets were striped the *length* of the goods because the colors came from the woolen warp threads woven tightly over weft "filler" threads of wool, hemp, or cotton. (See Plate 5.) Early-nineteenth-century Venetian carpets in America may have been imported from England or produced in the home, but by the 1830s, Pennsylvania factories were weaving striped Venetians and patterned ones known as "damasks."[56]

*The Workwoman's Guide* defined "common Venetian" as striped carpeting good for servants' rooms and schoolrooms in homes; "Venetian damask" it deemed appropriate for stairs and sitting rooms. Webster and Parkes's readers learned that Venetian carpeting belonged on stairs and in bedrooms because its flat, tight weave repelled dust better than other types of carpeting. Brass or iron rods generally held Venetian carpeting in place on stairs, and some authors even instructed readers to use rods with room-size carpeting. After seaming strips together to form the carpet, one sewed loops of strong tape or cases of linen along the perimeter underneath the carpet. Rods threaded through the loops or cases and fastened to brass rings or hooks in the floor at the corners of the room helped to keep the carpet taut.[57]

The third type of flat-woven carpet commonly used throughout the nineteenth century was ingrain, a reversible, patterned carpet woven on a multiple-harness loom. The weaving process actually produced two separate surfaces joined only where the colors reversed from one side to the other. Between those areas, an ingrain was separate pieces of fabric. Ingrains had several names, including "Kidderminster," "Scotch," "two-ply," and "three-ply," all of which serve to confuse modern readers. The first, "Kidderminster," referred to a town in Worcestershire, near Birmingham, where ingrains were first woven in the early eighteenth century. By the second quarter of the nineteenth century, ingrains were mostly manufactured in Scotland, hence the term "Scotch carpeting," or Yorkshire, which was sometimes distinguished as "English carpeting." The terms "two-ply" and "three-ply" denoted the number of *layers* of fabric in the finished carpet—two or three—and identified the technique employed to weave the material. "Three-plies" were also called "imperials"; they were developed by Thomas Morton of Kilmarnock, Scotland, in 1824 and were in use in America by 1833. The term "ingrain" was used chiefly in America, and referred to the process of dyeing the wool "in the grain" before weaving the carpeting.[58]

Even during the nineteenth century, the use of these terms was vague. Loudon made no clear distinctions, declaring "the kinds of carpets most suitable for cottages are chiefly the Scotch and the Kidderminster, on account of their cheapness." Within a few years, *The Workwoman's Guide* recommended Scotch carpeting for servants' rooms and Kidderminster for sitting rooms and stairs, sugesting that the latter, made in England, was "better" carpeting. By 1839, Ure's *A Dictionary of Arts, Manufactures, and Mines* defined Scotch carpeting as a three-ply imperial and shortly thereafter Webster and Parkes reported a "three imperial Scotch carpet" of superb texture, appearance, and durability woven in Kilmarnock, near Glasgow. Americans distinguished between "two-ply" and "three-ply," the latter considered better quality for its greater durability. Furthermore, three-ply carpeting could use a third color in the design and could have a different pattern on either side of the goods.[59]

From the middle of the eighteenth century, the colonies imported ingrains advertised as "English carpets" and manufactured in nine-, twenty-one-, thirty-six-, and fifty-four-inch widths. However, by the beginning of the nineteenth century, a number of carpet-weaving factories existed in America, particularly in the Philadelphia area. These firms employed mostly English and Scottish weavers working at handlooms. In 1804 a French inventor, Joseph Marie Jacquard (1752–1834), revolutionized the weaving industry by perfecting a loom attachment that could automatically weave a predetermined pattern. Still in use today, the "Jacquard attachment" uses thick paper cards punched with holes that are "read" by steel needles. As the needles pass through the holes they transfer information to hooks that raise and lower the harnesses of the loom, creating the pattern on the goods being woven and eliminating the need for a weaver's assistant. (It was the use of two Jacquard attachments that made it possible for three-ply carpets to have a different pattern on either side.) By 1825, Jacquard attachments were being used on carpet looms in Philadelphia. The American carpet industry remained small until the end of the first quarter of the nineteenth century,

*Cross sections of* (top) *two-ply and* (bottom) *three-ply ingrain weaves, illustrating the reversal of colors from one side to the other. From Fred Bradbury,* Carpet Manufacture. *(The Athenaeum of Philadelphia)*

*This anonymous portrait of a child from about 1830 quite clearly portrays an ingrain carpet on the floor and what must have been a common window treatment, a muslin panel and exterior shutter blinds. (Frank S. Schwarz and Son Gallery, Philadelphia)*

when protective tariffs raised import duties on finished goods, thereby encouraging American manufacturers. By 1832, the Lowell Manufacturing Company mill in Medway, Massachusetts, produced 110,000 yards of carpeting in one year. The Jacquard attachment enabled a single weaver to produce about seven or eight yards of intricately patterned two-ply carpeting a day on a hand-operated loom.[60] (See Plate 6.)

Another boost in production occurred in 1837 when Erastus Bigelow, an impoverished twenty-four-year-old medical student, invented a steam-powered loom for weaving decorative tapes. Within a few years he had adapted steam power to ingrain looms, and, abandoning his medical career,

Left: *An illustration showing the punching and stitching together of a set of cards for a Jacquard attachment. Each card controls the pattern across one weft from selvage to selvage, and a set governs the entire repeat of the pattern.* Right: *A loom to weave ingrain carpeting with two Jacquard attachments in place as illustrated in Andrew Ure,* A Dictionary of Arts, Manufactures, and Mines. *(The Smithsonian Institution, and The Athenaeum of Philadelphia)*

had gone into the carpet business. These early looms produced only a third more yardage per day than did hand-driven ones. However, they solved several problems inherent in handlooms. Machines—never tired, moody, or demanding—produced even selvages and consistent pattern repeats for better matching; they could be operated by less skilled workers who accepted lower pay. By 1841 Bigelow's newly improved power loom wove twenty-five to twenty-seven yards of carpeting per day, a fourfold increase over handlooms. Until the end of the nineteenth century, ingrain accounted for half the total carpeting made in the United States.[61]

Floor coverings denoted more than one's taste, as Alice B. Neal's short story "Furnishing; or, Two Ways of Commencing Life," published in *Godey's Lady's Book* in 1850, illustrates. Two young women, friends since school days, make household purchases prior to their marriages. Anne's fiancé is a struggling country doctor, while Adelaide will marry a promising New York merchant. Following their separate shopping expeditions, the women discuss their carpet purchases. Adelaide asks:

"And what sort of a parlor carpet did you get, *chérie?*"

"A beautiful three ply, wool colors, and green. I thought it would be cheaper, on the whole, than an ingrain."

"Dear me! Mamma chose a velvet at Orne's, and I have Brussels in my own room and the third story. I hate tapestry, they are so common."

"I think those in the parlors are beautiful."

"So I thought; but that was when they first came out. Now they are so cheap that everyone can afford them. A three ply! Why, what sort of chairs and tables are to go with such a carpet?"[62]

Anne chose a three-ply, more expensive than a two-ply but longer wearing and therefore more economical. Adelaide and her mother selected pile carpets, far more costly than Anne's. The production of Brussels, velvet, and tapestry carpets mechanized later than ingrains, keeping prices high—well beyond the reach of the wife of a young country doctor in 1850. (Pile carpets will be discussed in Chapter 2, covering the years 1850 to 1870, when their use became widespread in middle-class homes.)

Anne's three-ply in "wool colors" and green, presumably meant tans, creams, and green, the latter derived from natural—animal, vegetable, or mineral—dyes. Following the advice of critics mentioned earlier, Anne's carpet would have been the darkest value in the room to create balance and to hide soil; it would also be a different hue from the walls. Loudon advised readers, "the colours of the carpet and of the walls will form the principal masses in the composition, and will necessarily influence every other component part. If the floor and the walls were of the same colour, there would be a deficiency of force and of effect, from want of contrast; if they were of different colours, equally attracting the eye, the effect produced would not be that of a whole; because a whole is the result of the cooperation of different subordinate parts with one principal part." (See Plate 7.) To Loudon, color harmony meant a pleasing contrast in colors. He offered examples for his readers: a blue carpet with green walls was *not* in harmony, nor was a crimson carpet with scarlet walls. Instead, he suggested crimson carpeting with drab-tinted walls and draperies decorated with crimson borders and trimmings, or a bright blue carpet with white, yellow, or drab curtains and wallpaper with blue ornaments and borders. Other suggestions included green carpeting and black, red, or white curtains ornamented with green borders. Rooms with yellow carpeting might have black curtains trimmed in yellow and dark gray wallpaper with a yellow border.[63]

One wonders if Adelaide purchased hearth rugs to use in front of fireplaces to protect the carpeting from soil and sparks. Some manufacturers made hearth rugs in designs to complement the patterns of their more expensive products. While Adelaide may have purchased hearth rugs, Anne undoubtedly followed Loudon's advice and made one from a remnant of her three-ply, adding black or brown wool fringe to the edges. Loudon suggested that if no remnant were large enough, a piece of drugget bordered about two inches from the edge in a color used elsewhere in the room would suffice. If Anne further followed Loudon's advice, she chose a carpet with a pattern small in scale for economy and ease in matching seams and because smaller patterns generally fit the proportion of "cottage" rooms. She might even have carpeted two rooms identically so that one could be used to patch the other as they became worn.[64]

The author of *The Workwoman's Guide* offered equally sensible advice: when laying carpeting in a room with a projecting fireplace, slit the carpet on two sides and fold the excess under to expose the hearth. Then if the carpet must be moved to another room, there will be no awkward gaps. Lydia Maria Child told readers of *The American Frugal Housewife* to sweep carpeting with a broom when absolutely necessary; in order to reduce wear, she suggested sweeping crumbs with a hearth brush after meals and picking up sewing threads by hand.[65] These practical hints confirm that carpeting was treated with care to ensure it would last as long as possible. Child's description of a newlywed couple depicts the value assigned carpeting by midcentury:

> There is nothing in which the extravagance of the present day strikes me so forcibly as the manner in which our young people of moderate fortune furnish their houses.
>
> A few weeks since, I called upon a farmer's daughter, who had lately married a young physician of moderate talents, and destitute of fortune. Her father had given her, at her marriage, all he ever expected to give her: viz. two thousand dollars. Yet the lower part of her house was furnished with as much splendor as we usually find among the wealthiest. The whole two thousand dollars had been expended upon Brussels carpets, alabaster vases, mahogany chairs, and marble tables. I afterwards learned that the more useful household utensils had been forgotten; and that, a few weeks after her wedding, she was actually obliged to apply to her husband for money to purchase baskets, iron spoons, clothes-lines, &c.; and her husband, made irritable by the want of money, pettishly demanded why she had bought so many things they did not want. Did the doctor gain any patients, or she a single friend, by offering their visitors water in richly-cut glass tumblers, or serving them with costly damask napkins, instead of plain soft towels? No; their foolish vanity made them less happy, and no more respectable.
>
> Had the young lady been content with Kidderminster carpets, and tasteful vases of her own making, she might have put *one* thousand dollars at interest; and had she obtained six per cent., it would have clothed her as well as the wife of any man, who depends merely upon his own industry, ought to be clothed.[66]

# WINDOWS

"Next to carpets . . . nothing 'furnishes' a room so much as curtains to the windows," Downing wrote, "and this, not merely because they take away from the bareness of plain casings and subdue the glare of light, but because there are always pleasing and graceful lines in the folds of hanging drapery—even of the plainest materials."[67] During the 1830s and 1840s, many homes did not have the elaborate curtains and costly draperies seen in too many museum installations. Instead, English and American writers often recommended "blinds." For homeowners wishing to avoid window treatments that cover the woodwork or cost a great deal, some form of "blinds" may be the solution. But the term "blinds" causes endless confusion today, because at least seven different types of window coverings were so labeled.

## SHUTTER BLINDS AND VENETIAN BLINDS

Wooden blinds constituted a major category for discussion in the works of Loudon, Webster and Parkes, and Downing. All mentioned "shutter blinds" for instance, which they described as a combination shutter and Venetian blind. Loudon labeled them "folding Venetian blinds" in reference to the fixed or movable horizontal slats or "luffers" (louvres) fitted into frames hinged to the window casings. When closed, the shutter blinds allowed the passage of air while providing privacy, shade, and some protection from rain. Loudon encouraged their use, "as it is very desirable, in every house, whether of the poor man or of the rich, to preserve the colour of such expensive articles as window curtains and carpets, and to exclude flies, which totally destroy gilt picture-frames, and gnats, which are a personal annoyance, all houses that can afford it ought to have either shutter-blinds, or some description of outside blinds." English authors considered them for exterior use, but Downing believed that all American country houses should have "Venetian shutters" either inside or outside the windows, making curtains unnecessary from May to November. He added that the type of house determined shutter style. Exterior "Venetian shutters" were appropriate on Venetian, Tuscan, or Italian styles. Exterior shutters were generally considered inappropriate on "pointed" (domestic Gothic) or English styles (particularly if the windows contained Gothic tracery), chiefly because critics believed that shutters designed to cover pointed or arched windows looked peculiar when opened. In these cases, Downing proposed interior shutters which folded into the window casings when not in use. On the plain windows of a simple Gothic house, however, one could use exterior shutters, painted or stained a rich brown or dark oak color so as not to appear too "Venetian."

Other popular colors included green, stone, or cream.[68]

"Shutter blinds," "Venetian folding blinds," and "Venetian shutters" should not be confused with another type of window treatment with a similar name, "Venetian blinds." Oddly, Downing made no mention of this window treatment even though it had been used in America since the mid-eighteenth century. English writers suggested Venetian blinds inside or outside the windows of "better" cottages and villas. Chains linked the wooden laths of exterior blinds, and framing surrounded the entire blind to prevent it from blowing in the wind. Finally, a wooden cornice housed the pulley mechanism and the blinds when retracted. Interior blinds, of course, used cloth tapes and needed no framing; however, decorative cornices in wood or pierced tin often surmounted them. While green was a popular choice for interior blinds (see Plate 8), other colors were used; for example, a set painted terra cotta and yellow survives in the Wolcott House in Maumee, Ohio.[69]

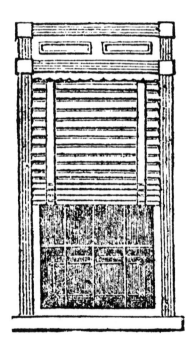

Left: *Wooden-slatted Venetian blinds complete with a decorative valance, as illustrated in Thomas Webster and Mrs. Parkes,* An Encyclopedia of Domestic Economy. Right: *A nearly identical version for exterior use, in the c. 1910 catalogue of the James G. Wilson Manufacturing Co., New York. According to the manufacturer, the blinds ran in grooves so they would not rattle in the breeze. (The Athenaeum of Philadelphia)*

## AWNINGS

Writers also characterized awnings as blinds. Loudon described one type made of wooden laths as a "Venetian fan blind," and another made of strong linen as a "bonnet blind" patented in 1826. Iron frames projecting on either side of the window held the cloth or laths steady; when not in use the blinds retracted into a cornice box at the top of the window. *Godey's Lady's Book* described the wooden variety in 1831 but added they were more common in France than in England or America, where shutters were more popular.[70]

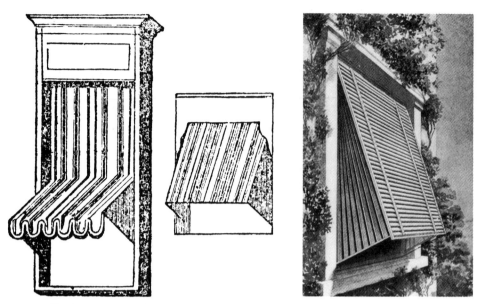

"Bonnet blinds" were also included in design books of the second quarter of the nineteenth century. Left: A canvas or linen blind illustrated in Webster and Parkes, An Encyclopedia of Domestic Economy. Loudon described blinds made of wooden laths, in An Encyclopedia of Cottage, Farm, and Villa Architecture and Furniture. The set illustrated here (right) is from the c. 1910 catalogue of the James G. Wilson Manufacturing Co., New York. (The Athenaeum of Philadelphia)

Fabric "bonnet blinds" on the residence of F. Cottenet, near Dobbs Ferry, New York, illustrated in Villas on the Hudson (New York, 1860). The tent roof over the second-floor window was painted to match. (Dornsife Collection of the Victorian Society in America at The Athenaeum of Philadelphia)

## WIRE BLINDS AND SHORT BLINDS

Loudon and Webster and Parkes wrote of "wire blinds," a term used to describe woven wire or wire gauze stretched in a wooden frame and placed at the window casing to exclude insects. Loudon identified such blinds as intended for use inside the windows of better cottages or villas. Because wire-mesh blinds would rust, these writers suggested that they be decoratively painted. Loudon proposed they be "ornamented with landscapes, figures, or other objects; or, in the case of a country tradesman, in a roadside cottage, they may exhibit the owner's name, or the implements or products of his trade." Downing made no mention of wire blinds, and American advertisements for them didn't begin to appear commonly until the fourth quarter of the nineteenth century.[71]

*One of a series of painted window screens located in the library and dining room of the Senator Justin Smith Morrill Homestead in Strafford, Vermont. The screens are thought to date from 1860, when additions were made to the house. (Vermont Division of Historic Preservation; photograph by Gordon Sweet)*

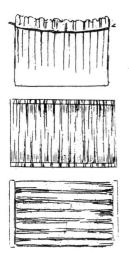

*Three different styles of "short blinds" illustrated in* The Workwoman's Guide. *(Dornsife Collection of the Victorian Society in America at The Athenaeum of Philadelphia)*

American homeowners of this period seem to have favored other techniques to exclude insects during the warmer months of the year, such as "short blinds" placed in the lower half of windows "to prevent seeing in." These curtains were hemmed at top and bottom and gathered onto brass rods fitted into brackets on either side of the window frame or simply threaded onto wire or string and fastened to brass hooks on either side of the window. One could make "short blinds" of muslin, gauze, chintz, or any "leno" fabric—meaning a loosely woven material in which each warp and weft thread interlock for dimensional stability. Loudon also suggested that housewives "net" them in white cotton or green worsted. Although Downing did not mention "short blinds," they certainly were used in America; *Godey's Lady's Book* printed many patterns for lace work and netting adaptable for this use. In the story "Country Boarding" by Timothy Shay Arthur, a husband whose family has taken rooms in the country for the summer rides back to the city to fetch "gauze frames for the window to keep out bats and bugs at night" after spending a sleepless night in a country house lacking such equipment. Since several other stories of the period contain such references, one suspects that "short blinds" appeared more often in city houses than in country ones.[72]

*A "short blind" hangs at the window in* The Image Pedlar *by Francis W. Edmonds (c. 1850–58). The bottle hanging nearby is probably a bug catcher filled with any one of a variety of mixtures guaranteed to be effective by countless columns of household hints in magazines such as* Godey's Lady's Book. *(The New-York Historical Society)*

## ROLLER BLINDS

Perhaps the most common window covering throughout the nineteenth century was the "roller blind." It was inexpensive, could be made at home, blocked direct sunlight, offered privacy, and gave some protection from insects. Comparing roller blinds to Venetian and wire blinds, Loudon praised them as cheaper and more suitable for "common cottages." Pulley-operated roller blinds were used through much of the nineteenth century, although spring-operated blinds date to the 1830s. Those with springs were more expensive and Webster and Parkes complained they were prone to malfunction. Since the first American factory producing spring rollers did not begin operation until 1858, the pulley method was the type most commonly employed in this country through the middle of the century. (See the illustration on page 99.) While linen was the most typical fabric for blinds, lawn, Holland, calico, painted print, green canvas, gauze, and calimanco were also used. *The Workwoman's Guide* gave the following directions for making roller blinds:

> If possible, procure the material of the exact breadth of the window, allowing for a good turning in, to herring-bone down, as the blinds wear and set far better without seams, and with the side herring-boned. They should have tape loops or a case for the rod to slip in, and not be nailed on, as the blind is so apt to wear and tear when taken off for washing. Sometimes a small ring is fastened to the blind at the bottom on each side, through which a cord runs, and is nailed tightly top and bottom of the window, this contrivance always makes the blind draw up straightly. A hem is made at the bottom, to admit of the stick, and a cord and tassel generally fastened to the middle, by which it may be drawn down. A cord moving round a pulley at the top, and window crank at the bottom, enable it to be drawn up and down at pleasure.

Throughout the nineteenth century, *Godey's Lady's Book* provided illustrated directions for crocheting roller-blind tassels.[73]

Downing recommended plain brown or drab linen as superior material for roller blinds, but many nineteenth-century examples were more ornamental. Loudon and Webster and Parkes all described linen shades decorated with designs painted in transparent colors. Loudon recommended imitations of stained glass and landscapes, to which Webster and Parkes added interior views of buildings or arabesque patterns. Surviving examples of American window shades from the 1830s and 1840s suggest that landscapes, perhaps inspired by scenic wallpapers of the time, were the most popular designs. Patterns at first covered the entire shade but by the 1840s decorative borders commonly framed the central design (see illustration on page 46). Downing condemned both types as "vulgar." He grumbled, "if they are badly painted, as is generally the case, they are . . . an offense to cultivated taste; if they are well painted, . . . they only hide . . . a more interesting view of the real landscape without. Such specimens of the arts as these may be tolerated in towns," he grudgingly admitted, "as they awaken a sentiment of nature in the midst of brick walls. . . ."[74]

Nineteenth-century householders sometimes substituted paper for painted fabric roller blinds. Manufacturers produced "curtain papers" in fairly standard widths of about thirty-five inches, containing a repeat of approximately 1½ yards. This product was cut and trimmed to fit roller blinds. Surviving examples suggest that householders may also have trimmed and pasted pieces of wallpaper onto paper strips, thus creating their own patterned shades. *Godey's Lady's Book* took note of these blinds when, reviewing the wonderful fabrics in a Philadelphia drapery shop, the writer commented they "would astonish the residents of villages, where wall-paper blinds are still in vogue."[75]

*A painted window shade, c. 1840, in which the landscape is framed by a decorative border rather than stretching edge to edge, as was generally the case earlier in the century. (Chester County Historical Society, West Chester, Pennsylvania)*

# A WORD ABOUT BLINDS

Exterior shutters are probably the most misunderstood element on the exterior of American buildings. To be practical they must be closable; yet many exterior shutters are now permanently affixed in the "open" position. Even if they were to close, the size of most replacement shutters prevents them from covering the window. The scale is incorrect and consequently the façade is ruined. When fitting Victorian houses with replacement shutters, many of today's homeowners also overlook the fact that most nineteenth-century houses used solid-paneled shutters on the ground floor—for security—and louvered shutters above that level for ventilation. Many homeowners unwittingly install the louvered shutters backward, so that if they were closed during a rainstorm the slant of the louvers would direct the rain into rather than away from the interior of the house!

Fewer problems are encountered with interior shutters. If there are indentations from hinges or an empty box recess on the interior window casing, the chances are the house once had interior blinds. Wooden shutter blinds can be found at suppliers of used building materials, and most custom planing mills will manufacture them. Once installed, the wooden shutter blinds should be stained to match the interior woodwork or painted so as not to be conspicuous from the outside of the house when covering the windows.

Fortunately, wooden-slatted Venetian blinds can again be purchased in widths varying from 1³⁄₈ to 2³⁄₈ inches, stained or painted a variety of colors, or custom finished. Cotton twill tapes also come in many colors and, of course, a more decorative tape can be stitched over those supplied by the manufacturer. The decorative cornices found over nineteenth-century Venetian blinds can be made today by any skilled cabinetmaker or tinsmith and painted to match the blinds.

Canvas awnings are also available and should be considered for the windows that receive the most direct sunlight. Striped materials are appropriate for Victorian houses since they imitate the desired "tented" effect. Nineteenth-century critics recommended "cool" colors, such as blues and greens, and generally avoided reds as appearing too "hot"; their advice is still good. Needless to say, plastic or aluminum awnings are not appropriate on nineteenth-century houses.

The common use of wire blinds (window screens) today eliminates part of the need for "short blinds" but city residents may still find them useful for privacy. The brass rods recommended by Webster and Parkes will probably be more appealing to most modern homeowners than wire or string, although museum houses should certainly consider the latter alternatives.

Finally, roller blinds made of muslin, rather than the opaque, plastic-coated styles so popular in recent years, can still be purchased. Today's spring-mounted blinds are fine for private home use but are not acceptable for a museum house of the first three-quarters of the nineteenth century; during that time pulley-operated blinds were used in America. Painted window shades are not manufactured today and the few old shades that survive are too fragile for use. New shades may be custom painted using transparent colors; or designs from wallpapers may be pasted onto the shades as was done during the nineteenth century.

## WINDOW CURTAINS

*Two examples of simple window curtains suitable for every cottage, "however humble," according to John Claudius Loudon. One pair of curtains has simply been tacked to the architrave of the window. Both pairs were illustrated in Webster and Parkes,* An Encyclopedia of Domestic Economy. *(The Athenaeum of Philadelphia)*

Curtains, wrote Loudon, "give such an air of comfort to a room, whether it be to the spectator from without, or to the occupant within, that we could wish no cottage, however humble, to be without them." And, he continued, "For the same reason, we should wish cottage windows to be large, that the curtains may be displayed without too much obstructing the light." The simplest curtain Loudon suggested was merely a piece of calico, sized to the window, hanging from small rings sewn along the top, threaded onto a cord nailed to either side of the window casing. One could even make it a draw curtain by using two cords—one hung from the leftmost ring while the second, also tied to that ring, was threaded through all the others and hung from the right side of the panel; the cord on the right drew the panel open while the one on the left closed it. For a fancier look, one might tack a "little frill or valance" at the top of the panel covering the rings and cords. Webster and Parkes also recommended inexpensive curtains made up of fabric panels tacked directly to the window architrave and looped back with a piece of cord. A second type was a "Venetian curtain," a style used in the eighteenth century, which operated much like a modern "Roman shade." Webster and Parkes's mention of them suggests that they, like swags, remained in use well into the nineteenth century.[76]

Today's homeowner, believing all nineteenth-century windows were heavily—if not overly—draped and being fearful of costs, should take heart from Loudon's suggestion. Of course, rich fabrics executed in wonderful, often French, designs hung at the windows of the homes of the affluent during the 1830s and 1840s. However, Loudon, Webster and Parkes, Downing, *The Workwoman's Guide,* and *Godey's Lady's Book* all addressed a middle-class readership who generally could *not* afford such window treatments. None-

*Three methods of covering windows employed during the eighteenth and early nineteenth centuries.* Left: *A "Venetian curtain," mentioned by Webster and Parkes in* An Encyclopedia of Domestic Economy. Center *and* right: *Festoons, later known as swags. The drawings show the placement of tapes and rings along the back of the fabric panels and the effect achieved when drawn up. (Drawings by Gail Winkler, adapted from a sketch by Jonathan Fairbanks)*

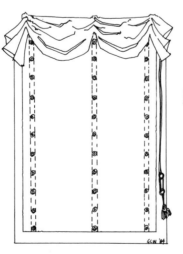

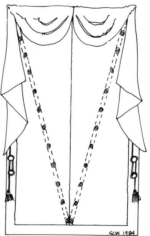

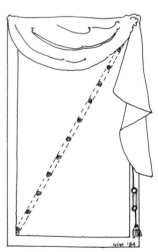

theless, Loudon encouraged his readers that "Window curtains give the mistress of the house an excellent opportunity for exercising her taste in their arrangement . . ." and suggested that, like the French, his readers might count on style, rather than expensive fabrics, to achieve superior effects. Muslins, cottons, and sheer leno weaves could all produce successful curtains; in the end, the manner of curtaining was more important than the material used.[77]

A fully draped nineteenth-century window consisted of a *cornice*, a *drapery* or *valance* (also spelled "vallance," "valence," and "vallens"), and one or more *curtains*. In the 1840s, the cornice was generally a painted, gilded, or stained pole or narrow decorative panel attached by screws to the molding or architrave at the top of the window. The fabric drapery or valance hung below the cornice—attached by rings, tacks, or tenterhooks—but over the curtain(s). Curtains were the panels of fabric hanging in front of the window and extending to the floor; they could be stationary or movable, depending upon the desires of the homeowner and the method of installation. Naturally, homeowners could omit one or more of these elements according to taste or finances.

The simplest treatment consisted of two curtain panels suspended from

*Curtains and valances illustrated in John Claudius Loudon,* An Encyclopedia of Cottage, Farm, and Villa Architecture and Furniture. *Bands are used to loop back the curtains shown at left, while pins with decorative heads serve that function in the picture on the right. In* The Architecture of Country Houses, *Andrew Jackson Downing illustrated a valance nearly identical to the one in the righthand picture, identifying it as "Gothic"; the type on the left, he explained, would be "Grecian"; while a valance with a rounded curve would be "Italian." (The Athenaeum of Philadelphia)*

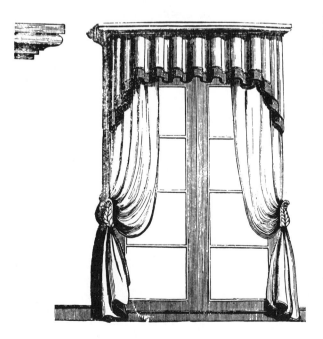
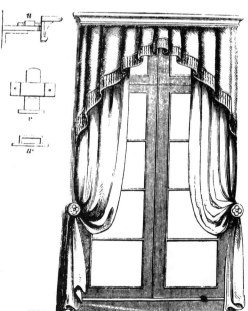

brass rings or bronzed iron rings threaded onto a round wooden pole supported by brackets that were screwed to the window architrave. The poles and brackets were often painted, stained, or grained to match the woodwork behind them. Each ring held an eyelet into which the curtain hook was inserted. Loudon estimated that the curtains for an average six-over-six double-sash window would require fourteen rings. One could draw these curtains across the window by hand or loop them back in graceful swags over brass bands, brass or wooden pins, or lengths of ribbon attached to knobs. A second set of curtain panels in sheer muslin was sometimes used next to the window. Illustrations frequently show this second set looped back, but since their use was to soften the sunlight, to prevent fading of colors in the room, and to exclude insects, the muslin curtains probably hung over the windows in daily use.[78]

Nineteenth-century sources indicate that these simple curtains required a minimum of fabric. *The Workwoman's Guide* recommended two widths of fabric for a six-over-six window, while a larger window, four or five panes wide, needed 2½ or three widths. Since early-nineteenth-century fabrics were commonly twenty-two to thirty-six inches wide, the curtains described required less fabric than modern practice dictates.[79] One reason was the general absence of pinch pleats, which were not used on curtain panels until the end of the nineteenth century; instead, pins were inserted vertically into the unpleated fabric along the top of the curtains. When drawn back, the fabric fell into natural folds; when drawn over the window, the fabric stretched nearly straight. *The Workwoman's Guide* suggested that the finished length

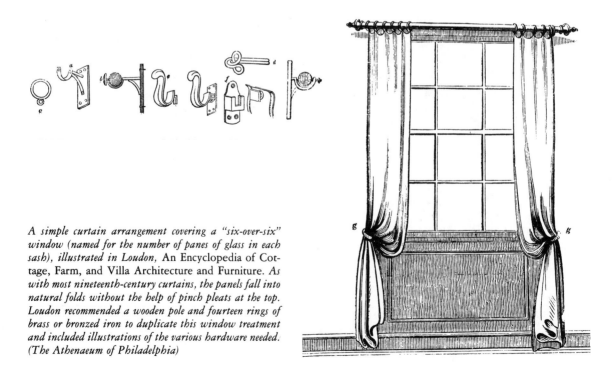

*A simple curtain arrangement covering a "six-over-six" window (named for the number of panes of glass in each sash), illustrated in Loudon,* An Encyclopedia of Cottage, Farm, and Villa Architecture and Furniture. *As with most nineteenth-century curtains, the panels fall into natural folds without the help of pinch pleats at the top. Loudon recommended a wooden pole and fourteen rings of brass or bronzed iron to duplicate this window treatment and included illustrations of the various hardware needed. (The Athenaeum of Philadelphia)*

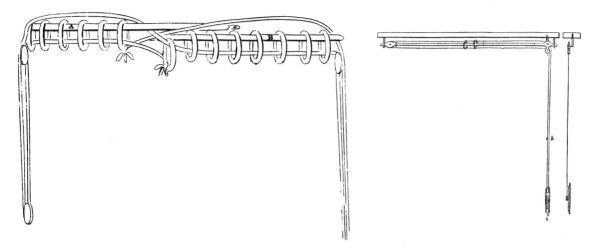

*Pulley rods of the type used throughout the nineteenth century, from* (left) The Work-woman's Guide *and* (right) Loudon, An Encyclopedia of Cottage, Farm, and Villa Architecture and Furniture. *(Dornsife Collection of the Victorian Society in America at The Athenaeum of Philadelphia)*

of a curtain should be "six to eight nails" *longer* than the distance from pole to floor (a "nail" is 2¼ inches). The additional thirteen to eighteen inches enabled the bottom hem of the curtain just to skim the floor *when looped back.* The extra material "puddled" on the floor only when the curtains were drawn over the window to help block drafts.[80]

Most curtains were drawn by hand. Beginning about 1800, however, households willing to pay more might purchase a "French rod," which operated by a pulley system much like modern theater curtains. The curtains hung from hooks attached to rings on a brass, iron, or hardwood pole suspended under the window architrave. A cord passing over the pole attached to the innermost ring of the right panel, passed through a pulley on the left side of the pole, and returned to the right side, where it attached to the innermost ring of the left panel. Pulling the cord made the curtain panels open or close simultaneously. The method was slow to take hold; as late as 1845 Webster and Parkes argued that a pulley system was the "best method" while admitting that a pole with rings was the "general method at present, in the better sort of rooms."[81]

A still more ornate window treatment required a cornice and valance or drapery above the curtains—incidentally covering the unattractive pulley system. There were other considerations as well. Loudon, quoting the English designer and architect A. W. N. Pugin, explained that the purpose of curtains—to exclude drafts—could not be accomplished while space remained at the top of the curtains allowing cold air to circulate. He urged householders to attach a "boxing of wood" above the curtains "in front of which a valance is suspended to exclude air."[82]

Here we must consider two important—and potentially confusing—terms:

"valance" and "drapery." Both hang above curtain panels. Nineteenth-century critics termed fabric hanging in vertical folds from a pole or cornice a "valance" and fabric draped over a pole to lie in somewhat horizontal folds parallel to the floor a "drapery." Draperies required the skill of an upholsterer; consequently critics addressing a middle-class audience disapproved of them. Loudon again cited Pugin on the subject: "All the modern plans of suspending enormous folds of stuff over poles, as if for the purpose of a sale or of being dried, is quite contrary to the use and intentions of curtains, and . . . abominable in taste; and the only object that these endless festoons and bunchy tassels can answer is, to swell the bills and profits of the upholsterers, who are the inventors of these extravagant and ugly draperies, which are not only useless in protecting the chamber from cold, but are the depositories of thick layers of dust, and in London not unfrequently become the strongholds of vermin."[83]

Webster and Parkes attributed draperies to France, noting they were "introduced some years ago, as being much richer and more elegant than ours," but adding, *"one inconvenience in the elegant French draperies* was the great skill and taste required to put them up well; and it is said that the cutting out of this part of upholsterer's work was kept as much as possible a secret, and seldom taught, even to their apprentices." They concluded, "valances are more generally put up" than draperies.[84]

While valances required less labor and less material than draperies, they were not as easy to produce as advocates claimed. A flat piece of material attached to the cornice was the easiest, as cutting patterns included in *The Upholsterer's Accelerator* by Thomas King, an English draper and upholsterer, illustrate. During the 1830s and 1840s, this style was variously labeled "straight" or "plain" or "geometric" valances. By midcentury, Americans used the term "lambrequin" when describing these valances. Householders also hung another design, the "piped valance," from rings or cornices. Whether hung from rings or cornices, the fabric fell in easy folds much like curtains. However, when using a cornice, the fabric was first arranged in folds and then nailed to a lath, which was attached to the inside of the cornice, or else the fabric was attached directly to the cornice by tenterhooks. The results were termed a "plaited drapery or valance." By the 1840s, "piped valance" was the usual label.[85]

While many critics took a strong stand against draperies, many magazines and books illustrated them along with valances. *Godey's Lady's Book* printed four hand-colored plates of fashionable draperies over curtains in 1839 but nine years later published Loudon's examples of piped valances. Downing, a disciple of Loudon, included only piped valances in *The Architecture of Country Houses.*

One nineteenth-century rule regarding window coverings survives today. The height of the window should determine the length of the drapery or

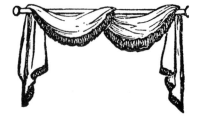

*Webster and Parkes labeled this drapery a "festoon" in* An Encyclopedia of Domestic Economy. *They explained, "the festoon itself is called the* swag, *and the end that hands down is termed the* tail." *Critics agreed that draperies such as these required the skill of an upholsterer to execute. (The Athenaeum of Philadelphia)*

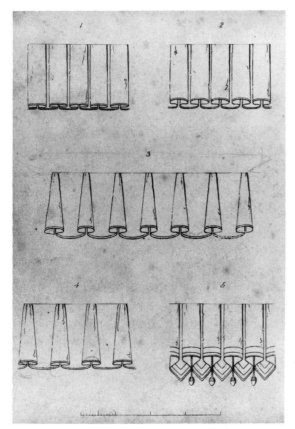
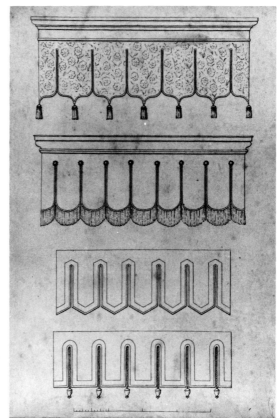

*Valances of the type recommended by Loudon, Webster and Parkes, and Downing, including* (left) *"piped valances" and* (right) *"geometric valances," known in America as "lambrequins." These valances were illustrated in Thomas King,* The Upholsterer's Accelerator *(c. 1830–1840), which Webster and Parkes mention in* An Encyclopedia of Domestic Economy. *(The Henry Francis duPont Winterthur Museum Library, Collection of Printed Books)*

valance; a short valance tops a short window so as not to exclude light or view; a longer valance suits the proportions of a taller window. To achieve the effect of high windows, the valance may be carried above the window architrave. Modern owners of old houses often avoid this technique in the misguided belief that the window architrave should always be exposed to view. The original owners of the house probably had no such values and covered the window surround with curtains and draperies, unless the architrave was exceptionally ornate and obviously intended to be seen.

As to whether a valance or drapery is the more appropriate choice, *either* technique is correct for a house built in the 1830s or 1840s. Naturally the style should fit the architecture of the house; Downing believed that curtain style—Gothic, Grecian, or Italian—basically depended upon the molding profile of the cornice or the cut of the valance. (See the illustration on page 49.)

The curtain and drapery hardware should also be considered. Grand houses

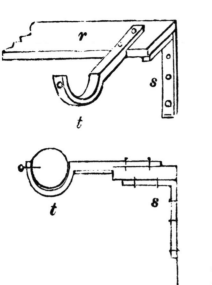

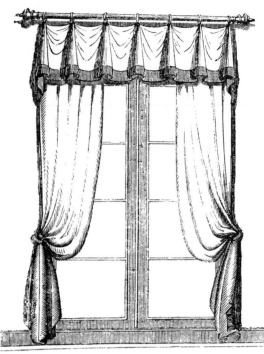

*A window treatment employing a "piped valance" suspended from a rod attached to the boxing (as shown in the two line drawings on the near right) recommended by Loudon (and Pugin) to prevent drafts. Illustrated in Loudon, An Encyclopedia of Cottage, Farm, and Villa Architecture and Furniture. (The Athenaeum of Philadelphia)*

often had pressed brass or gilded gesso (plaster of Paris) finishes, while average homes used painted, stained, or grained cornices or poles, to match the other woodwork in the room. Whatever the modern homeowner elects to do, modern traverse rods are *not appropriate* for houses erected before the second quarter of the twentieth century. If it is important to have draw curtains, one might recreate the original hardware or simply draw the curtains by hand, a technique common throughout the nineteenth century. Wooden rings and rods are readily available today and may be finished with paint, stain, graining, or even metallic pastes to replicate bronze or gilt finishes.

## CURTAIN MATERIALS

Window curtains, draperies, and valances were produced in a variety of materials, all employing natural fibers—linen, silk, cotton, and wool. Since silk was quite expensive, and the woolen industry lagged behind the cotton industry in America until the second half of the century, most middle-class houses probably used more cotton fabrics than other fibers at windows.

A limited number of fibers did not indicate a limited number of weaves or finishing techniques. During the first half of the nineteenth century, frequently mentioned materials for draperies and curtains included damask, satin, moreen (a woolen fabric pressed between rollers to achieve a watered appearance), lustring or lutestring (a crisp, glossy silk fabric), tabaret (another silk fabric with alternating satin and watered-silk stripes), chintz (cotton printed in five or more colors and often glazed), dimity (a bleached cotton generally woven in stripes), and calicoes (printed cotton), in addition to muslin curtains, which hung at the window under the heavier curtains.[86]

The best rooms in the best houses obviously called for the richest materials, such as the damask draperies with "bullion" fringe containing silk drops illustrated by Loudon for villas. Less affluent households used moreens, calicoes, chintzes, and dimities—Webster and Parkes warned readers to avoid stiff, highly glazed fabrics that would not drape well—and embellished them with fringes or borders in colors harmonizing with those already selected for the room. Loudon instructed his readers that fringes should only be applied at the edge of the fabric, since the origin of fringe was the tying of cut edges of selvages to prevent further unraveling. Fringe was suitable on moreen or dimity; on chintz or calico, writers recommended a border composed of strips of single-colored, glazed calico about 1½ inches wide sewn on about two inches from the edge. These borders were removed before laundering the drapery since many nineteenth-century dyes were not colorfast.[87]

Part of the rich appearance of nineteenth-century curtains depended upon proper lining and interlining. The interlining was a layer of flannel that furnished extra protection from the sun, blocked winter's drafts, and contributed to the proper "hang" of the curtains. Interlining was most common on heavier weaves, such as damask, velvet, and the like—and on the most expensive fibers, such as wool and silk. It was rarely used with cottons.

An important shift in fabric choice and use occurred between 1830 and 1850. In 1833, Loudon urged that the window fabrics should be *identical* in color and pattern to the other fabrics in the room, such as upholstery or bed hangings. In libraries or dining rooms where there were no other fabrics, the colors at the windows should match the woodwork; Loudon suggested that red, brown, or scarlet went well with mahogany furniture, while light-colored fabrics were better with oak. However, by 1844, Webster and Parkes stated that the fabrics at the windows should *not* be *identical* to those elsewhere in the room. They recommended that the window fabrics should accord in richness and "harmonize" with the others, which did "not mean they should correspond, or be the same but that there should not be any violent contrasts, and that the colours should agree with each other." Downing suggested that window hangings harmonize with other colors in the room, specifically those on the wall and in the carpet.[88]

## *Where to Hang Curtains*

As to where curtains hung in the house, *The Workwoman's Guide* advised, "it is desirable to have as little window drapery as possible to family or secondary rooms, particularly nurseries and servants' rooms, on account of their liability to catch fire, especially as toilet tables are so often situated within the window. In an upper story, curtains might be dispensed with, using only the valance." However, parlors, dining rooms, and master bedrooms were likely to have draperies and curtains; the last perhaps a holdover from the eighteenth-century practice of entertaining guests in the best bedchamber. There were also rules governing the fibers used in curtains. Most writers recommended using only cotton fabrics in cottage bedrooms. Loudon was adamant: "Moreens and other woolen stuffs should never be used . . . as they have not only too heavy an appearance for a small room, but are liable to harbour dust and vermin." Through most of the eighteenth century, woolens had been the most popular fabrics for bedrooms, possibly because they are naturally fireproof—wool smolders but will not flame once the source of the fire is removed. However, since shrinkage made cleaning of wool difficult, woolen curtains were seldom laundered, encouraging the problems Loudon mentioned. The Victorian discovery of flame-retardant processes for cotton—such as rinsing in a solution of alum and water—popularized washable cotton fabrics, such as chintz and dimity, for bedrooms.[89]

### Bed Hangings

In England and America, the best bedsteads—the wooden frame holding the mattress—were either four-posts, tents, or "French." All three required hangings matching the color, fabric, and style of the window treatments. *The Workwoman's Guide* advised, "beds that are furnished with thick drapery,

## FIBERS AND WEAVES

All materials consist of some sort of *fiber*. Before the twentieth century and the advent of synthetic fibers such as rayon, nylon, and polyester, all materials consisted of natural fibers, the most common being cotton, linen, wool, silk, and horsehair. If one is striving for an absolutely authentic restoration, materials made of natural fibers must be selected. However, where authenticity can be sacrificed for appearance or must be sacrificed for price, materials made of modern fibers offer successful substitutes. For instance, rayon can imitate the sheen of silk for far less money.

All fabrics are made by one or more *construction techniques*. During the nineteenth century, these were: single-element weave, two-element weave, and three-element weave. A single-element weave consists of a single continuous strand, such as knitting, crocheting, netting, and some laces.

Two-element construction produces a woven fabric in which the warp threads (running the length of the loom) and the weft threads (running the width of the loom) interlace at right angles to one another. The most common two-element weave is called "plain" or "taffeta" weave, in which one warp thread crosses one weft thread, producing, for example, muslin. If two warp threads cross two weft threads the result is a variation of the plain weave known as basket weave, as in hopsacking. If extra strands are added

*The three most popular "best" bedsteads during the years 1830 to 1850 were identified by Loudon as (left) the "four-post bedstead," (center) the "French bedstead," and (right) the "tent bedstead." These bedsteads were not universally used in England or America: the vast majority of people probably slept in simple, uncurtained bedsteads. The illustrations are from Loudon,* An Encyclopedia of Cottage, Farm, and Villa Architecture and Furniture. *(The Athenaeum of Philadelphia)*

in only the warp or the weft, the resulting fabric appears ribbed in one direction, producing a fabric such as rep or grosgrain. A two-element weave in which the warp and weft threads float over two or more strands produces a diagonal interlace across the material known as twill. Most twills are woven at a forty-five-degree angle that may move from right to left or left to right on the face of the goods. A regularly spaced reversal of a twill weave produces a "herringbone." Finally a two-element weave in which warp threads float over a number of weft threads and under one produces satin.

Three-element weave uses either two wefts and one warp or the reverse. The extra weft or warp creates a pattern supplemental to the basic weave of the cloth. Velvets and brocades are examples of three-element construction.

In addition to a variety of construction techniques, certain *finishing techniques* are used to create specific fabrics. Woolens, for example, are finished by "fulling" (shrinking), "calendaring" (pressing through rollers), or "napping" (brushing). The method of application of each technique results in a specific fabric. For example, woolens pressed between two hot, embossed rollers results in a self-patterned fabric known as "moreen." Cottons may be "glazed," a technique using wax or resin and hot rollers and producing a shiny finish typical of polished cotton and most chintz.

such as stuff, moreen, damask or linens, seldom, if ever, require linings, while chintzes and sometimes dimities are lined with glazed calico, in which case, care should be taken that the colour of the lining harmonizes not only with the bed-furniture, but with the papering of the room. The fringe, tassels, ribbons, cord, and other decorations, should match in colour with the lining. The pattern of the material should also be a consideration. Stripes or small patterns are suitable for small rooms, while large flowers or patterns best accord with large ones."[90]

Curtaining a bedstead required a large amount of material. A fully draped four-post bed used over fifty yards of fabric and a tent bed forty-three yards. The hangings—called "bed furniture"—of a four-post bed included a head-cloth, valance, tester (canopy), and side panels that could be drawn completely around the bed. A drapery or ornate valance generally hung along the outside of the bed, attached by rings to metal rods, covering the tops of the curtains. However, a "straight" valance or one made of deep fringe might hang inside the cornice, requiring an ornate rod of larger diameter to hold the curtains. Optional linings and trimmings also added to the cost of these bed hangings.[91]

Labor was another consideration. Some beds were easier to drape than others; a householder could drape a tent bed or "French bed" with a pole attached to hold the panels, particularly if the material was unlined. The draperies for a four-post bed might be more complex, as were the ornate coronets over some French bedsteads; both required the skills of an upholsterer to execute well. Since 85 percent of the American population lived in the country at midcentury, and only a handful of urban residents could afford such services, we can assume that fully draped four-post beds and ornately composed French bedsteads were the exceptions, not the norm, in most American houses in the 1830s and 1840s.

*The hangings for the tent bedstead in the Towne House at Old Sturbridge Village, Sturbridge, Massachusetts, required about forty-three yards of twenty-five-inch fabric, according to nineteenth-century sources. (Old Sturbridge Village; photograph by Henry E. Peach)*

*The bedsteads, bed furniture, and bedding illustrated in* The Workwoman's Guide *give some indication of the variety available. The bottom row pictures various methods of supporting a mattress of hair or straw. (Dornsife Collection of the Victorian Society in America at The Athenaeum of Philadelphia)*

## 2

# THE 1850 TO 1870 PERIOD

At the turn of the century, the United States was not yet a global power, though it had become a nation far different from Thomas Jefferson's land of yeoman farmers. But much change was in store for the United States between 1850 and 1870. The country described as a "magnificent spectacle of human happiness" by the *Edinburgh Review* (1824) had, by 1865, endured a bitter civil war in which more Americans died than in any war in our history. In this era America lost its innocence and launched into a period of unprecedented growth in all sectors of life—growth accompanied by cynical optimism.

"Manifest Destiny," a phrase first used in 1845 to justify the annexation of Texas, captured the public's imagination and became the cry for the westward expansion demanded by a growing population. Between 1850 and 1870 the population nearly doubled, from 23 million to 40 million, with immigration accounting for only a quarter of that number. The urban population slowly increased to about 20 percent of the total, while the number of places classed as urban rose dramatically, from 392 to 939 between 1860 and 1870 alone. Oregon and Minnesota becames states, followed by Kansas, Nebraska, Nevada, and West Virginia, making thirty-seven in all by 1870.

Urban growth notwithstanding, the frontier was never far away. In September 1850, the Swedish writer Fredrika Bremer reached Chicago in her tour of the United States. She described the city in a letter to her sister, reporting that it had a population of twenty-five thousand. Bremer was staying in a villa along the shores of Lake Michigan, but one day she and some friends traveled eighteen miles into the countryside by wagon, where they visited the inhabitants of a log cabin. Bremer described the year-old cabin as "tolerably open to the weather, but clean and orderly within."[1]

Travel in many parts of America remained difficult. After visiting Chicago

*The stair hall of the Ebenezer Maxwell Mansion in Philadelphia. (The Ebenezer Maxwell Mansion, Inc., Germantown, Philadelphia, Pennsylvania; photograph by Louis Meehan)*

Bremer went north to Milwaukee by lake steamer and then set off to Water-town, Wisconsin, by coach. She wrote of this leg of the journey:

> I was shaken, or rather hurled, unmercifully hither and thither upon the new-born roads of Wisconsin, which are no roads at all, but a succession of hills, and holes, and water-pools, in which first one wheel sank and then the other, while the opposite one stood high in the air. Sometimes the carriage came to a sudden stand-still, half overturned in a hole, only to be thrown into the same position on the other side. . . . Sometimes we drove for a considerable distance in the water, so deep that I expected to see the whole equipage either swim or sink altogether. And when we reached dry land, it was only to take the most extraordinary leaps over rocks and stones. They comforted me by telling me that the diligence [public stage coach] was not in the habit of being upset very often![2]

Although roads remained primitive, America at midcentury ushered in the age of the railroad. Canals had carried twice as much as railroads in 1852; however, by 1859 railroads carried two billion ton-miles (a measure meaning a ton of freight moved one mile), and surpassed canals by 25 percent. No new canals were built after this decade, although those in operation continued to carry goods. Railroads could be constructed cheaper and faster than canals; they were not as limited by geography, nor as impeded by winter weather. Railroads were generally safer than steamboats; fully 30 percent of the steamboats built before midcentury were lost, mainly in explosions. (In fact, Andrew Jackson Downing, the architectural critic so often quoted in Chapter 1, lost his life in 1852 when the steamboat *Henry Clay* burned while racing the *Armenia* on the Hudson River.)

By 1870 America had 52,922 miles of track, 43,901 laid after 1850. On May 10, 1869, the Central Pacific and the Union Pacific lines joined at Promontory Point, Utah, to complete the first transcontinental railroad. The echoes of Leland Stanford's silver hammer striking the last spike (made of gold) reverberated in American mills, shops, and homes from coast to coast. The host of goods that had already homogenized the look of American homes east of the Mississippi—ready-mixed paints in resealable cans, richly cast lighting fixtures, inexpensive machine-carved furniture, bedsprings, iron stoves, power-sawed millwork—could now move west with ease. Henry Dinwoodey, a Salt Lake City furniture dealer and cabinetmaker, reported that he planned a shopping expedition to "New York at the time the last spike was driven which connected the Union Pacific with the Central Pacific Road." Knowing the railroad was completed, "I bought a considerable quantity and variety of furniture which I could not manufacture" and shipped it back to Salt Lake. It was, he added, "the first imported furniture for sale in the Territory." The furniture was delivered to Ogden, a stop along the rail line, but from there the shipment had to be moved by ox team to Salt Lake City thirty-nine miles away.[3]

Technological advances wrought wondrous changes inside American homes. Following the Civil War, gas and kerosene were increasingly used for illumination. Because gas derived from coal required a generating plant and a distribution network, its use was restricted mainly to urban areas or houses of those able to afford private gas generators. Kerosene, however, became plentiful after the opening of Pennsylvania's oil fields in 1859 and could be used anywhere. Because kerosene lamps had the advantage of being portable, many urban residents used both forms of lighting, thereby raising the level and flexibility of illumination in their homes. Plumbing made slower advances. New York City recorded a population of 629,904 in 1856 but only 1,361 bathtubs and 10,384 toilets. American design critics urged readers to adopt these conveniences. Catharine Beecher and Harriet Beecher Stowe informed readers of *The American Woman's Home* (1869), "water-closets . . . cost no more than an out-door building, and save from the most disagreeable house-labor."[4]

As the railroads increasingly carried the mail for the U.S. Post Office and packages for express companies, information and fashionable goods moved inland more rapidly than ever before. When *Godey's Lady's Book* began in 1830, a subscriber generally paid fifteen cents in postage for each issue. By 1852, those rates had been reduced to 1½ cents per issue and the publisher boasted that among his nearly 150,000 subscribers were readers in Kearney City, Nebraska, and at Fort Scott in the Kansas Territory. With cheaper rates, a larger population, and expanded service, problems arose. Major cities that served as distribution points for the mail were inundated. Louis Godey complained in 1854 that according to reports from the *Galena Jeffersonian*, "There are now in the Chicago post-office more than two hundred bags of mail matter undistributed; and they are daily accumulating!" The problem remained unsolved until 1865 when the postal service introduced special cars on trains to sort and distribute mail en route, thus alleviating the congestion at central distributing points and further enhancing service.

The demands on the U.S. Post Office reflect changes within American society. In 1840, four-fifths of all children did not go beyond the primary grades and less than three-quarters of one percent went to college. Few states had public schools (in the sense that we use the term today) and funding for such schools came slowly. However, as states eliminated the property restrictions that limited suffrage, many of the newly enfranchised voters saw education as the primary path of upward mobility for their children and voted funds for the support of public schools. As the movement for universal education slowly grew, so too did literacy. An increasing number of Americans could turn to books, magazines, and newspapers for information about their world.

By midcentury the decoration of the home had become primarily the woman's responsibility. Magazines and books instructed their readers in good taste and the latest fashions. *Godey's Lady's Book* was joined in 1842 by Charles J. Peterson's *Ladies' National Magazine* (known as "Peterson's") and in 1852 by T. S. Arthur's *Home Magazine*. All these magazines contained short stories, fashion plates, and household decorating hints directed toward women readers. Furthermore, Godey introduced a "buying service" in 1852, which shipped goods from New York and Philadelphia firms to his readers throughout the country; this service was the precursor of mail-order companies. Architects also wrote manuals that included interior-decorating ideas, while the works of Loudon, Webster and Parkes, and Downing continued to be reprinted and widely read. Fredrika Bremer made a point of meeting Downing and was invited to stay at his home on the Hudson River. A friend told her that Downing's books "are to be found every where, and nobody, whether he be rich or poor, builds a house or lays out a garden without consulting Downing's works. Every young couple who sets up housekeeping buys them." When asked about his popularity, Downing modestly replied, "It happens that I came at a time when people began universally to feel the necessity of information about building houses and laying out gardens."[5] The influence of Loudon, Webster and Parkes, and Downing continued until the 1870s when other writers such as Charles Eastlake, Clarence Cook, and Harriet Spofford gradually replaced them.

In addition to new magazines and books on architecture and interior decoration, advertising began to grow in importance during the period 1850 to 1870. In the first half of the nineteenth century, when the demand for goods outstripped the supply and shipping any distance overland was extremely difficult, advertisements were rare. By the time of the Civil War, the total income from advertising realized by *all* American magazines was about twenty-five cents per person. But between the Civil War and 1880 there was a threefold increase in advertising, signifying changes in the production and distribution of goods, as well as individual purchasing power, all of which affected the interior design of the middle-class American home. The average annual wage during this period was $590. But averages can be misleading: unskilled laborers received about $1 a day in midcentury, while foremen might earn $2; bookkeepers earned $600 to $800 a year, and accountants received about $1,300. One historian suggests that "middle-class incomes" ranged between $800 and $5,000 in 1860. Observers at the time felt America was increasingly a better place for all its citizens. The Reverend Henry W. Bellows opened the New York Exhibition in 1853 with the words "Luxury is debilitating and demoralizing only when it is exclusive. . . . The peculiarity of the luxury of our time, and especially of our country, is its diffusive nature; it is the opportunity and the aim of large masses of our people; and this happily unites with industry, equality, and justice."[6]

# WALLS AND CEILINGS

Many American interiors during the years 1850 to 1870 continued to reflect the recommendations of Loudon and Downing, possibly because no new critics of such commanding stature emerged to replace them. In 1846 *Godey's Lady's Book* began a monthly series containing perspective drawings, floor plans, and brief descriptions of "model cottages" for farms, towns, and suburbs. The first houses in this series came from Loudon's *An Encyclopedia of Cottage, Farm, and Villa Architecture and Furniture* (1833). But American architects were also publishing books of house plans and interior-decorating advice aimed at the middle class. Lacking the national appeal of Downing, these author/architects nonetheless managed to reach a wide audience. By the 1850s, the *Lady's Book* was publishing their work, thus keeping subscribers abreast of contemporary designs. These architects assumed their audience was female, reflecting the prevailing belief that the house was the woman's sphere and she should have a hand in planning it. Few went as far as Calvert Vaux, who urged women to start careers in architecture, suggesting that anyone who could lay out complicated needlework could design a house.[7]

By midcentury, interior and exterior color preferences were changing. William H. Ranlett, architect and author, noted in *The Architect* (1849) that the prevailing color of a room affected the eyes, the minds, and the behavior of the occupants. "Cheerfulness and amiability could hardly be compatible with a dark blue ceiling and dingy brown walls, yet it is very common in country houses to see sitting-rooms and bed-chambers so colored that they impart a sensation of oppressed solemnity to the feelings," while "pure white walls, so common in our city houses, . . . are painfully distressing to the eye, and must have an injurious effect upon the sight," in addition to being "cheerless" and "liable to stains." Ranlett's comments seem directed at "straw men," since earlier critics had urged readers to employ a variety of colors in their houses. His alternatives included brownstone color, sage, slate, violet, lilac, peach blossom, salmon, bronze green, and orange. He included the basic ingredients to create each color, acknowledging that "the gradation of shades produced by a varied proportion of these colors is almost indefinite," since housepainters still mixed colors on-site. Ranlett also provided an estimate of costs using as an example drab (dull yellowish-brown) oil paint:

painter's fee . . . . . . . $1.75/day
glue sizing . . . . . . . . $0.20/pound
lampblack in oil . . . . . $0.40/pound
chrome yellow in oil. . . $0.30/pound
linseed oil . . . . . . . . $0.80–$0.90/gallon[8]

Gervase Wheeler, an English architect who practiced briefly in America, pleaded for an antidote to "the cold, hard, white walls, whose severe surfaces are illy reconciled with . . . gaudy carpets and brilliant scarlet or purple upholstery." In *Homes for the People* (1855), he argued that the only appropriate use for white paint was "in portions of the internal wood-work that stand out in relief against a tinted background, such as a painted or papered wall affords." The April 1857 issue of *Godey's Lady's Book* contained a "recipe" for whitewash with the guarantee it had been used on the east end of the "President's house" in Washington. One could tint the solution with Spanish brown (for red or pink); Spanish brown and clay (for lilac); lampblack (for slate); yellow ocher or chrome yellow (for yellows). Greens were not available, claimed Godey, because the lime destroyed the color and the finish would crack and peel. The depth of color depended upon the quantity of pigment used.[9]

The shifting fashion in color did cause comment. In *House-painting: Plain and Decorative* (1868), John W. Masury cautioned:

> We must now guard against the . . . extreme, and not suffer our houses to be streaked with colors and tints laid on by unskilled hands, without regard to harmony or tasteful arrangement. The fashion for compound hues, neutral tints, grays, and other so-called quiet colors, is giving place to a preference for combinations of red, blue, yellow, and other colors of the prism. It has been the custom to decry these colors as gaudy. It is only when they are put together without due regard to their suitableness to each other, and their relative quantities in the arrangement they require, that they appear gaudy and glaring.[10]

Writers began to specify rules for interior color choice and placement. Most relied upon the work of David Ramsay Hay of Edinburgh, Scotland, a housepainter and author of *The Laws of Harmonious Colouring* (1828), mentioned by Loudon and Downing. Nearly every article on the subject of color during the 1850s and 1860s referred to Hay's work, including pieces in *Godey's Lady's Book*. Most American householders with tasteful aspirations probably had a passing knowledge of Hay's theories, although an American edition of his work did not appear until 1867. John W. Masury included Hay's theories in *House-painting: Plain and Decorative* describing two approaches to color harmony. The first was "harmony by analogy," using those colors *next* to one another on the color wheel. Masury's examples included crimson and purple, yellow and gold, crimson and rich brown. The second was "harmony by contrast," employing those colors *opposite* one another on the color wheel, such as scarlet and blue, orange and blue, yellow and black, white and black.[11]

"Harmony by contrast" was the more popular approach to selecting in-

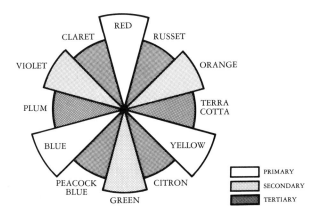

*A color wheel depicting primary, secondary, and tertiary colors. Complementary or contrasting colors are those opposite one another on the wheel (e.g., red-green and orange-blue). Analogous colors are those next to one another on the wheel (e.g., yellow-citron-green). (Drawing by Richard A. Votta)*

terior colors throughout the 1850–1870 period. When the architect John Bullock mentioned Hay's color harmony in *The American Cottage Builder* (1854), he included *only* the contrasting harmonies. He recommended the following schemes: crimson and green; red and bluish-green; reddish-orange and greenish-blue; orange and blue; orange-yellow and indigo blue; yellow and purplish-indigo; and yellowish-green with violet. Bullock maintained that three principles applied to these schemes. First, each pair would remain in harmony regardless of the values (tints or shades) of the individual hues. Pale green with dark crimson was just as harmonious as dark green with pink. Second, if the pair of colors in each scheme was mixed together, they would form a neutral tint that could be included in the scheme. Third, if both colors were of the same intensity, the result was an "exciting" contrast; if of different intensity, they resulted in a feeling of "repose." Bullock added it was "less evil to be unable to find excitement, than to be unable to find repose." Samuel Sloan, a Philadelphia architect whose work frequently appeared in *Godey's Lady's Book*, also preferred "repose," noting in *Homestead Architecture* (1861) that one hue should predominate but it should not be too intense or bright. He urged caution in choosing the finishes for walls and floors because they were the largest areas of color in a room. He recommended placing the darkest value on the floor with walls and ceiling progressively lighter, following Loudon's advice of thirty years earlier. Even the popular press favored repose. An article entitled "Color—in Dress, Furniture, and Gardening" in the December 1862 issue of *Godey's Lady's Book* gives the following suggestions regarding color harmony in various rooms of the house:

> The paper, the curtains, the carpet, the sofa, and the tablecover, etc., should not "fight," but either harmonize or contrast; and I must confess I am puzzled as to which is the best rule to follow. Perhaps in boudoir and bedroom, and generally in small rooms, harmony should be the rule;

in drawing and dining-room, and generally in large rooms, contrast. There must be no contrast, of course, in a library or picture-gallery. Bright colors best become a northern aspect; paler colors all the rooms which receive much sunlight. A warm tone should pervade a winter room, where the hearth is always glowing.[12]

Most writers' examples contained only *two* colors to be distributed throughout the room on the walls, window, and floor coverings. Masury, however, prepared far more complex schemes, ranging upward to eight combinations, such as blue, crimson and yellow with black, white and brown, plus orange and purple.[13] Not all colors were distributed in equal amounts in such complex schemes; blue might predominate, followed by crimson and then yellow, with lesser amounts of the other colors. The effect was a unified arrangement of color, seeking "repose" rather than "excitement." For example, the triad blue-red-yellow and the paired colors orange and purple achieve harmony by contrast; yet, when used together, the five colors are adjacent on the color wheel, thus introducing harmony by analogy into the scheme. It is important to keep in mind that *colors were not used indiscriminately* in the nineteenth century.

In addition to color theory, midcentury critics began to experiment with more decorative painting techniques on walls. In *Homes for the People*, Wheeler suggested using additional colors on walls to harmonize with the woodwork. A dining room with dark woodwork, for example, might have walls painted a light tint of sage green. Then a strip of bright red paper about one-sixth inch wide could be applied on the walls approximately two inches from the woodwork and cornice throughout the room. If the woodwork was light oak or white, and sage green was still preferred, a four-inch width of "pearly green" paper, bordered on both sides with pure blue paper one-sixth inch wide, and having a pure red strip one-eighth inch wide in the middle, could be used on walls around the woodwork and cornice. In either case, one could enrich the corners of the room using borders cut into "curving knot" or "rectangular fret" designs. For a library with dark wooden bookcases, Wheeler suggested deep, rich blue walls covered in a diaper pattern composed of fine lines in brilliant red, orange, or light blue; the effect of color contrast using red or orange would be warmer than that of color harmony using light blue.[14]

## WALLPAPERS

By the 1850s, American wallpaper manufacturers employed the technological advances mentioned in Chapter 1: using continuous rolls of paper made on Fourdrinier or Gilpin machines and printing these papers with raised cylinders developed by English manufacturers in the 1840s. So immediate was the American response to these innovations that by 1857 imported

*A twelve-color wallpaper printing machine illustrated in the November 26, 1881, issue of* Scientific American. *Machines like these revolutionized the industry and altered the way in which average householders decorated their rooms. (The Athenaeum of Philadelphia)*

papers accounted for only 5 percent of the domestic market. However, cylinder printing dictated its own aesthetic. Whereas pattern sizes ("repeats") in block printing were limited by what an individual printer could manipulate, pattern sizes in cylinder printing were limited by the size of the cylinder. Cylinders were rarely larger than six inches in diameter and created design repeats less than eighteen inches in length. Furthermore, blocks were "inked" with rather viscous pigments producing large areas of solid color in the patterns. Cylinders carried colors in raised felts that had to be fairly small in order to remain in place. The felts held thinner colors, however, which dried rapidly and permitted multicolored papers, printed with many cylinders, each laying on one color. Consequently, cylinder-printed papers normally boasted more colors, finer lines, and smaller repeats than most of the block-printed papers made before midcentury. Mechanization led to standardization: by the 1850s machine-made papers in England were twenty-one inches wide and twelve yards long, in France eighteen inches by nine yards, and in America eighteen inches by eight yards.[15]

The best wallpapers continued to be printed on cotton-fiber paper, although hemp, straw, and wool were used to produce lesser grades. As the demand for paper increased, experimenters sought abundant and cheaper alternatives to use as a base. English researchers first made paper from wood pulp in the early 1850s, followed by American manufacturers by 1855. The use of wood-pulp paper then grew slowly throughout the period until, by the 1880s, it was the base for most commercial wallpapers.[16] As wood-pulp paper ages, it becomes brown and quite brittle. The pigments printed on the paper also discolor because of the acids that are part of the papermaking process. If such paper survives today in an old house, it almost certainly dates no earlier than the 1860s and rarely can be color-matched accurately by sight.

The wallpaper industry profited from the successful pursuit of artificial

*Even with advances in printing technology, the wallpaper industry continued to rely on hand labor for tasks such as winding the printed paper into rolls, as illustrated in the November 26, 1881, issue of* Scientific American. *(The Athenaeum of Philadelphia)*

pigments and dyes during the 1850–1870 period. Traditional sources of pigments included various earths (for reds, yellows, and browns), vegetables (madder root for reds and indigo for blues), and animals (cochineal for reds and prussic acid made of dried blood, horns, and hoofs for blues). However, Masury described new pigments deriving from sources such as chemical reactions with metals, which produced red from iron, green from copper, yellow from chromium, blue from cobalt, and green from arsenic. These pigments created brighter colors than many of the natural sources and resulted in more varied and intense hues on wallpapers, but not without attendant problems. In 1860, for example, *Godey's Lady's Book* warned that the apple-green color printed on some wallpapers was poisonous and "dangerous to life" if used in bedrooms. The warning probably referred to Sheele's green or Schweinfurt green, both derived from copper arsenite.[17]

Despite the new technology and changing notions of color harmony, wallpapers popular during the 1830s and 1840s remained in use. In reviewing the collection available at James S. Griffith's Philadelphia establishment in 1857, *Godey's Lady's Book* listed three types of papers most in demand: statuary papers, French scenics, and imitations of wood (mahogany, oak, rosewood, and others). Griffith's scenics included Zuber's "Eldorado" and "Views of North America," the former first issued about 1848, the latter in

## IDENTIFYING OLD WALLPAPERS

Should a remnant of old wallpaper be discovered, there are a few simple tests to determine its age. First, with a large enough sample, it can be determined whether it was printed on a continuous roll or glued together from smaller (handmade) sheets. Continuous-roll paper is undoubtedly from the second half of the nineteenth century or even later. If the sample is small, break off a piece. If it breaks to a straight edge, the paper was probably made by machine; if it breaks to a crooked edge, it was probably made by hand. Next, examine the color and texture of the fragment. Wood-pulp paper from the nineteenth century will be brown and brittle. If the fragment appears creamy or gray and in fairly good condition, it may be earlier rag paper. Look closely at the pigments. Test a small area with a

drop of water; if the pigments do *not* run, the paper has either been varnished (in which case you will see a shine) or was printed toward the end of the nineteenth century, when insoluble pigments came into common use. Finally, examine the pattern under 10X magnification. If the surface is pitted, the paper was block-printed using thick pigments common early in the nineteenth century. If each color seems more intense at the edges of the pattern, it was probably printed by roller, which causes the pigments carried by the brass edges to appear heavier than those trapped by the felts. (For more tricks on identification, see Catherine Lynn Frangiamore's *Wallpapers in Historic Preservation* (Washington, D.C.: National Park Service, 1977), particularly pages 3–6.)

1834, confirming that once the blocks were cut, wallpaper designs remained in production for a long time. Griffith's also sold scenic papers by Délicourt including "La Grande Chasse" (identified in the *Lady's Book* as "Grand Chase Subjects") exhibited at the Great Exhibition in London in 1851. Readers were assured, if "persons ordering [Griffith's papers] will give the size of the room and mention the colors they would prefer, . . . they can be suited almost as well by letter as by personal application."[18]

The 1859 billhead of Josiah F. Bumstead, a Boston manufacturer and importer of paper hangings who was mentioned in Chapter 1, listed long-popular papers: statuary, scenery, and grained papers, as well as the columnar

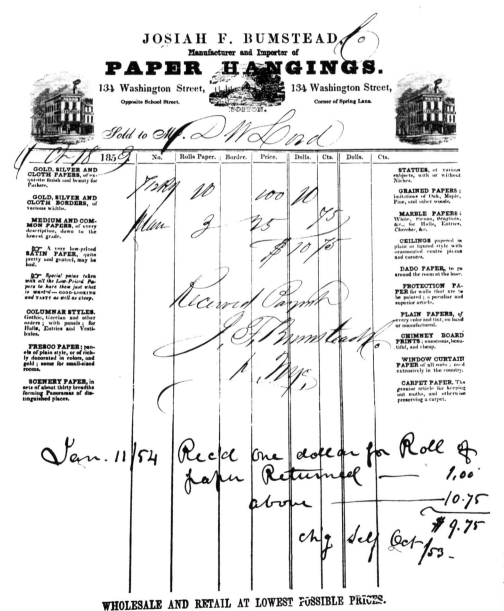

*An 1859 billhead from Josiah F. Bumstead of Boston, a manufacturer and importer of wallpapers. His stock is listed along both margins. (The Athenaeum of Philadelphia)*

styles and dado papers—all used in the years before 1850. Bumstead also advertised fresco, plain, marble, satin, gold, and silver papers, and "medium and common papers of every description down to the lowest grade."[19]

Bullock's *The American Cottage Builder*, which provided designs ranging from $25 cottages to $25,000 villas, gives an indication of the widespread use of wallpaper. "The commoner sorts of paper now being so cheap . . . the walls of every cottage living-room, at least, should be covered with it, as conducing much to the cheerfulness and comfort of the inmates." As for new designs and colors, it seems that most people chose patterns deemed "inappropriate" by the authors of books on architecture. Bullock, for example, urged readers to select designs in two colors, one the ground and the other the pattern; he appealed to no less an authority than Augustus Welby Northmore Pugin, as had earlier writers. Apparently few homeowners chose to listen, for Bullock decried "the most expensive modern papers consist of a set of unmeaning patterns, or direct imitations of flowers, animals, parts of buildings, &c., in as many colors as the price of the paper admits of, and commonly without the least regard to harmony of arrangement. Those who are unable to produce a beautiful and harmonious effect by the use of two colors are not very likely to succeed by the use of ten or a dozen,—the difficulty of producing a fine and harmonious effect increasing in a geometric ratio (so to speak) with every additional color employed."[20]

If critics no longer favored the Baroque or Rococo patterns of flowers, asymmetrical cartouches, undulating stripes, S- and C-curves, and pseudo-architectural designs, the general population continued to purchase them in every imaginable color throughout the period 1850 to 1870. In September 1852, *Godey's Lady's Book* gently offered a few hints for decorating with such papers. The scale of the room should determine the scale of the paper; large patterns were suitable only in large rooms. Diagonal trellis patterns and stripes appeared to heighten low rooms; wavy stripes were deemed most graceful. Small, geometric patterns would hide soil in high-traffic areas such as sitting rooms, stairs, halls, and passages; those based on "Elizabethan" designs, such as quatrefoils, were particularly good. Marble papers in light gray or yellow were also recommended for passages; they could be cut into blocks to resemble ashlar and varnished to withstand water. Bedrooms required cool and quiet papers.[21]

Ten years later, the same magazine offered further suggestions, and thus recorded changes in taste during the intervening years. Except for dining rooms, where the use of dark, rich, warm colors still prevailed, most rooms should use papers printed on light grounds and in more subtle colors than previously. Yellow, light-green, and light-blue papers were all recommended, depending on the kinds of woods the furniture in the room was made of: blue with light woods and yellow with dark woods. In bedrooms, where repose was desirable, strong contrasts were avoided; and papers with

Top: *This lithograph published by "N. Currier" in 1847 is entitled* Battle of Cerro Gordo April 18th 1847, *after a battle in the Mexican War in which sixty-three Americans were killed.* Bottom: *There seems little doubt that the designer of this wallpaper took inspiration from the Currier lithograph for his unusual subject, framing the soldiers with curved borders and flowers. The critics would not have admired this effort. (The Athenaeum of Philadelphia)*

grounds of white, light grays, or pastels with simple patterns in blue, yellow, or green were preferred.[22]

By 1866, nearly forty years after Pugin's comments deriding realistic patterns, the popular press reflected the end of realism and the beginning of smaller, abstract designs that became increasingly popular over the next two decades. An article in *Godey's Lady's Book* that year recommended diaper patterns of two colors, always subdued, or of gold or silver on a colored ground. "Ordinary sized" rooms used six- to eight-inch repeats and bedrooms

## WALLPAPER SELECTION TODAY

Hunting for wallpapers that are historically appropriate for your old house can be a frustrating and expensive task, particularly since manufacturers alter their lines constantly. In *Wallpapers for Historic Buildings* by Richard C. Nylander, updated and reissued by the National Trust for Historic Preservation in 1983, you will find the most current information regarding what is available.

Some companies do manufacture papers that reproduce designs used during the nineteenth century. It is possible to purchase scenics, for example, although the price is quite high. Flocked papers are also available, but in making your selection, care should be exercised regarding pattern, pile height, and color —too many of the flocked papers are inaccurate in these details. A few ashlar papers are manufactured that closely resemble those of the 1850s. In addition, several companies produce papers with overall patterns appropriate for houses of 1830 to 1900—some of these were produced under the auspices of organizations such as the National Preservation Institute, restorations such as Old Sturbridge Village, and institutions such as the Society for the Preservation of New England Antiquities. Papers are available today only in limited selections. Only two firms currently produce a "rainbow paper," and that in just one pattern. One company will custom-color

it, however, to suit your needs. The process is not cheap. As more owners of nineteenth-century houses demand appropriate papers, however, the market will respond with more designs at affordable prices.

A few flocked borders are on the market. If you can't find one you like, as a substitute, you might purchase a roll of striped, flocked paper in colors appropriate for your needs, and trim it to achieve the effect of a nineteenth-century border. You could go one step further, and stencil a pattern onto the border in colors that complement the other wallpaper. Another substitute can be created with one of the borders appropriate for houses of 1830 to 1850 that several companies are producing. Choose one of these and, using a thick, flat paint, touch up certain areas of the border. When hung at ceiling height, the matte finish of those areas will closely resemble the shallow flock typical of flocked borders of the first half of the nineteenth century.

Only a few architectural papers are available, although architectural borders are common. You could choose such a border and use it around the cornice, baseboard, and architectural features in the room. Or, taking a hint from Downing, purchase plain papers in corresponding colors and create architectural features such as those in Acorn Hall.

even smaller ones. Ivy, oak, maple, and fig-leaf patterns, if "conventionally treated" in two colors, also made "excellent decorative forms." The article concluded, "we will not venture to lay down any definite rule for the choice of patterns, but would earnestly deprecate all that species of decoration which may be included under the head of 'scroll' ornament. It will be easily recognized from its resemblance to the so-called carved work round modern drawing-room mirrors, and is sure to be of bad style."[23] Thus did the press trumpet the end of the popular taste for the Rococo.

There were several acceptable ways to use wallpaper in houses of the 1850–1870 period. One could paper walls from cornice to baseboard, using a fairly narrow border at the cornice and baseboard. During most of the period, the color of the borders contrasted with the dominant hue of the paper on the wall. For example, following Hay's theory of color harmony, a blue or violet border should be paired with a yellow paper.[24] This technique echoed the taste prior to the middle of the century.

Fresco papers, which remained popular during the period, were generally printed in keeping with Baroque or Rococo designs with ornate columns, fanciful flowers, and even landscapes in cartouches. They were applied to parts of the wall, with the remainder of the surface finished in paint or encaustic paper (solid-colored paper) that gave the effect of a finely painted wall.[25]

Architects offered several other treatments. By midcentury moldings (or paper resembling moldings) were applied to walls to create panels that could be papered or covered with a rich fabric in imitation of Louis XVI style. (See Plate 9.) Calvert Vaux provided illustrations of such walls in *Villas and Cottages* (1857), Gervase Wheeler recommended the same treatment for the parlor of a country villa in *Homes for the People*, as did C. P. Dwyer, architect and author of *The Economic Cottage Builder* (1856). Illustrations in *Godey's Lady's Book* attest to the popularity of this treatment during the 1850s. It was short-lived, however, for by 1866 the *Lady's Book* despaired: "Recently a fashion prevailed of arranging paper in panels round a room, and enclosing them with narrow strips of the same material stained and shaded in imitation of wood. This style of decoration had its admirers, but, though attractive from its novelty, it was false in principle, and no one need regret that it has fallen into disuse."[26]

## WOODWORK

During this period, critics began to recommend actual hardwood wainscoting used in conjunction with wallpapers for the walls of certain rooms. Gervase Wheeler, in a design entitled "The Homestead" from *Rural Homes* (1851), patriotically proposed that all the woodwork in the house be "national" in character, such as Southern pine, black walnut, American oak, and chestnut.

In two of his other home designs, Wheeler recommended hardwood wainscoting in the entry halls and also suggested oiling the wood (rather than varnishing) with a mixture of linseed oil, beeswax, and turpentine, rubbing it with flannel, and repeating the process several times to achieve the degree of polish desired.[27]

Architects also reintroduced chair rails. In *The Economic Cottage Builder*, which included plans ranging from a $180 log cabin to a large house for $3,000, C. P. Dwyer proselytized:

> Although it has, for half a century, been customary to omit what were once called *sur-bases* in rooms, that is, a moulded band running parallel with the base or wash board, and some two feet above it, we would most strongly recommend their being introduced once more, if it were for nothing but their actual utility, at even a sacrifice of appearance. House-

*Calvert Vaux included these six designs for walls employing panels, wallpaper, and fabrics in* Villas and Cottages. *These suggestions closely resemble the actual wall treatments in the double parlors at Acorn Hall, built in 1853 in Morristown, New Jersey (see Plate 9). (The Athenaeum of Philadelphia)*

*This engraving from* Godey's Lady's Book *of November 1857 clearly illustrates the paneled wall treatment, "approved" midcentury carpet pattern, and simple curtain treatment employing only rings and a pole. From periodicals like the* Lady's Book, *readers throughout the country learned the latest fashions. (The Athenaeum of Philadelphia)*

wives will surely bear us out in this opinion when they consider how destructive to walls are the effects of chair-backs, or, worse still, of the heads of gentlemen who find a luxury in assuming an inclined posture of the body by tipping back their chairs. Room-papering will always be found to have had more hard usage at the one point just indicated than at any other in the whole height of the room. These sur-bases might be elegantly moulded, and should always be two and a half inches projection from the face of the wall.[28]

Calvert Vaux addressed a more prosperous audience in *Villas and Cottages* with designs of houses ranging in cost between $3,000 and $60,000; however, his advice was similar to Wheeler's and Dwyer's. He opposed graining as "a sham and pretense," estimating that it cost as much to apply graining over white pine as it would have cost to use a better wood from the start. He specified wainscoting for the entry hall and library of several plans, suggesting yellow pine, black walnut, and oak. Even Catharine Beecher and Harriet Beecher Stowe, pioneers in domestic science, praised oiled woodwork of butternut, chestnut, or pine in *The American Woman's Home* as being cheaper, more handsome, and easier to keep clean than painted finishes.[29]

These authors' views notwithstanding, most midcentury homes did not contain hardwoods or wainscoting. Samuel Sloan praised walnut and rosewood for doors in the "best" houses, while admitting white pine remained the most common wood because it was light, rigid, and easily worked, even if it required "the painter's art . . . to render it at all presentable."[30] So, while some architectural books of the years 1850 to 1870 hinted at the beginning of interest in hardwoods—an interest that would peak during the last decades of the nineteenth century—most midcentury houses contained painted or grained woodwork.

It is not surprising that these early proposals favoring natural woods coincided with the erosion of interest in the late Neoclassical style—which favored marbleized and grained finishes—and the beginnings of the lumber industry in the hardwood forests of the upper Midwest. Lewis F. Allen, architect and author of *Rural Architecture* (1852), derided the ornate carving found in some Neoclassical interiors for yet another reason. "None but the initiated can tell the affliction that *chiseled* finishing entails on the housekeepers in the spider, fly, and other insect lodgment which it invites. . . . Bases, casings, sashes, door—all should be plain, and painted or stained a quiet *russet* color—a color natural to the woods used for the finish, if it can be, showing in their wear, as little of dust, soiling, and fly dirt as possible." He concluded, "There is no poetry about common housekeeping."[31]

# FLOORS
During the period from 1850 to 1870, architects continued to specify softwood floors—often pine—laid as planks or with tongue-and-groove joints. They rarely mentioned hardwoods or the parquet that would become popular in the decades to follow. Yet never before had so many Americans had such a wide range of choices in floor coverings; some early types remained in popular use, while entirely new products also appeared. From among these materials nineteenth-century householders made choices based on cost and availability, as well as aesthetics and practicality.

## PAINTED FLOORS

Painted floors remained popular. In kitchens, halls, and occasionally bedrooms, paint sealed the softwood floors, making cleaning easier: painted floors did not stain or absorb grease, and could be cleaned by wiping rather than scouring. Paint was a good floor "covering" for a homeowner who could not afford oilcloth or carpeting. Evidence suggests the practice of decoratively painting floors continued for many years, especially along the frontier. For example, a recently completed study of Texas interiors found painted floors dating to as late as the first decade of the twentieth century.[32]

A description of floor painting is found in "The Unexpected Visitor," a short story published in 1859 and set in "a large, handsome house, about five miles from Dayton, a town in the far West." The head of the family, Mr. Melville, had been a merchant in New York City; having made a "handsome fortune," the family "emigrated to the West, from a love of novelty and a wild country life." They purchased a large house in Ohio, only partially completed by a bankrupt speculator, and finished as many rooms as the parents, five children, and a maiden aunt required, "leaving several large, handsome apartments entirely unfurnished." The story concerns preparations for the impending arrival of a visitor. The maiden aunt, who we are told came originally from New England, assumed responsibility for the preparations. One of her first directives was to her nephew to paint the floor of the room to be used by Aunt Fannie: "To-morrow, you must drive to Dayton, Albert, purchase some pearl-colored paint, enough to put two coats on the floor, and some green, enough for a border. Take a sheet of tin, mark three large leaves in a group upon it, and take it to the tinman. Tell him to cut out the leaves like a stencil letter; and you can, by putting it down and painting over it, make a handsome border of green leaves for your carpet."[33]

Presumably, the rest of the house had genuine carpeting. Perhaps time or money prevented the purchase of carpeting for this room; painting the floor was the best solution. Undoubtedly, households in similar circumstances did the same thing if only as a temporary measure. Furthermore, the instructions were so precise that any reader of *Godey's Lady's Book*, in which the story was printed, could follow them.

## OILCLOTHS

Floorcloths, generally called "oilcloths" by midcentury, offered an alternative to paint or carpeting. Americans could choose from English and domestic products. Two American makers, Woodcock of Brooklyn, New York, and Albro and Hoyt of Elizabethtown, New Jersey, exhibited at the Great Exhibition in London in 1851. However, most critics agreed that the English products, though double the price of "an equally showy American product," wore twice as long. Furthermore, importers would cut the pieces "any desired width or length, so that the floor is covered by a single piece." A Philadelphia auction catalogue recorded the room-by-room sale of a row house in 1856 containing seventy-three square yards of "oil cloth" in the parlor and thirty-two square yards in the dining room, all of English manufacture. *Godey's*

*Lady's Book* provided directions for making an oilcloth to a reader in Forest House, Wisconsin, noting "it is by all odds cheaper to buy the oil-cloth, where it is possible; still, there may be situations where this is impossible."[34]

By the 1850s, oilcloths most frequently appeared in areas of hard wear, such as halls and kitchens. Miss Leslie instructed readers of *The Lady's House Book* (1854), "there is no better covering" for kitchen floors "than a coarse, stout, plain oil-cloth, unfigured, or all one color; for instance, dark red, blue, brown, olive, or ochre yellow." Oilcloths were more common in the kitchens of English than American homes, but Miss Leslie urged readers to purchase them because "they save the trouble of scrubbing the floor, it being only necessary to wash them off with a wet cloth; and as they are impervious to damp, or to cold from open cracks between the boards, they make the kitchen as dry and warm as it could be rendered by a woollen carpet; and they have the advantage of collecting and retaining no dust or grease."[35]

No less authorities than Catharine Beecher and her sister Harriet Beecher Stowe concurred; they provided readers of *The American Woman's Home* (1869) with instructions on making oilcloths. "To procure a kitchen oilcloth as cheaply as possible," they advised, "buy cheap tow cloth [cloth made from flax, hemp, or jute], and fit it to the size and shape of the kitchen. Then have it stretched, and nailed to the south side of the barn, and, with a brush, cover it with a coat of thin rye paste. When this is dry, put on a coat of yellow paint, and let it dry for a fortnight. It is safest to first try the paint, and see if it dries well, as some paint never will dry. Then put on a second coat, and at the end of another fortnight, a third coat. Then let it hang two months, and it will last, uninjured, for many years," they assured their readers. "The longer the paint is left to dry, the better. If varnished, it will last much longer."[36]

In halls, oilcloths substituted for more expensive tiles or carpeting, but critics continued to warn that oilcloths should never be used on stairs because they were slippery. Nonetheless, an 1850s catalogue from Cunningham's Emporium in Providence, Rhode Island, advertised oilcloths in all widths and all patterns, including for stairs and stair covering, although the latter might refer to the practice of nailing a small strip of oilcloth to each stair tread to protect the carpet underneath from wear.[37]

## TILE FLOORS

Use of encaustic and geometric tiles in vestibules, first-floor hallways, and sometimes on verandas, increased during these decades. Bullock's readers learned that such tiles were durable, easy to clean, and fireproof, albeit expensive; he predicted an increased demand would reduce the price. Wheeler praised their "lively effect" and their durability, which he described as greater

Middle Age, *from "The Four Seasons of Life" series, published by Currier and Ives in 1868, depicts a stair hall with papered walls, carpet rods on the stairs, and an animal-skin mat to trap soil and protect the carpet or oilcloth on the floor. The window is "curtained" with plants in a manner illustrated by Catharine Beecher and Harriet Beecher Stowe in* The American Woman's Home *(1869). (The Library of Congress, and The Athenaeum of Philadelphia)*

than that of marble. The Willows, a home built for the Revere family in Morristown, New Jersey, in 1854 and modeled on a Wheeler design, has buff, red, and black encaustic tiles in the large first-floor hall; this was possibly one of the earliest residential uses in America. The Philadelphia architect John Notman also used encaustic tiles manufactured by the English firm of Minton & Co. on the floor of the octagonal stair hall in Fieldwood, built for Richard S. Field in Princeton, New Jersey, about 1855. Nor was their use restricted to the East Coast. Geometric tiles were laid in the vestibule of the McDonnell-Pierce House built in Madison, Wisconsin, in 1858.[38]

Samuel Sloan illustrated in *Homestead Architecture* six English geometric tile patterns available from S. A. Harrison of Philadelphia in black, terra cotta, gold, and blue at prices varying from thirty-two to forty cents a square foot, excluding the cost of installation. (See Plate 4.) Sloan recommended tiles for libraries and conservatories as well as for vestibules or

*The entry hall of The Willows, built in 1854 by the Revere family in Morristown, New Jersey, after a plan by Gervase Wheeler. The walls are painted in trompe l'oeil paneling and the encaustic-tile floor of plain "geometrics" is one of the earliest residential uses of the material in the United States. (Morris County Park Commission)*

first-floor halls; he intended to use them on the floor of the rotunda in "Longwood," the ill-fated octagon house begun on the eve of the Civil War for Dr. Haller Nutt of Natchez, Mississippi. The tiles would have formed a design consisting of a central flower, five feet in diameter, with additional patterning radiating out to the walls.[39]

## MATTING

Grass matting remained in use as a seasonal or year-round floor covering. For seasonal use, *The Lady's House Book* suggested, "in the middle and eastern section of America, it is best not to put down the matting, and arrange the rooms for summer, before the middle of June; and it should be taken up and replaced with the carpets before the middle of September." Although shops such as Cunningham's Emporium in Providence, Rhode Island, advertised checked Canton matting during the 1850s, Miss Leslie found the effect "common and ungenteel"; she recommended plain matting for the better rooms in a house. She instructed readers to sew the matting strips together to create a rug and to bind the edges with colored worsted, cotton, or linen tapes, preferably the latter two, which were impervious to moths. Tape colors were to harmonize with the other furnishings in the room.[40]

Matting covered gaps between poorly laid plank floors, thus giving any floor a neat appearance and offering some insulation from sound and cold. Samuel Sloan despaired that while most carpenters knew how to lay a floor with tight joints, "owing to the present fashion of covering all floors with carpets and oil-cloths, [it] is considered by many as scarcely worth attention."[41] Households that could not afford carpeting, but could afford matting, gained wall-to-wall floor covering for less money. Consequently, matting remained popular for middle-class parlors and bedrooms, two areas that received little wear in most homes. When M. Thomas & Sons auctioned the contents of the Philadelphia row house in 1856, yards of matting were found in second- and third-floor chambers.[42]

If matting was the only floor covering in a room (except perhaps for a small rug), Catharine Beecher and Harriet Beecher Stowe approved tacking it to the floor. They estimated in *The American Woman's Home* that "good matting" cost fifty cents a yard, permitting one to carpet an average-sized room for a mere $15. They added, "We are here stopped by the prejudice that matting is not good economy because it wears out so soon. We humbly submit that it is precisely the thing for a parlor, which is reserved for the reception-room of friends, and for our own dressed leisure hours. Matting is not good economy in a dining-room or a hard-worn sitting-room; but such a parlor as we are describing is precisely the place where it answers to the very best advantage." As an example, they described "our friends, who lived seven years upon matting, contrived to give their parlor in winter an effect

*This midcentury bedroom is fitted out for summer with grass matting on the floor, a "bug bar" over the bed, and the light fixture "bagged" against fly specks. (Campbell House Museum, St. Louis, Missouri; photograph by James K. Mellow)*

of warmth and color by laying down, in front of the fire, a large square of carpeting, say three breadths, four yards long. This covered the gathering-place around the fire where the winter circle generally sits, and gave an appearance of warmth to the room."[43]

## DRUGGET

Estate inventories occasionally listed druggets during the years 1850 to 1870, but few authorities discussed them. *The Lady's House Book* urged that drugget or coarse matting be used as a padding *under* better carpeting, a technique superior to the usual practice of laying carpets over straw, which could hardly remain smooth. Miss Leslie also recommended drugget "in an eating-room," where "the carpet should be protected from crumbs and grease-droppings by a large woollen cloth kept for the purpose, and spread under the table and the chairs that surround it; this cloth to be taken up after every meal, and shaken out of doors; or else swept off carefully as it lies. It will also require occasional washing. A crumb-cloth may be of drugget, finished round the edge with carpet-binding; of thick green baize; or very strong, stout brown linen." She condemned the "unsightly" practice of laying a strip of drugget up the middle of a staircase to protect the carpeting, observing tartly that from "the pains . . . taken by many persons . . . one might suppose that a stair-carpet was of all articles of furniture the most costly."[44]

Other evidence for crumbcloths is scanty. Walraven's, a Philadelphia emporium, advertised them in an 1860 issue of *Godey's Lady's Book*, and an 1862 photograph of Titian Peale's home in Washington, D.C., shows a striped oilcloth under the dining-room table, undoubtedly to protect the wall-to-wall carpeting. The inventory of James S. Smith of Philadelphia taken in 1857 included a three-dollar oilcloth in the dining room protecting the ten-dollar carpet. Nonetheless, the use of crumbcloths apparently declined steadily throughout the second half of the nineteenth century.[45]

## CARPETING

Between 1850 and 1860 the production of carpeting in America increased 45 percent; as a result, more households than ever before were carpeted. Improved production techniques increased the supply and lowered the costs to consumers who, recovering from the panic of 1857, created the demand. The 1860 census recorded thirteen million yards of carpeting manufactured in that year at an average value of fifty-nine cents a yard.[46]

Carpeting began to be viewed as a basic household furnishing rather than a luxury. C. P. Dwyer told the "toiling millions" to whom he dedicated *The Economic Cottage Builder*, "as it is customary in this country to carpet every room in the house, flooring need not be laid with a view to appearance. It is cheap to lay down an undressed floor, covering the joints with slips of brown paper, and then spreading old newspapers, instead of straw, under the carpet." As finer carpeting became affordable, cheaper carpeting, such as list and Venetian, was relegated to inferior uses. Miss Leslie informed readers that Venetian carpeting was "rarely used, except for stairs and passages."[47]

During the 1850s and 1860s, ingrain and three-ply carpeting accounted for 80 to 90 percent of all the carpeting manufactured in the United States and undoubtedly for most of the carpeting used in middle-class homes.[48] For the wealthy, however, several other types of carpeting were available in America by midcentury, including Brussels, Wilton, and tapestry. Like ingrains and Venetians, these carpets were woven in narrow widths that were seamed together to cover a floor wall to wall. (See Plates 6 and 7.) Unlike

*The wallpaper, window treatment, and Venetian car-peting in* Grandmother's Delight, *by Charles Cole Markham (c. 1860), are decidedly old-fashioned and would not have been found in a stylish middle-class home of the period. (Frank S. Schwarz and Son Gallery, Philadelphia)*

ingrains and Venetians, however, these carpets had pile only on one side and consequently were not reversible.

Brussels carpets originated in Belgium in the early eighteenth century and were produced in Kidderminster, England, by the 1740s and in Philadelphia by the 1820s. The weaving process required the insertion of wires over which the face wool passed; when the wires were removed, loops remained, forming a "level-looped pile," as manufacturers call it today. The size of the wires determined the depth of the pile, while the number of loops per inch indicated the quality of the carpet—six loops being a coarse grade and twelve a superior one. Most Brussels carpets contained up to six colors, and strands in each color ran throughout the length of the carpet, caught by two weft threads, alternating as face pile or filler, depending upon the pattern. By the 1820s Brussels looms with Jacquard attachments wove carpeting in standard twenty-seven-inch widths. However, it was only in midcentury, after power looms reduced costs, that many households could afford Brussels carpeting.[49] (See Plate 10.)

Wilton carpeting, a variation of Brussels, was first woven in Wilton, England, only a few years after the first Brussels were produced in Kidderminster. The carpets differed in two ways. First, Wilton carpeting had a *cut pile* formed by weaving over a wire that had a small knife at one end, which

*The parlor of* The Family of Deacon Wilson Brainerd, *painted by Erastus Salisbury Field (c. 1858), is quite stylish, with ingrain carpeting, lace curtains, and furniture in the Rococo style popular at the time. (Old Sturbridge Village; photograph by Henry E. Peach)*

cut the loops as the wire was withdrawn. Second, a Wilton carpet used three weft threads to lock in each warp strand, thus creating a carpet slightly stronger than the Brussels.[50] In other respects, a Wilton and Brussels carpet were similar; the carpet industry today identifies a Brussels as a "level-looped Wilton."

The term "tapestry" actually described a method of making two different products known as *velvet* or *tapestry Wilton* and *tapestry Brussels* (as distinct from *body Brussels*). A level-looped pile is called a "tapestry Brussels"; a cut pile is a "velvet." The tapestry method was developed by Richard Whytock of Edinburgh, Scotland, who, in an attempt to reduce the costs of carpeting, experimented in 1831–1832 with weaving carpeting using preprinted warp threads wound on large drums, each holding enough woolen yarn for a single warp along the entire length of the carpet, thus forming both pattern and pile at once and reducing the amount of wool required. Because the threads were preprinted, the number of colors used in a tapestry carpet was virtually limitless, which permitted a variety of subtle shadings needed to achieve the

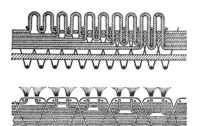

Top: *Cross section of a Brussels carpet, showing the loops that make up the face pile.* Bottom: *A Wilton carpet, in which the pile is cut. Both are illustrated in* A Century of Carpet and Rug Making in America. (The Athenaeum of Philadelphia)

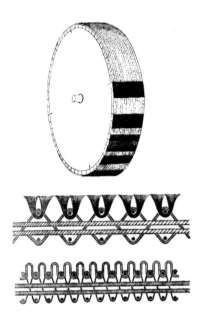

*A tapestry drum (top) and the carpets it could produce—a "velvet" or tapestry Wilton (center) and a tapestry Brussels (bottom). In both carpets, the pattern runs along the top of the carpet; the face yarns are not carried underneath, as they would be in a "body Brussels" or standard Wilton weave. The double parlors in Acorn Hall are carpeted with an unusual imported tapestry Wilton (see Plate 9). (The Victorian Society in America, and The Athenaeum of Philadelphia)*

naturalistic effects so popular at the time. This weaving technique was introduced to America in the 1840s. Tapestry carpets were more expensive than ingrains but less expensive than body Brussels. Charles Pearson purchased tapestry Brussels at $1.70 a yard for his new house near Trenton, New Jersey, which was completed in 1850.[51]

Throughout the 1840s, English manufacturers exported large quantities of pile carpeting to America. Cunningham's Emporium in Providence, Rhode Island, was advertising *English* Brussels, tapestry, and Kidderminster carpeting in the 1850s. However, by 1847 Erastus Bigelow began work on power looms to make such carpets in America. In 1850 he wove Brussels carpeting on a power loom and even exhibited his product at the London Exhibition of 1851. Unfortunately, the loom and five-frame samples arrived too late for the formal judging; nonetheless, the committee noted the products were "better and more perfectly woven than any hand-loom goods that have come under the notice of the jury." Power looms for weaving Wilton and tapestry carpets followed shortly thereafter.[52]

A variety of sources—critics, magazine fiction, and inventories—give us a good sense of what carpets were used in which rooms during the 1850 to 1870 period. As one might expect, the more costly the carpet, the more likely its use in the formal areas of the house. The 1856 auction catalogue of M. Thomas & Sons listed the furnishings of a Philadelphia row house by room. The parlor contained eighty-three yards of tapestry carpet and a slightly smaller amount of English oilcloth, while the dining room had twenty-eight yards of ingrain carpeting and another piece of English oilcloth, possibly used as a drugget. Venetian carpeting covered the hall and stairs; thirty-three flat, brass stair rods held the stair carpeting in place. The front chamber contained sixty-one yards of ingrain carpeting and fifty-eight yards of Canton matting, while the back chamber had thirty yards of ingrain and a Wilton rug. The third-floor chambers and the attic used only matting and the kitchen floor one "lot oil cloth &c."[53]

The Philadelphia inventory of James S. Smith taken in June 1857 evaluated—but did not identify—the floor coverings in each room. The parlor carpet was valued at $70, the entry at $8.40, the dining room at $10, and the "best chamber" at $3. These figures suggest a pile carpet in the parlor and ingrains or older carpeting recut to fit the other rooms. Other floor coverings included druggets of oilcloth in the entry and dining room, valued at $6 and $3, and stair carpet valued at $18 and the rods to hold it in place at $12.[54]

Another inventory taken during November 1867 in Germantown, a suburb of Philadelphia, reflected the use of more expensive carpeting in better rooms. The parlor contained seventy-five yards of velvet carpet while the dining room and library had Brussels. The dining-room carpet was estimated at $1.25 a yard and that in the library at $2.25; both rooms had druggets at $3 each. The stair carpeting may have been a Brussels or a three-ply, since it too is valued at $1.25 a yard and the stair rods at $10. The kitchen contents included a rag carpet of minimal value since all kitchen furnishings—four chairs, three tables, and equipment—were estimated at $100. With the exception of the master bedroom, containing Brussels carpeting at $1.75 a yard, all the other bedrooms used ingrain or unspecified floor coverings valued between fifty cents and $1.50 a yard.[55]

These inventories are in accord with the suggestions of the critics of the period. In 1855, *Godey's Lady's Book* described proper floor coverings for various rooms in the house. For the vestibule or floor of the stair hall, marble or encaustic tiles were preferred; if tiles were used, they were to be topped by a single width of carpeting—velvet, tapestry, or Venetian. If the vestibule floor was of softwood, it was to be "entirely covered" by oilcloth. Stairs were to use velvet or tapestry with "flat stair-rods, from one to three inches in width, of brass or silver plate." The article also recommended Brussels or

## CARPET SELECTION TODAY

Venetian carpeting was made in Carlisle, Pennsylvania, as late as 1953; for many years after the Pennsylvania factory closed it was impossible to purchase new Venetian. Recently, however, it is again being woven by one major manufacturer and is even marketed under the name "Venetian." Small companies are also producing it but generally do not label it as Venetian. While most of these products are excellent copies of the nineteenth-century product, they are hardly inexpensive floor coverings. However, Venetian is essential to many house museums and others seeking an authentic restoration. All of these new products are striped; none have designs of the damask Venetians.

Ingrain carpets are also manufactured today in a limited number of patterns. Like Venetians, the cost is high and the product does not long survive in high-traffic areas. One solution to this dilemma for owners of old houses is to use a pile carpet woven in an ingrain pattern, thus getting the correct design coupled with a much more durable floor covering. Several companies carry such patterns in their lines with the added benefit of custom coloring. Museum houses, however, may find this alternative unacceptable and will have to use ingrain in their restoration.

Wilton and Brussels carpeting are still in production, although the latter is now known in the trade as "level-looped Wilton." These are available in wool and wool-nylon blends, and these carpets wear extremely well. They may be custom-colored to fit specific requirements. A museum restoration may require custom-designed and -manufactured carpets that can be had in Wilton or Brussels pile.

Unfortunately, tapestry carpets, with their enormous variety of colors, are no longer manufactured. Attempts to reproduce "tapestry Brussels" or "velvets" using modern looms are generally not satisfactory because the weaving process is limited in its use of color.

tapestry for libraries or sitting rooms, Brussels or ingrains for dining rooms, and ingrain for bedrooms.[56]

In "A Word for Carpets" published by Godey in 1859 and aimed at "moderate housekeepers, living within a thousand or twelve hundred a year," readers were informed that "a bright ingrain or three-ply carpet adds twice as much to the cheerfulness of an ordinary sitting-room as a threadbare Brussels or dingy tapestry . . . ; a firm, fine ingrain carpet, costing a dollar a yard, will last, with ordinary wear and care, on a chamber, for six or eight years, and even then respectable bedroom pieces may be cut from it." Furthermore, a Brussels carpet's "original cost is fully one-third more than the best three-ply," and since "it is much narrower, usually wastes more in cutting, and cannot be turned." The author condemned all tapestry carpeting, which might appear more elegant at first "from the richness of the dyes and the grace of the designs, but it defaces sooner and gives nothing like the same wear" as a Brussels.[57]

Catharine Beecher and Harriet Beecher Stowe in *The American Woman's Home* gave similar advice, recounting the story of a woman who set out to purchase an ingrain for her parlor and instead selected a Brussels, which had been reduced by "a dollar and a quarter less a yard than the usual price" because the pattern was unfashionable and the storekeeper wished "to close it off." Unfortunately, she bought "the Brussels carpet, which, with all its reduction in price, is one third dearer than the ingrain would have been, and not half so pretty." They concluded that the hapless shopper now owned "a homely carpet whose greatest merit it is an affliction to remember— namely, that it will outlast three ordinary carpets."[58]

Similar tales appeared throughout the period. In Alice B. Neal's "The Tapestry Carpet; or, Mr. Pinkney's Shopping," a shoemaker from Rhinebeck, New York, journeyed to New York City to purchase an ingrain for the parlor. The shoemaker and his wife had saved for three years in order to afford a carpet. A disreputable clerk informed Pinkney that ingrains were appropriate only for chambers or dining rooms, explaining that "Nobody uses 'em for parlors," and persuaded him to purchase a tapestry that cost more per yard and was narrower, hence requiring additional yardage. When delivered to Rhinebeck, the carpet's brilliant colors made the rest of the parlor furnishings appear shabby, and Mrs. Pinkney's reaction was that her husband must have been mad to purchase a carpet with only "one side" so that it could not be turned. Fortunately, this sensible woman managed to sell the carpet to a doctor's wife and with the proceeds purchased an ingrain, some dress material for herself, and a shawl for their daughter. The moral appears to be that shoemakers' families cannot afford tapestry carpets.[59]

In "The Story of a Carpet" by Alice B. Haven, Mr. and Mrs. Lambert went to New York City to select a carpet for their home in Brooklyn.

Lambert, a bookkeeper earning $1,400 a year, and his "sensible" wife planned to use their old parlor carpet to replace the matting in the bedroom and purchase new carpeting for the formal room. Once again, a crafty salesman tried to convince them that nobody used ingrain anywhere except bedrooms and "even for dining-rooms we generally sell three-plys," which "wear twice as long and . . . are all copied from the Brussels." The Lamberts still decided that three-plys, ranging in price "from ninety cents to a dollar twelve and a half," were appropriate for their needs and their budget, and they selected one for the parlor. Their pleasure was diminished, however, when the salesman casually mentioned that he had just sold such a carpet to Mr. Hastings, Mr. Lambert's coworker, for use in a bedroom and that Hastings had purchased Brussels for his stairs and velvet tapestry for his parlor! Although Mrs. Lambert was envious and wondered how Hastings could afford such style, she sensibly chose a three-ply suiting both room and budget. Once installed, the carpet looked wonderful. Of course, within a few months, Hastings was found guilty of stealing from the firm to pay for his "elegant tastes and expensive habits."[60] Apparently the family of a cashier making $1,800 a year cannot afford tapestry carpets either.

As for carpet designs, the frequency with which critics condemned patterns displaying brightly colored, naturalistic representations of flowers suggests that many homeowners preferred them, a fact supported by surviving nineteenth-century photographs. In an article entitled "Some Advice to Ladies Purchasing Carpets," *Godey's Lady's Book* suggested, "A carpet should always be chosen as a background, upon which the other articles or furniture are to be placed, and should, from its sober colors and unattractive features, have a tendency rather to improve, by comparison, objects placed upon it, than command for itself the notice of the spectator. It should vie with nothing, but rather give value to all objects coming in contact with it. Composed of sombre shades and tones, and treated essentially as a *flat* surface, it exerts a most valuable, though subordinate influence upon all the other decorations of the day."[61]

Most critics agreed on a few guidelines. First, they condemned realistic shading—giving the effect of three dimensions on a two-dimensional surface—as being in poor taste. They insisted that carpet patterns be "flat," meaning they were to have no realistic or trompe l'oeil effect. "Carefully shaded flowers, wreaths, and other vegetative decoration always appear out of place upon the floor to be trodden on," wrote Gervase Wheeler in *Rural Homes*, for "crushing living flowers under foot, even to inhale their odor, is a barbarity, but to tread on worsted ones, odorless, and without form, certainly seems senseless." Instead he preferred "that indescribable mosaic that, whether floral or geometric, never offends the eye by its imitation of flower or foliage."[62]

Silliman and Goodrich, authors of *The World of Art and Industry*, analyzed products displayed at the New York Exhibition of 1853–1854 and heartily condemned the design of an Axminster carpet manufactured by James Templeton and Company of Glasgow, Scotland, as being too realistic. "One is almost afraid to walk here, lest his inadvertent foot should crush the delicate beauty of the roses, or tread out the purple juices of the grapes . . . ; good taste forbids the confused and indiscriminate intermingling of the ornaments of different arts. We do not strew bouquets or pile fruit upon our parlor floors to decorate them, nor should we find it convenient to walk over bronze scrolls, or carved panels and mouldings; and common sense should teach that the pictures of these things are in the same places equally inappropriate. Indeed the impropriety increases as the imitation becomes more deceptive and exact." Instead, the authors suggested, "both the makers and buyers of carpets may profitably refer to the practice of those eastern countries where carpets had their origin. There a strict mosaic principle prevails throughout, and no fac-simile or relievo ornaments being employed, the carpet is smooth and flat in appearance as well as in reality. Turks, Persians, and Hindoos, are commonly classed among barbarous, or at least half-civilised nations, but in the matter of decorating carpets they exhibit a refined taste and correct perception of the fitness of things, such as is rarely seen in the manufactures of Europe."[63]

A second rule advanced by nineteenth-century critics was that a carpet with limited colors was better than one with many. No doubt this rule was

*The dining room of the James Rush house at 17th and Chestnut streets, Philadelphia, drawn about midcentury. The paneled effect of the wallpaper, the pattern of the wall-to-wall carpeting, and the suggestion of the window treatment are quite stylish. The room is set up for a party. (Library Company of Philadelphia)*

a reaction to the colorful effects achieved in tapestry carpets. Miss Leslie cautioned that carpets with "a great variety of different and gaudy colours are much less in demand than formerly." She suggested "two colours only, with the dark and light shades of each, will make a very handsome carpet. A *very light* blue ground, with the figure of shaded crimson or purple, looks extremely well; so does a salmon-colour or buff ground, with a deep green figure; or a light yellow ground, with a shaded blue or purple figure." Even one color could create "the most truly chaste, rich, and elegant carpets . . . where the pattern is formed by one colour only, but arranged in every variety of shade." She included as examples "a Brussels carpet entirely of red; the pattern formed by shades or tints varying from the deepest crimson (almost a black) to the palest pink, almost a white. Also, one of green only, shaded from the darkest bottle-green, in some parts of the figure, to the lightest pea-green in others. Another, in which there was no colour but brown in all its various gradations, some of the shades being nearly black, others of a light buff. All these carpets had much the look of rich cut velvet."[64]

A third rule was that the scale of the pattern should conform to the size of the room—small rooms required small patterns, and so forth. Small patterns were also more economical because they wasted less yardage than large ones when matching the pattern and sewing the widths together.

A fourth rule—and perhaps the most important—was to exercise care regarding the overall effect of the carpet's dominant color in the room. There were two possible approaches. One was the use of a variety of shades and values of one color throughout a room, but this approach, which echoed past fashion, was deemed unfashionable by the 1860s. *Godey's Lady's Book* noted in 1859 that the use of one color was fashionable only for bedrooms. The magazine regretted the change in taste because the technique was "not only in good taste, but saves trouble, as the different apartments may then be generally designated as 'the blue,' 'the green,' 'the red room,' instead of 'my room,' 'the southwest chamber,' 'the room your grandmother had last summer,' etc. etc."[65] The second approach, the use of many colors in a room's scheme, had generally supplanted the use of a single color. The *Lady's Book* referred to Hay's "Treatise on Harmonious Coloring" and then advised readers:

> Taking a room as a whole, and considering its effect as a picture, the colors of the carpet and of the walls form the chief masses in the composition, and necessarily influence every other component part. If the floor and the walls be of the same color, there will be a deficiency of force and of effect from want of contrast; and, on the other hand, if of different colors, equally attractive to the eye, the effect produced would not be that of the whole, because a whole is the result of a co-operation of different subordinate parts with one principal part. While, therefore, they should not be of the same color, they should be of colors that

harmonize, or, in other words, look well together. For example, a very brilliant color, such as crimson, in a carpet, may have a drab or other subdued color in the curtains and paper; but then there should be a portion of the brilliant color introduced in both, as bordering or ornaments.[66]

# WINDOWS By midcentury, homeowners who could afford the lavishly draped windows illustrated in magazines had a variety of styles to choose from. Louis A. Godey, publisher of the *Lady's Book*, claimed credit for introducing these fashions to his tens of thousands of subscribers and through them to all of America. Yet, simpler window coverings hung in most households.

## SHUTTERS, SHUTTER BLINDS, VENETIAN BLINDS

Between 1850 and 1870, critics mentioned window shutters more than any other window treatment. The practice of excluding light from rooms extended back to eighteenth-century America; it had often drawn comment from foreign visitors. Fredrika Bremer observed shutters everywhere during her two-year tour of the United States. Writing in the spring of 1850 from a home along the Hudson River, she reported, "here, as in many other places, I observed how they exclude the daylight from the rooms. This troubles me, who am accustomed to our light rooms in Sweden, and who love the light. But they say that the heat of the sun is too powerful here for the greater part of the year, and that they are obliged as much as possible to exclude its light from the rooms." When Bremer spent July in Washington, D.C., even she conceded that in her room "all is kept cool by the green Venetian shutters."[67]

By 1850 most critics agreed that two types of exterior shutters were useful. The first type, panel shutters, was suited for basement or ground-floor windows to furnish protection against what Samuel Sloan identified as "light-footed agents."[68] Second- and third-story windows, presumably beyond the reach of robbers, used shutters with stationary louvers or, a more recent development, with movable louvers, which offered ventilation, protection from rain and sun, and some privacy. These shutters containing louvers were often identified as "Venetian shutter blinds"—the important word here is "shutter."

By midcentury, critics began to argue in favor of interior shutters, stressing that exterior shutters could be awkward to manipulate and were not particularly attractive on the pointed or arched windows of Gothic cottages or Italianate residences popular at the time. Describing even a simple farmhouse, Lewis F. Allen allowed that "outer blinds may be added . . . but it is usually better to have these *inside*, as they are no ornament to the outside of the building, are liable to be driven back and forth by the wind, even if fastenings are used, and in any event are little better than a continual annoyance."[69] Architects offered two solutions. "Sliding shutter blinds" required hollow wall construction with "pockets" to contain the shutters. This technique increased construction costs, and some writers argued that sliding shutter blinds were often likely to need repair. For these reasons, critics preferred folding shutter blinds that fit into boxes along the interior trim of the window.

The movable louvers on both interior and exterior shutters were attached to a single vertical wooden rod that controlled the angle of tilt within the frame; the rod could also be fastened at one end to tightly shut the louvers. The motion of the louvers in the frame led to these shutters being variously known as "pivot-blinds" or "Venetian rolling blinds." While exterior shutters were commonly painted green, interior ones might be any number of colors. Since they were "intended for convenience rather than for ornament," Miss Leslie cautioned readers, "it is not necessary that Venetian blinds should, like curtains, have a conspicuous effect in the room. On the contrary, it is better that their colour should as nearly as possible match that of the wall."[70]

Interior shutters, with or without louvers, that folded into "boxes" at the sides of the window gradually replaced the hanging Venetian blinds used in the eighteenth and early nineteenth centuries. Fredrika Bremer observed "the stars shining through the Venetian shutters" of her bedroom in Brooklyn, New York; a phenomenon possible only with movable louvers.[71] Other styles persisted, however. For example, the 1859 Ebenezer Maxwell Mansion built in Germantown, Pennsylvania, contains interior folding paneled shutters, while earlier houses continued to use blinds rather than shutters. Philadelphia inventories taken in midcentury generally give low appraisals for Venetian blinds (in contrast to "Venetian rolling blinds"), confirming they were no longer stylish nor salable.

## SHORT BLINDS AND WIRE BLINDS

Writers continued to offer solutions to combat flying insects. Wheeler recommended that all doorways, internal and external, of a "Southern House," be fitted with two doors, "one being a close-panelled, ordinary door, and the other with slats that will open to admit a current of air, and at the same time give seclusion to the room." In addition, "all doors and windows should, for comfortable habitancy of the house, be provided with folding-frames,

*The parlor of the Browne House, 907 Clinton Street, Philadelphia, photographed in 1865. The wallpaper and floral carpeting are in the Rococo style, as is the tall, narrow pier glass between the windows. The absence of any window coverings other than Venetian blinds, and the fireboard and table placed in front of the mantel, suggests spring or summer; however, the photograph is dated December. (Library Company of Philadelphia)*

lightly made, and covered with netting, either of wire, gauze, or muslin, to exclude those flying torments that infest a southern Home." Bremer confirmed the need to follow Wheeler's advice. In Charleston, South Carolina, she wrote, "during the whole meal-time, one of the . . . boys or girls stands with a besom of peacocks' feathers to drive away the flies."[72]

In a short piece of fiction that contains the ring of truth, Mary W. Jarven described a miserable night spent in "Hyacinth Cottage" by a family whose summer home lacked "mosquito-bars," a term for netting used at either beds or windows. As night descended, Mrs. Woodner ordered her child's nurse to "put out the light, Ann, after you have driven out all you can; and then drop your window curtain." The story continued, "An hour later, silence had spread her mantle over Hyacinth Cottage; silence, save the shrill, small 'winding horn' of the insects that roamed the 'stilly night'; but sleep had not yet brought her blessed dew to seal the eyelids of all beneath that roof. 'Maria,' said Mr. Woodner, turning restlessly on his pillow, 'I advise that you cage and train one of the biggest of these mosquitos, in case you want a carrier dove to bear any neighborly dispatches to Mrs. Harrison," the friend whose idea it had been to rent the summer house in the first place.[73]

Writers continued to describe "short blinds" covering the lower sash, which Miss Leslie identified as "very useful in obviating the inconvenience of being seen by persons passing the windows, or of being exposed to the view of opposite neighbours." She never mentioned insects. "For sitting-rooms, chambers, &c., the blinds generally in use are of white muslin. Those of plain unfigured Swiss or Scotch muslin look much the best, but are more easily seen through than when the muslin is striped or cross-barred [stripes running on the horizontal]; if the latter, let the cross-bars be small and close. Large cross-bars give muslin a very ungenteel look for all purposes, even for window blinds." Her directions for making short blinds echoed Loudon and Webster and Parkes. "Two yards of [fifty-four inch] muslin will generally be sufficient for a pair of blinds. They should reach to the top of the lower sash, and descend to the window sill. Hem the bottom of each blind, and make a case in the top, through which run a tape, (securing it by a few stitches in the middle,) and leaving long ends of tape to wrap tightly round the nails which fasten the blind on each side to the window frame. There should be two sets of blinds, as they will frequently require washing. It is well always to starch them a little."[74]

*Godey's Lady's Book* also included directions for making "dwarf blinds." However, the writer conceded, "blinds of wire gauze stretched in a frame are the best that can be used; they last a long time, and are free from the objections peculiar to the Venetian and muslin. But any attempt to disfigure them by absurd ornaments should be rigidly avoided. A plain band of one or two colors, running round, about an inch or two from the edge, is, in general, the most suitable decoration for wire blinds. Beside the wire gauze made in England, there is a kind imported from China which has a very fanciful appearance, with its grotesque paintings, and which suits well with the style of certain old-fashioned rooms." Catharine Beecher and Harriet Beecher Stowe's advice regarding mosquitoes (included in a section entitled "Modes of Destroying Insects and Vermin" in *The American Woman's Home*, which provided methods for exterminating ants, cockroaches, crickets, bed-bugs, and flies) concluded with the suggestion that "close nets around a bed are the only sure protection at night," thus attesting to the rarity of window screens in America at the time.[75]

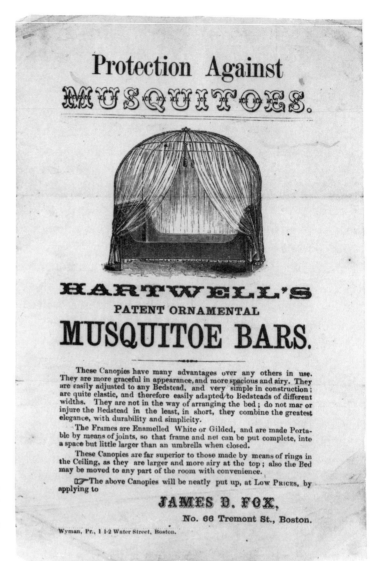

*A mid-nineteenth-century advertisement for "bug bars," illustrating a canopy much like that in the Campbell House Museum in St. Louis. The use of "bug bars" in all parts of the country suggests window screens were rare. (The Athenaeum of Philadelphia)*

## WINDOW SHADES

While architects praised interior louvered shutters, women writers continued to recommend fabric roller blinds, generally called "window shades" by the 1850s. Unlike Venetian blinds that "should every day be dusted with a small brush or a turkey wing, and wiped with a soft dry cloth," Miss Leslie preferred shades because they "soften the glare of the sun without excluding the light" and were easier to maintain. She restricted paper blinds to "common bedrooms, for attics, and for kitchens." Fabric shades, considered far superior, might be the only window cover in the hall, dining room, and library, or they might be combined with curtains, which they protected from the sun, in the parlor and best chamber.[76]

Householders did make their own roller blinds at home, using Holland (a fine linen) or "various kinds of ginghams, and fancy patterns, and transparencies, any one of which may be chosen according to taste or other circumstances." *Godey's Lady's Book* warned, "in cutting them out, pains should be taken to have the top and bottom perfectly square, and the edges perfectly straight; and the needlework required upon them should be so neatly done as to leave the material free from crease or wrinkle; indeed, the blind should present the appearance of not having been touched at all with fingers. The side hems should be lightly herring-boned, this being the only method which leaves the sides sufficiently free to run up and down without a bias." The magazine stessed that "pains should be taken to keep blinds clean as long as possible, because they never look or run so well as before after being washed. A very good way to preserve them, is the practice to make the tuck which receives the lath at the bottom sufficiently large to receive the roller, so that every time the blind is washed it may be changed end for end when it is put up again, and thus be made to last much longer than by keeping the same end always downwards."[77]

While "various contrivances, by spring rollers and otherwise, to make blinds run up and down as well as the usual line and rack-pulley"[78] were being sold by 1860, many homeowners undoubtedly made their own, as in the story "The Unexpected Visitor," which was mentioned earlier. Preparing for a visitor, Aunt Lorrie organized her nieces and nephews to furnish a bedroom. She covered the windows with "roller curtains" and while lacking cords and rollers, she contrived a successful substitute:

> "Albert, can you nail a strip of wood across each window, a little below the top of the framework, leaving room for a cord to pass over?"
>
> "Now drive a hook in the centre of the framework, at the top, and another at the right-hand side. Now, Minnie and Cora, cut off some of that chintz, enough to make a curtain for each window, allowing for a hem broad enough to pass a lath in."
>
> When the curtains were made, the top part was nailed to the strip at the top of the window, and a large cord was securely fastened to the same strip under the curtain. A lath was put into the hem, the cord was carried down, then carried up on the outside of the curtain, passed over the hook at the top, then over the one at the side, and then fastened to a brass knob driven into the side of the framework, within reach of the band. When the cord was drawn the curtain rolled up, when it hung down the curtain hung over the window.[79]

*A homemade window shade illustrated in "The Unexpected Visitor," a story in the January 1859 issue of* Godey's Lady's Book. *A pulley system operated the shade in lieu of the spring-mounted mechanism familiar today. (Historical Society of Pennsylvania)*

Commercially manufactured shades were sold in America by the 1850s. Subscribers to *Godey's Lady's Book* kept abreast of current fashions carried by the Philadelphia shop of Mr. W. H. Carryl, which sold the latest French imports. In 1853, Carryl's had painted and buff-colored Holland shades, which the *Lady's Book* proclaimed were "now used in almost every house in the city." By 1858, Carryl's stocked "gold border window-shades, so indispensable for excluding the sun, of any required size, and in a variety of ornamental and plain patterns . . . of American manufacture. The gold leaf is tastefully arranged on fine cambric, of plain colors, to combine durability and elegance. They are sold from one dollar and a half to eight dollars each, with suitable trimmings and fixtures complete." The most "desirable" colors according to the magazine were buff, stone, ashes of roses (a grayish-pink), pearl, and rose.[80]

Mid-nineteenth-century shades employed borders and centers instead of the overall landscapes that had been popular earlier. The borders were often complicated arrangements—architectural moldings entwined with flowers, or Rococo patterns with decorative motifs in each corner—while the centers often held medallions of flowers, landscapes, or architectural scenes. Carryl's charged from $2 to $20 for shades in 1854, depending on how ornate the painting and gilding. Although Carryl's carried ornate designs, *Godey's Lady's Book* preferred plain shades, declaring "the most tasteful are of perfectly plain buff Holland, with cords and tassels of the same shade. They are much more stylish than the most costly Venetian or painted shades, as they are subdued in color, and can be made to harmonize with any style of furniture. Gothic patterns, painted shades, are sometimes used for halls or libraries; but sprawling bouquets, or flower baskets in gaudy colors, are not considered in taste." Cost and availability, as well as taste, determined what shades a homeowner employed. Like Aunt Lorrie, many women probably made their own or relied on "window curtain paper" advertised as late as 1859 by Josiah Bumstead in Boston, who claimed they were "used extensively in the country."[81]

## CURTAINS

The decoration of museum rooms and historic houses often misleads modern owners of old houses into believing that rich, heavy draping was nearly universal in the nineteenth century. It was not. Even proponents of the fashion confessed it was not common. Louis A. Godey bemoaned in 1851, "almost the first thing noticed by a stranger, on arriving in Philadelphia, is the prevalence of a uniform style of stone-colored or green window blinds, which give a cold, unwinking, unwelcome stare to the passer-by from half the domiciles in our principal streets." He pleaded for the use of heavy curtains at windows: "Picture to yourself, dear reader, the difference between a winter's sun striking coldly through the slats of a stone-colored blind, and the same radiance lighting up the heavy folds of a crimson curtain! and, of all things on a winter's evening, with a light fire in the grate, and a shaded centre lamp lighting the merry home gathering." Godey enlisted practical as well as aesthetic considerations in his crusade:

> When the candles are lit and the shutters closed, a room has rather an unfinished appearance unless the breaks in the wall, caused by the windows, are covered with curtains, and, in rooms where there are no shutters, the curtains are of material service in preserving warmth; for as the glass is kept cool by the air on the outside of the house, the air of the room is chilled by coming in contact with it, and descends with a steady current from the ceiling to the floor. In this way some of the unaccountable draughts felt by those who sit near a window are to be explained; they do not always come from the outside. This cannot take place where there are curtains, as their substance prevents the flow of the air of the room towards the glass, and effectually excludes all unwelcome currents of air that may enter by the windows. Curtains and drapery, therefore, are not merely ornamental; they serve an important purpose. And what an air of snugness and comfort they impart to a room.[82]

*Godey's Lady's Book* claimed credit for creating a demand for curtains in homes across the country. According to Godey, curtains had been "confined to the houses of the wealthy few," but now their use "has spread rapidly where new villages grow into flourishing towns, and the township gives place to a city charter; city halls, State houses and hotels, springing up as if by magic on the lake shores, and along the Upper Mississippi; the very saloons of the floating palaces that convey the summer traveller thither to wonder and admire, are gorgeous with draperies from Carryl's rich importations, and fashioned from designs such as he has furnished for our pages from time to time." According to the *Lady's Book,* Carryl's establishment supplied curtains for the Pennsylvania State House in Harrisburg—crimson India damask lined in white silk—and the statehouse at Austin, Texas—"rich brocatelle hangings, diversified with emblems and mottoes of the Southern State of the Gulf, all finished in superb style." Carryl's also sent curtains and draperies to Western and Southern merchants and undertook commissions for individual homeowners who sent dimensions, a description of the room, and the amount of money they wished to spend. Whether cottage or mansion, the *Lady's Book* assured readers, Carryl's work would meet with satisfaction, with costs of an entire room estimated at $25 to $200.[83]

By 1850, a fully equipped parlor window might include a shade, a valance or lambrequin, an "undercurtain" next to the glass, and a pair of heavier curtains. For pairs of windows, fashion dictated a large mirror be placed on the pier between them and finished with a cornice of stamped brass or gilded wood matching the cornices over the windows. Godey identified this fashion

Godey's Lady's Book *identified this method of treating windows and pier mirror as "a recent innovation of Parisian taste," in October 1851. This particular illustration was printed twice in the magazine, once in August 1854 and again in August 1858. When the curtains were drawn back, their hem just touched the floor. (The Athenaeum of Philadelphia)*

(which replaced the earlier pier table and matching looking glass) as "a recent innovation of Parisian taste."[84] The general effect was a profusion of ornately draped and embellished fabric covering windows, moldings, and much of the wall.

Ornately patterned, gilded wood or stamped metal (brass) cornices replaced the architectural cornices or Neoclassical poles popular earlier. Carryl's stock ranged from "the light metallic stamped cornices to the heaviest wood-carvings covered with burnished gold," at a variety of prices. Such cornices generally employed a valance known as a "lambrequin" that bore some resemblance to the "straight," "plain," and "geometric" valances illustrated in Chapter 1. By midcentury, lambrequins were an integral element of fashionable designs for window coverings. *Godey's Lady's Book* defined them as "a fall of the same material as the curtain, edged with rich gimp [a

*By midcentury, simple geometric valances had become convoluted lambrequins. The more ornate example (left) was illustrated in the September 1852 issue of* Godey's Lady's Book, *while the simpler one (right) appeared in Catharine Beecher and Harriet Beecher Stowe,* The American Woman's Home. *(The Athenaeum of Philadelphia)*

flat, braided trimming used on upholstery and curtains], and usually ornamented by heavy cords and tassels depending from the points of scallops."
However, lambrequins were not always the same fabric as the curtains. The
August 1851 issue of the *Lady's Book* carried descriptions of two designs
available at Carryl's. The first had a lambrequin of plain crimson brocatelle
over a curtain of patterned crimson brocatelle, while the second used a
crimson lambrequin edged in gold over a curtain of gold with a crimson
border. While earlier nineteenth-century valances favored pleats evenly spaced
across the pole, midcentury lambrequins often placed pleats only at the
center and edges, leaving the remainder of the material either flat or slightly
draped.[85]

Various gimps, cords, and tassels increased the rich effects of lambrequins;
gimp was appliquéd in ornate patterns, fringe sewn along the hem, and tassels
"depended from" specific points in the design. These garnishings might also
appear alone, creating a lambrequin of deep fringe attached directly to the
cornice, with cords looped from one side to the other, and tassels added to
the ends. Carryl's advertised exotic garniture such as "one very elegant set,
of green and gold, with the most spider-like delicacy of weaving, and threaded
with large bead moulds, covered with the same, adding twofold to its elegance . . . in the style of Louis IV, and valued—the tassels and cords alone—
at thirty dollars. Others may be had, however, ranging from five dollars to
twenty dollars."[86]

Undercurtains—also called "glass curtains"—hung next to the window.
One 1852 source instructed readers that "no heavy curtains are now in use
without one of lace or muslin to soften the effect." Undercurtains were
shirred onto a rod and either hung straight to the floor or were looped back
during the day. If the first course was followed, the hem just reached the
floor; however, if the undercurtain was looped back, it was cut longer so
that the hem touched the floor during the day but "puddled" at night when
drawn closed. The same cord might loop back both the undercurtains and
the heavier curtains or one could select separate cords in colors coordinating
with the entire ensemble; magazines such as *Godey's Lady's Book* illustrated
both techniques at midcentury.[87]

Next came the heavier pair of curtains suspended from tenterhooks behind the cornice or from a pole hidden by the lambrequin. While iron or
brass rings remained common, sets made of gutta-percha, a plastic gum
obtained from Southeast Asian trees, were preferred by many because they
made less noise as the curtains were drawn. One sewed the rings directly
onto tape at the top of the curtain or attached them to hooks imbedded in
the tape. Curtains remained unpleated with folds depending on the weight
and amount of material used in each panel. As before, curtains were drawn
by hand or by a pulley system, the latter preferred "where the room is lofty,

or the curtains heavy." In either case, the outermost rings were attached to hooks at the edges of the window molding, which prevented the outer edge of the curtain from slipping toward the inside of the window as the curtains were drawn.[88]

The drapery poles were generally attached to the window moldings. However, in low rooms, critics recommended placing the cornice and lambrequin at the ceiling to avoid covering the window glass. And in cases where the windows were unusually narrow the poles were extended six to eight inches beyond the moldings to make the windows appear wider and to admit as much light as possible.

Various considerations determined the amount of fabric needed for the curtains. Critics continued to recommend a finished length *eighteen to twenty-four inches longer* than the actual distance from the rod to the floor; otherwise, "when looped up during the day, their lower edges will be so far above the floor as to give them a very mean appearance. They should be of such a length as to reach the floor when looped up, and, when drawn at night, this extra length rests on the floor in a heavy mass of folds." However, the finished width of the curtains "must depend somewhat on the purchaser's means and inclination: but if too scanty, there is not only a poverty of effect, but also a loss of protection, for small curtains do not exclude draughts. For ordinary windows, three feet or three feet six inches wide, not less than two breadths should be taken, and this quantity may be increased at pleasure, according to taste or to differences in width." Keep in mind that most fabrics used for curtains during the mid-nineteenth century were twenty-two to thirty-six inches wide.[89]

Adjusting curtains required some skill. One critic instructed that "when the curtains are looped up in the morning, some pains should be taken to make the folds fall gracefully; some people take no pains in this particular. The curtains may be suspended over the band or loop, either towards the window or away from it; or it may hang straight up and down." The author concluded, "indeed, there are almost as many ways of arranging the curtains as of folding napkins for the dinner-table, and they may all be found out by a little ingenuity." *Godey's Lady's Book* suggested, "One method is by a long loop of silk or worsted cord, with or without a tassel, suspended from a hook three or four feet above the floor, which is the usual height. Bands of bronze or brass, too, are much used, fixed either upright or horizontally, as may be tasteful and convenient. The upright bands are generally found most suitable for small rooms. Curtain pins—that is, handsome rosettes of wood or metal—are also used for the same purpose; but, at the present time, they are not so well liked as the bands or loops." Another midcentury device for looping back curtains were pairs of glass pins in the shape of "some well-known fruit or flower, in Bohemian glass, mounted on a rich gilt foliage;

*This illustration from an advertisement in the October 1866 issue of* Godey's Lady's Book *shows two ways to loop back curtains using the same cords, tassels, and pins. The illustration had been published in the magazine in September 1859 by Carryl's, the shop later bought by Walraven's, which ran the same advertisement again. (The Athenaeum of Philadelphia)*

tulips, lilies, and fuchsias being among the favorites, given in different tints of glass, to correspond with the curtains—as dead white, pale emerald-green, etc."[90]

### Curtain Materials

Writers of the 1850s and 1860s suggested that window coverings should fit the style of the furnishings—rather than the architectural style of the house, as Downing had earlier recommended—and described curtains as "classical," "Louis IV," "Louis XIV," or, more commonly, "elegant" and "in the latest fashion," terms generally descriptive of the Rococo Revival and Renaissance Revival styles popular at the time. The only fabrics available for use at windows were composed of cotton, flax (linen), wool, and silk. The last remained beyond the budget of most families; *Godey's Lady's Book* noted that silk "brocade, damask, satin, taffeta, tabaret, plush, serge, and velvet . . . produce the richest possible effects, but . . . need not be further entered upon here" because they were so costly. However, a limited number of *fibers* did not imply a limited number of *fabrics*. Midcentury households used the fabrics mentioned in Chapter 1, in addition to several others. One was satin, made of silk or a less expensive wool-and-silk blend known as "satin laine"; both had a smooth, shiny surface created by "floating" warp threads over five to eight weft threads, followed by calendaring. Silk satins from India cost up to $10 a yard, while Carryl's estimated an entire window might be curtained in striped laine (a woolen material) for $25 to $45 depending upon the trimmings. Writers recommended these fabrics for parlors, dining rooms, and libraries.[91]

Carryl's advertised brocatelles—a fabric whose pattern, created in one type of weave, stood out in high relief against a background formed of another weave—in *single colors* (including crimson, green, blue, light rose, and dark rose), *two colors* (including blue and gold, garnet and crimson, gold and green, purple and gold, blue and fawn), and *three colors* (including gold with two shades of green, maroon with two shades of crimson, gold with two shades of blue, and crimson with maroon and gold). This material cost more than satin laine. Carryl's charged $90 to $120 for a set of "plain" curtains in French silk brocatelle.[92]

Damask—a fabric consisting of plain and satin weaves creating a pattern that reverses from one side of the material to the other—was available in wool ("merino"), silk, and cotton. Although wool and silk created superior fabrics for window coverings, homeowners could purchase less expensive products such as cotton damask or "union damask," made of cotton and wool. Carryl's advertised "union damask" curtains at $10 a window and all-cotton German damasks at fifty cents to $1 a yard.[93]

In general, mid-nineteenth-century writers recommended specific fibers for specific rooms in the house. With silk beyond the reach of most middle-class households, critics preferred woolens for parlors, dining rooms, and libraries. In addition to satins, brocatelles, and damasks, woolen fabrics included velvets, brocades, reps (solid-colored or printed), plain weaves, and "watered moreens." Cotton remained the choice for bedrooms, with chintzes and calicoes popular, although by midcentury "chintz" had come to mean any glazed, printed cotton—previously it had referred specifically to a cotton textile printed in five or more colors on a white or colored ground.[94]

"Tamboured" (embroidered) muslin or lace undercurtains were available at various prices depending upon pattern complexity and country of origin. Carryl's advertised lace pairs from $15 to $50 or muslin sets bordered in Swiss lace from $3 to $30.[95] *Godey's Lady's Book* also included patterns and instructions for netting undercurtains at home.

In choosing the colors of curtains, mid-nineteenth-century households probably relied on Hay's theories of color harmony espoused by the critics. They employed *harmony by contrast* when furnishing public rooms such as parlors and dining rooms; the walls, upholstery, floor and window coverings each provided an area of correctly contrasting color in the room. Sloan told readers "a good contrast is more pleasing than sameness, even though the material be rich." The selection required care. Masury recommended the walls of the room provide the color contrast to all the fabrics and suggested they harmonize with one another *by analogy*. As an example, Masury described a room in which the upholstery, window coverings, and floor coverings were reds, browns, crimsons, scarlets, and perhaps an "admixture" of orange or gold against walls finished in greens. For bedrooms, however, most authors agreed that harmony *by analogy* was best, with one hue in various tints and shades throughout the room. Critics also suggested using the same fabric in bedrooms to curtain the windows and the bed and upholster any furniture, a technique not acceptable for parlors and dining rooms at midcentury.[96]

*This advertisement of W. H. Carryl and Brother, which appeared in the June 1859 issue of* Godey's Lady's Book, *is particularly interesting because it pictures a method of curtaining a bay window with two curtain panels and one valence. (Historical Society of Pennsylvania)*

W. H. CARRYL & BROTHER,
IMPORTERS AND DEALERS IN CURTAIN MATERIALS.
NO. 719 CHESTNUT ST., MASONIC HALL, PHILADELPHIA, PENNA.

CURTAINS AND TRIMMINGS.

FURNITURE COVERINGS.
Every style and description.

LACE AND MUSLIN CURTAINS.

CURTAINS MADE AND TRIMMED IN THE NEWEST STYLE.

GOLD BORDERED WINDOW SHADES.

FRENCH BROCATELLES.
All colors.

FRENCH SATIN DAMASK, AND BROCADES.

SATIN DE LAINES.

UNION DAMASKS AND REPS.

WORSTED DAMASKS FOR CHURCHES.

TASSELS, FRINGE, GIMPS, CORD, ETC.

GILT CORNICES.
All styles.

BANDS, PINS, ETC. ETC.

CURTAINS FOR A BAY WINDOW.

*This engraving of an English parlor has all the familiar midcentury touches on the walls, windows, and floors and includes Rococo-style furniture. The illustration appeared in C. H. Savory,* The Paper Hanger, Painter, Grainer, and Decorator's Assistant, *published in London in 1879, but the style of the interior is years earlier. (The Athenaeum of Philadelphia)*

A fully draped and curtained parlor window—complete with cornice, rich fabrics for lambrequin, curtains, undercurtains, shade, and cords, tassels, gimp, and drapery pins—might easily cost hundreds of dollars during the nineteenth century. Middle-class households with incomes of $1,000 a year could not easily afford such window treatments, which cost more than many floor coverings. On the eve of the Civil War, *Godey's Lady's Book* stressed economy, warning readers, "a room which has been some time used may be made to look shabby all of a sudden, with all that is in it, by new and showy window curtains, when hangings of a quiet character would have harmonized and given a tone of relief and cheerfulness to the whole." The magazine suggested, "In addition to the question of taste, there is one of an economical nature; and that is the use to which a room is to be put. If it is already overcrowded with furniture, or if it be the common family room where the children pass most of their time, it would be a mistake to trim the windows with a large mass of hangings. The aim should be to have that which is most suitable in all respects—not to shut out too much light nor to hinder ventilation."[97]

The full-blown window treatments illustrated in *Godey's Lady's Book* probably appeared only in the most formal rooms of any house. Significantly, Fredrika Bremer, who frequently commented on windows and ventilation

**Old Age,** *from "The Four Seasons of Life" series, published by Currier and Ives in 1868, depicts grandparents in their sitting room. The foliated pattern of the wall-to-wall carpeting and the window treatment, resembling those in* Godey's Lady's Book, *are both fashionable. Not everything is current, however. The sofa with the bolster pillow to the left of the fireplace was stylish decades earlier. (The Library of Congress)*

in American homes, never mentioned such curtains and draperies in her record of her American travels; most houses undoubtedly had simpler window coverings. For example, the *Lady's Book* described a "summer drapery" in this fashion: "the cornice is of a lighter style, the long curtains of delicate French lace embroidery, and the lambrequin . . . with its heavy garniture of fringe, cords, tassels, and gimp" forming the only truly ornate note. This mode was "especially suited to country houses, used chiefly in the summer season, and usually more lightly furnished than a town residence."[98] It may also have appeared year round in a great many homes where the cost of heavier draperies was prohibitive. Furthermore, the *Lady's Book* advised:

> The question here arises whether the high-priced or the low-priced is to be preferred; but we think, with regard to hangings, that, as a rule, the low-priced should be chosen. The best quality of damask, or drapery material of any kind, will last a lifetime; on the other hand, the common qualities may be purchased two or three times in the same period for the same cost. We, therefore, should decide for cheap hangings, and

afford ourselves the pleasure of seeing our rooms newly decorated at least once in ten years. There is more economy in the plan than appears at first sight. Cleanliness, and consequently health, are promoted, and frequent opportunities are offered for the exercise and gratification of taste.[99]

Many middle-class homes of the 1850s and 1860s undoubtedly followed this advice, or continued to use the simpler window coverings popular in the preceding decades. (See Plates 11 and 12.)

# THE 1870 TO 1890 PERIOD

On the eve of the American Civil War, the immigrant artist Emanuel Leutze mounted a scaffold in the United States Capitol to begin his grand allegorical-historical mural, *Westward the Course of Empire.* The inexorable drive to dominate a continent faltered only momentarily as North and South clashed. The drive quickly resumed in the late 1860s, sweeping aside the native Indians and wrenching wealth from virgin soil to satisfy the rapacious needs of an emerging industrial nation. Between 1870 and 1890 the American frontier virtually disappeared. Seven states entered the Union within those two decades: Colorado, the Dakotas, Wyoming, Montana, Idaho, and Washington; the nation's population increased by 23 million (nearly a third of them immigrants) to a total of almost 63 million. The urban population continued to grow at an even faster rate than the rural: by 1890 a third of the American people lived in towns and cities of more than 2,500 residents. Twenty-eight American cities had populations of over 100,000, while New York, Chicago, and Philadelphia exceeded a million each.

Between 1870 and 1890 the federal and state governments enticed the railroad companies to open routes through sparsely populated areas. The miles of track doubled, encouraging the settlement of Western lands, and bringing an end to the frontier. Railroads changed the living standards of most Americans by forging the links necessary for a national economy and a mass market. The railroads made it possible for a smaller percentage of farm workers than at any time in history to feed the growing urban work force. The transformation from an agrarian/mercantile society to an industrial one accelerated in the post–Civil War years. New industries, such as the canned food industry, which was spawned in part by the California Gold Rush, flourished. Encouraged by the need to provision armies during the Civil War, companies like those of Philip Armour and Gail Borden grew

*The entry hall of the Bullard-Hart House, Columbus, Georgia. (Courtesy of the Bullard-Hart House; photograph by Joe Maher)*

quickly. The first refrigerated railroad cars appeared in the 1870s and made possible meat-packing firms such as the one founded by Edwin and Gustavus Swift in 1878. By 1884, refrigerator cars carried meat, fish, fresh fruits, and vegetables across the continent and to the home "icebox"—a term coined around the year 1860.

Dry-goods and furniture manufacturers competed for the national market and a place in the urban "department store," a new creation in the decades after the Civil War. In 1823, an Irish immigrant, Alexander T. Stewart, opened a small store in New York that eventually became the first American department store, A. T. Stewart & Co.; John Wanamaker of Philadelphia, Marshall Field of Chicago, and others throughout the country imitated Stewart with varying degrees of success. To reach distant consumers, thirty-one-year-old Aaron Montgomery Ward parlayed $2,400 into a mail-order business in 1872. Postwar American industry created surpluses in consumer products, which gave the average individual a choice of products and brands, something previously available only to the rich.

As railroads changed the standard of living for Americans scattered across the continent, urban transportation networks altered the lives of city residents. By the 1870s, horse-drawn trolleys were replacing omnibuses. The faster, more reliable trolleys helped determine the outward thrust of urban growth. For those residents with sufficient means, the trolley lines meant a chance to live in new suburban areas beyond the crowded city centers. The middle class's exodus from cities began in the 1870s.

And what of the American home? It too felt the effects of new technology. As municipal sewage systems struggled to keep pace with growing urban populations, Charles Harrison patented the now familiar oval-shaped toilet bowl, which broke up the centrifugal force of flushing water and eliminated the need for the ominously named "save-all tray" previously considered standard equipment. By the 1880s some American writers on interior decoration began to reflect the public acceptance of bathrooms as places of pleasure, rather than mere "necessaries," and offered suggestions to make them "pretty and cheerful."[1] And in Menlo Park, New Jersey, in 1879, Thomas Alva Edison brought together all the complex elements necessary for a successful, practical electrical lighting system.

It is likely, however, that the name most familiar to Americans of taste in this period was that of an Englishman, Charles Eastlake (1836–1906). In 1872, Eastlake's work *Hints on Household Taste in Furniture, Upholstery & Other Details* (1868) was first printed in America, and the author attained a level of influence previously achieved only by Andrew Jackson Downing, who had died nearly twenty years before. By 1878, echoing Fredrika Bremer's praise of Downing a generation earlier, Harriet Spofford, herself a writer on household design, told readers that Eastlake's book met "a great want" in America. "Not a young marrying couple who read English," she maintained, "were to be found without *Hints on Household Taste* in their hands, and all its dicta were accepted as gospel truths."[2]

The popularity of Eastlake's book served to spread the reform movement in design throughout the United States. Charles Eastlake did not arrive at his reform theories in a vacuum, however. By midcentury, several British designers, architects, and critics, such as John Ruskin (1819–1900), A. W. N. Pugin (1812–1852), and Owen Jones (1809–1874), were at work. Eastlake and these other British critics would profoundly influence British and American design; their influence can be seen in the work of the designers and writers of the 1870–1890 period, including Christopher Dresser (1834–1903), Walter Crane (1845–1915), William Morris (1834–1896), and Louis Tiffany (1848–1933), to name but a few.

Eastlake deplored the ornate, highly decorated and polished furniture associated particularly with the Rococo Revival; he described these furnishings as poorly made items designed only to capture a market temporarily ensnared by their novelty. He urged readers to purchase simple furniture lacking veneers, lustrous finishes, and excessive ornamentation. *Hints on Household Taste* illustrated pieces with something of a medieval quality, a style praised by William Morris and other British designers associated with the Arts and Crafts Movement, who employed the new aesthetic in all aspects of decoration including wall, floor, and window coverings.

A spate of American design critics, all claiming to be disciples of Eastlake, emerged to influence the decorating choices of homeowners. Even as the rapidly expanding American economy rattled through a serious depression and several economic panics, the income of the average family grew in real terms, increasing the money for nonessentials—embellishments and home furnishings, for example. Nearly ten million Americans, almost a quarter of the population, traveled to Philadelphia in the summer of 1876 to celebrate the national Centennial. If nineteenth-century authors are to be believed, Americans returned to their homes both infatuated with the exotic tastes of foreign cultures and imbued with a missionary zeal to spread the new aesthetic they had encountered. The novelty was quickly disseminated in other ways as well. For instance, the Mitchell and Rammelsburg Furniture Company of Cincinnati, Ohio, whose products were displayed at the fair, redesigned several of its showrooms after the Centennial, importing, according to a Cincinnati newspaper, "an artist in household decoration" from England who "supervised the fitting up in the store of three rooms illustrative of the dispensation of aestheticism." According to the reporter, these newly appointed reform rooms "quietly revolutionized the interior decoration of the homes of wealth in the valley of Ohio."[3] In the pages that follow, we will explore how that revolution changed the interiors of American houses.

# WALLS AND CEILINGS

### THE TRIPARTITE WALL

Changes in taste during the 1870–1890 period transformed the treatment of walls. Eastlake dismissed two popular midcentury wall treatments. He condemned the fashion of arranging paper in vertical panels around the room as "attractive from its novelty" but "false in principle," concluding, "no one need regret that it has fallen into disuse." The second treatment, covering a wall "all over with an unrelieved pattern of monotonous design," he labeled "the most dreary method of decorating the wall of a sitting-room." Eastlake favored instead the use of three-foot-high wainscoting around the walls of the principal rooms, both for visual interest and to protect the walls from "careless fingers" and contact with chairs.[4]

The use of wainscoting had its admirers before Eastlake; architects such as Gervase Wheeler and E. W. Godwin had recommended it for halls, entries,

*Wainscoting in the stair hall of a design published by Henry Hudson Holly in* Modern Dwellings in Town and Country. *(The Athenaeum of Philadelphia)*

and kitchens. Eastlake, however, greatly popularized wainscoting, or its imitation, in *all* rooms of the house. And in his use of wainscoting, he introduced the new three-part horizontal treatment of wall surfaces, which remained stylish for two decades. This division included a wainscoting or dado at the bottom of the wall, a frieze or cornice at the top, and a field between the wainscoting and frieze. The top of the wainscoting was generally thirty-six to forty-two inches above the floor. The English designer Christopher Dresser suggested that the "proportion which is most pleasing will be found to be of a subtle character; four to four is bad; four to three or five to eight is better." Consequently, wainscoting occasionally reached heights of sixty inches or even level with doorway architraves, although the most common treatment was to divide the wall at less than half its height.[5]

American critics echoed Eastlake. In *Modern Dwellings in Town and Country* (1878), the architect Henry Hudson Holly hailed the dado for resolving the decorating conflict that arises because "furniture and costume show to a better advantage when the walls of an apartment are dark, while pictures look well upon a light background." The three-part treatment of wall surfaces resolved this problem: "The dado, or lower three feet of the walls, may be dark in color; the surface, where the pictures are to be hung, of a neutral tint; while in the cornice and ceiling any number of brilliant hues may appear." Holly firmly believed "it would be well if this arrangement of colors were to be made the rule in decorating apartments."[6]

Other writers hailed the dado for different reasons. In *How to Furnish a Home* (1882), Ella Rodman Church, a writer on household decoration, favored the dado "to break the monotony of an unrelieved pattern the whole height of the room." Clarence Cook, an influential writer on decoration whose columns appeared in *Scribner's Monthly*, wrote in *What Shall We Do With Our Walls?* (1881) that wallpaper was more beautiful when "sparingly used," and wainscoting naturally reduced the amount of paper. He condemned "the old style [which] was, to cover the walls with one vast expanse

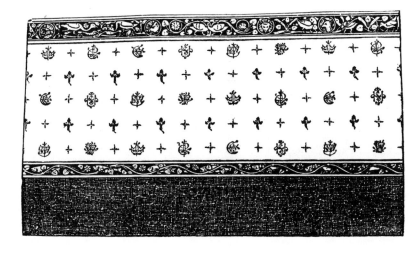

*A design for a tripartite wall in Charles L. Eastlake,* Hints on Household Taste *(Boston, 1877), follows the advice of Christopher Dresser that decoration should never divide a wall in half. In this example, the dado and dado rail occupy only one-third of the wall. (The Athenaeum of Philadelphia)*

of paper, from end to end, and from cornice to mop-board." He added, "it would be hard to say which had the more disheartening effect upon the visitor, the sight of this desert when the paper was of a pale tint just off the white, or when it was of a dark ground with a sprawling design, or else with a very set pattern profusely relieved with gold."[7]

In addition to visually lowering ceilings, R. W. Shoppell suggested in *Modern Houses, Beautiful Homes* (1887), dadoes gave continuity to a room, and the wall above the dado supplied a less decorated surface suitable for hanging pictures. In keeping with the new horizontal emphasis, critics recommended hanging pictures at standing eye level (by which they meant at a height of five feet, six inches) in a single row around the room and never "skyed" (placed high up, one above another) as they had been hung in the past. Critics recommended hanging pictures on hooks and cords from a picture rail just under the frieze to avoid defacing plaster walls and to permit greater flexibility in positioning; most preferred unobtrusive cords corresponding in color to the wall.[8]

There were several ways to achieve the tripartite division. The most expensive employed wood paneling designed specifically for the room. Few households could afford this treatment for all rooms; often it appeared only in entry halls and dining rooms, where it would be least hidden by furniture. By the 1880s, however, several companies offered *ready-made* wooden wainscoting one-quarter inch to seven-eighths inch thick and glued onto heavy cloth for easy installation. The least expensive of the ready-made wainscoting

*The recommended method of hanging pictures involved cords, hooks, and a picture rail generally placed below the frieze. A Gothic interior (right) from Harriet Spofford,* Art Decoration Applied to Furniture, *depicts the effect of using the sort of hardware (above) illustrated by Clarence Cook,* The House Beautiful. *(The Athenaeum of Philadelphia)*

*The tripartite wall division was not restricted to Gothic interiors; exotic styles such as Moorish and Japanesque, pictured here in Cook,* The House Beautiful, *also employed it. (The Athenaeum of Philadelphia)*

used plain vertical boards—perhaps of two different woods to create a custom appearance—which was finished with a wooden cap, making installation and fitting fairly easy.[9]

Of course, a simpler solution was to attach a molding strip to the wall about thirty-six to forty-two inches above the floor, and apply paint or paper to the surfaces on either side, a treatment favored by William Morris. One could use either calcimine or oil-based paints. Henry T. Williams and Mrs. C. S. Jones, the authors of several books on home decorating, assured readers of *Beautiful Homes* (1878) that painting in calcimine was so simple that "a number of ladies" had applied it themselves, touching up areas they had missed after the surface was dry. That claim was dubious; *House Painting and Decorating,* a trade magazine begun in 1885, warned its professional readership that "care must be taken to have no patches requiring to be gone

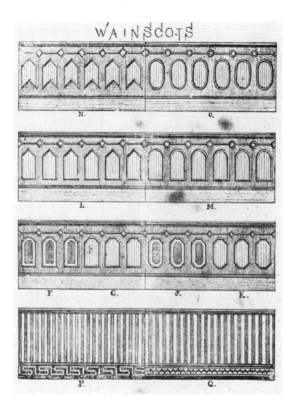

*Ready-made wainscoting available from the c. 1880 catalogue of the Decorative Wooden Carpet Company of Warren, Illinois. (The Athenaeum of Philadelphia)*

over" because it was nearly impossible to paint spots missed without altering the color. All writers agreed, however, that calcimine was less expensive than oil paints and many favored the "softer" matte finish to glossier oil surfaces. Williams and Jones described "tints the most lovely and delicate, or deep and full-toned with a finish far softer and more beautiful than [oil] paint can be obtained with, but (comparatively) small outlay of money, and with less labor than either paper-hanging or painting." Because calcimine was water soluble, it was reserved for walls, while oil-based paints covered the wainscoting. The permanence of oil-based paints recommended them in an article entitled "Sanitary Decoration in the Home," which appeared in *House Painting and Decorating* in 1886.[10]

The tripartite wall could also be achieved without the application of wood moldings by using sets of wallpaper imitating dado, field, and frieze patterns. Many companies and well-known designers—Christopher Dresser, E. W. Godwin, and Walter Crane, to name a few—created such papers. Henry Hudson Holly urged householders to purchase them, in part because he deplored the skills of most housepainters, about whom he wrote, "it is scarcely too much to say that those possessing positive skill can almost be counted on one's fingers. Wall-papers are a simple remedy for this difficulty," he suggested, "as, when the selections have once been made, all that is then necessary is to find a man who can properly apply them."[11]

*Sets of wallpapers forming dado, field, and frieze designed by* (left) *Christopher Dresser,* (center) *E. W. Godwin, and* (right) *Walter Crane. All were illustrated in Henry Hudson Holly,* Modern Dwellings in Town and Country. *(The Athenaeum of Philadelphia)*

Lincrusta-Walton was another alternative that became popular during the 1880s. In 1877, Frederick Walton—who created linoleum in 1863—patented the process for embossing semiliquid linseed oil, backed with heavy canvas or waterproofed paper. Five years later, using Walton's patents, Frederick Beck and Company opened the first American factory to produce Lincrusta, in Stamford, Connecticut. By November 1885, *House Painting and Decorating* informed readers the product was "sold by dealers in decoration in most cities." A brochure from Beck and Company recommended Lincrusta for dadoes because "its solid substantial appearance . . . harmonizes with and relieves the richest papers, and protects the walls from injury when they are most liable to harm from blows, the backs of chairs, children playing, and such like minute perils, against which a careful householder will desire to guard."[12]

Although Lincrusta was a thick, heavily embossed material, it was applied much like wallpaper. When heated it became soft and easy to shape, which allowed it to conform to corners and curves. Available in a few colors or plain, it could be further painted or highlighted once installed to resemble wood, leather, or metals. Households unable to afford those better finishes turned to Lincrusta. Its durability and variety of designs made it especially popular for entries, halls, and dining rooms.

Householders of the 1870s and 1880s might choose other new embossed products, including Japanese leather paper, anaglypta, and Tynecastle tapestry. Japanese leather paper, as its name implies, was made in Japan to imitate the appearance of hand-tooled leather. It was created by embossing thick rolls of paper, eighteen or thirty-six inches wide by twelve feet long, with designs generally finished in gold metallic with or without a second

*Lincrusta-Walton came in a variety of patterns suitable for various uses, as pictured in the catalogue of Frederick Beck and Company, c. 1884. Beck and Company opened in Stamford, Connecticut, in 1882 as the first American manufacturers of Lincrusta. (The Athenaeum of Philadelphia)*

color. Anaglypta was a thick, embossed paper first patented in England in 1887 by Thomas J. Palmer, manager of the Lincrusta-Walton Company. Not as durable as Lincrusta, anaglypta was suitable for wall, frieze, and ceiling decorations; it was colored or glazed to fit the scheme of the room. Tynecastle tapestry, less expensive than Lincrusta-Walton, was canvas stiffened with glue and embossed with a pattern while still wet; the designs were in greater relief than those on Lincrusta. Less exotic alternatives included so-called cartridge papers with designs printed onto thick, smooth surfaces; ingrain (or oatmeal) papers where the pulp was dyed before the paper was made (producing a color "ingrained" in the paper); and "sanitary papers" printed in washable oil-based pigments.[13]

## THE DECORATED CEILING

Ceilings were increasingly decorated by the 1880s, and the practice remained fashionable for decades. Critics labeled white ceilings "crude and harsh" and in terrible contrast to stylish dark walls. Cook declared them "disagreeable to everybody" and the decorator Almon Varney happily informed readers of *Our Homes and Their Adornments* (1885), "walls and ceilings are no longer left in monotonous white where even the presence of a soiled spot affords relief for the eye, but are now beautiful in many ingenious ways to relieve the dreary expanse." By the 1880s, white ceilings were fashionable only if the rest of the room was also white.[14]

Ceilings, commonly eight to fourteen feet above the floor, utilized a variety of decorative treatments. Williams and Jones suggested first tinting a ceiling three shades lighter than the walls and then adding some ornamentation to arrive at a "simply enriched" effect. Recommended colors included violet, lavender, blue, peach blossom, straw color, and gray. A simple ornamental technique was "pencil striping," in which colors were applied in various widths, none smaller than one-eighth inch, around the edge of the cornice. Another was stenciling, which gave the householder a chance to create unique decorations suited to specific rooms and taste.[15]

Three-dimensional ornaments in wood, plaster of Paris, or papier-mâché were also used to decorate ceilings. By the 1880s, several American companies carried center medallions for use above hanging light fixtures, ornate cornice moldings, and details for corners. French & Co. of Philadelphia advertised all styles in 1888, from "the flat Wall Centre for frescoing, to the heavy Moorish drop." Tin ceilings also produced ornamental effects. Bakewell & Mullins of Salem, Ohio, stressed that such ceilings were cheaper, lighter, and more durable than stucco and cast work. They were shipped from the factory in "lustreless white" to resemble plaster ceilings and once installed could "be painted and ornamented to suit the taste of the purchasers,

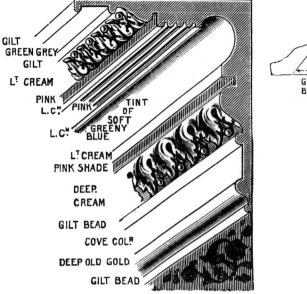

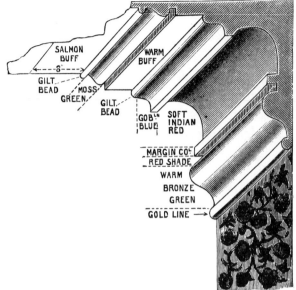

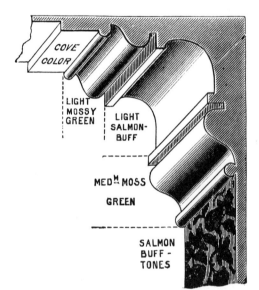

*Suggestions for painting the cornices in: (top left) a parlor, (top right) a dining room, and (right) a bedroom. Although these illustrations first appeared in* House Decoration, *in 1894, the colors recommended are distinctly part of the 1870–1890 palette. (The Athenaeum of Philadelphia)*

and to correspond with the style and decoration of the room where used."[16]

The easiest way to obtain a decorative ceiling was with wallpaper. Because most housepainters could not execute decorative ceilings, Cook confessed "wallpaper is the only substitute that is within the means of most people." (See Plate 13.) Fred Miller, an English decorator, also found the result of papered ceilings satisfying. In his book, *Interior Decoration* (1885), he told readers, "it is a somewhat modern innovation to put pattern papers on ceilings, but it has much to recommend it, since a paper can be cleaned with bread [wiping with slices of bread removed the grime but not the pigment]

*Two examples of painted ceilings from* Interior Decoration *by Fred Miller, who described them as being "of a simple character that might be produced almost, if not entirely, by stencilling." (The Athenaeum of Philadelphia)*

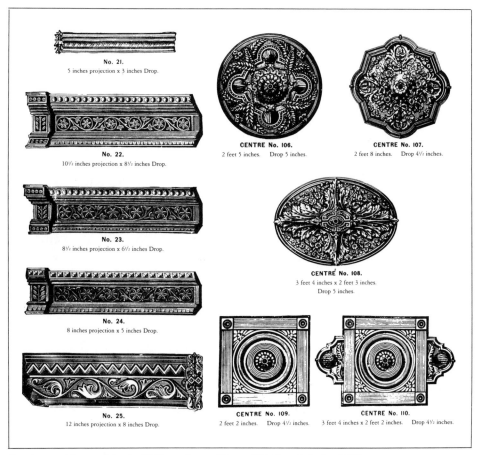

No. 21.
5 inches projection x 3 inches Drop.

No. 22.
10½ inches projection x 8½ inches Drop.

No. 23.
8½ inches projection x 6½ inches Drop.

No. 24.
8 inches projection x 5 inches Drop.

No. 25.
12 inches projection x 8 inches Drop.

CENTRE No. 106.
2 feet 5 inches.    Drop 5 inches.

CENTRE No. 107.
2 feet 8 inches.    Drop 4½ inches.

CENTRE No. 108.
3 feet 4 inches x 2 feet 3 inches.
Drop 5 inches.

CENTRE No. 109.
2 feet 2 inches.    Drop 4½ inches.

CENTRE No. 110.
3 feet 4 inches x 2 feet 2 inches.    Drop 4½ inches.

*Cornices and "centres" in the 1882 catalogue of Samuel H. French & Co., Philadelphia. Centre No. 108 cost $5.50 and Cornice No. 25 was forty-five cents a foot. (The Athenaeum of Philadelphia)*

*A ceiling design using wallpapers illustrated in* Modern Houses, Beautiful Homes *(1887), by R. W. Shoppell, who recommended papers with simple, nondirectional patterns as the most appropriate. (The Athenaeum of Philadelphia)*

and brightened up two or three times, and will last much longer than a distempered ceiling, besides being richer in effect, and more in harmony with the other surroundings than would be the case with a plain ceiling." Ceiling papers were not the same as wallpapers, however; critics recommended nondirectional patterns that appeared the same from all parts of the room. They also preferred "conventional" (that is, stylized) to realistic patterns.[17]

In their book, *Interior Decoration,* published in 1887, the architects Arnold W. Brunner and Thomas Tryon continued to recommend ceiling ornaments. Presaging a treatment popular in the last decade of the nineteenth century, they suggested that cove molding be used to join the walls and ceiling. If the ceiling was *too high,* wall and frieze colors traveled over the cove onto the ceiling where they met a separate treatment; if *too low,* the treatment was reversed and colors carried from the ceiling over the cove to meet the wall decoration.[18]

## WOODWORK

Whatever material a householder chose for the walls and ceilings, fairly standard rules determined color placement: the ceiling was the lightest color, the walls and dado darker, and the woodwork darkest. Critics generally recommended staining hardwood trim in some natural color and painting softwood to correspond with the overall color scheme of the room. Some traditional finishes lost favor: white paint was declared "objectionable" by Ella Rodman Church, and graining was a sham that was "never very good; every scratch or mar reveals the color of the true wood, and there is a tendency for the paint to peel off in spots, giving the surface a most disagreeable eruptive appearance." Perhaps the most telling evidence of the decline in graining appeared in the trade magazine *House Painting and Decorating,* where writers admitted few painters could do it well without using stencils.[19]

Woodwork, if not stained and varnished, was painted to coordinate with other colors in the room; except in bedrooms, the finishes were far more vibrant than the less complex hues previously used. Constance Cary Harrison, an accomplished writer and leader of New York society, recommended black, maroon, chocolate brown, orange-green, dull India red, dark Antwerp blue, and bronze-green as appropriate colors for woodwork, in *Woman's Handiwork in Modern Homes* (1882). Several hues, or several values of one hue, created interesting variations. In *Interior Decoration,* Fred Miller suggested painting doors and window shutters gold on black, India red on black, or cream-ivory on black, using the lighter color of each pair for the panels and the darker for the stiles and rails surrounding the panels. A more complex arrangement entailed painting the baseboards and the molding around the door the darkest value, the stiles and rails of the door and of the dado a middle value, and the panels the lightest. One might paint or gild the beads around the panels or draw a simple line on the stiles about three-eighths of an inch out from the panels, although Miller cautioned "it is seldom necessary to introduce more than three colours onto woodwork." Miller was English, but American critics recommended similar schemes; Henry Hudson Holly described several in *Modern Dwellings in Town and*

*Stencils and rollers sold for graining during the fourth quarter of the nineteenth century; apparently, the average housepainter had not acquired the skill to produce such finishes freehand. This set of tools was illustrated in J. J. Callow,* Perforated Metallic Plate Graining Tools & C. *(Cleveland, Ohio, 1906). (The Athenaeum of Philadelphia)*

*One suggestion for painted door panels, illustrated in Constance Cary Harrison,* Woman's Handi-work in Modern Homes *(1882), and, five years later, in R. W. Shoppell,* Modern Houses, Beautiful Homes. *(The Athenaeum of Philadelphia)*

*Country* as did the Sherwin-Williams Company in its 1884 catalogue.[20]

Critics also proposed using painted, stenciled, or wallpapered decorations on the panels of doors and shutters. Harrison praised them because open doors were too often "inharmonious" with the rest of the decoration. The designs critics recommended included flowers or, in nurseries, paintings taken from children's rhymes, "foliage," " 'Queen Anne' decoration, swags and festoons," and "quaint renderings of beasts, birds, and fish" for which "the designer cannot do better than go to the Japanese for ideas and suggestions." Painted panels appeared in American houses—as in the chambers of the Ebenezer Maxwell house in Germantown, Pennsylvania, redecorated in the 1870s—but the fashion was short-lived; by 1887, the architects Brunner and Tryon labeled it "a waste of effort."[21]

## PAINT TECHNOLOGY AND COLOR THEORY

Fashionable colors during the years 1870 to 1890 differed dramatically from those of the preceding period, chiefly because of developments in paint technology as well as in color theory. An article in the November 1885 issue of *House Painting and Decorating,* entitled "What the Art of House Painting

Owes to the Manufacturers of Ready-Mixed Paints," explained that "as soon as ready-mixed paints, or paints ready for use, began to be introduced a field of new and rich design was opened to the painter and owners of property, which circumstances had previously barred. Shades and tints of color were prepared, which had hitherto been beyond the painters' reach." Sample cards quickly followed, "which enabled tints and shades of color to be *seen* and their effect in combination determined." The writer concluded, "the ladies of a household are now enabled to exercise their proverbial taste, and have a voice in the selection of colors for the beautifying of their dwellings."[22]

Sophisticated studies of the effects of adjacent colors on one another also influenced the palette used in the home. The most significant of these was the work of Michel Eugène Chevreul (1786–1889), long-lived Director of Dyes for the Gobelins tapestry works. His text *The Principles of Harmony and Contrast of Colors* was published originally in France in 1839, and followed by an English translation in 1854. Chevreul's principles appeared in America in *The Painter, Gilder, and Varnisher's Companion,* which ran to sixteen editions between 1869 and 1873. The magazine *House Painting and Decorating* found Chevreul's work so important it urged readers to consult the English translation because "It is an error, of course, to suppose that the art of arranging colors so as to produce the best effects in painting is entirely dependent on the taste of the operator; for harmony of coloring is determined by fixed natural laws." The magazine stressed that the fashions required more knowledge by the trade because "the increased demand for fine decorative or ornamental work renders it of considerable importance to the painter to make himself acquainted with these laws; as without some attention to them, the most elaborate and elegant designs of the architect, and the finest colors that can be produced, may yield but an indifferent, if not a decidedly unpleasing result."[23]

From his work with tapestry dyes, Chevreul observed that adjacent to some hues certain colors appeared to shift in hue or value while the same colors adjacent to other hues might intensify. Chevreul was not the first to witness these phenomena, but he was the first to record them systematically. For instance, he discovered that complementary colors adjacent to one another in patterns appeared more intense because the retina of the eye produces an "afterimage" of the complement of each color. For example, the afterimage caused by looking at red is green, and of green, red—in both cases the complements. (*Complements* are those colors opposite one another on the color wheel, *analogous colors* are next to one another.) The human eye has this response to all colors; thus yellow will cause a purple afterimage and orange will cause blue. Because of the afterimage, two colors adjacent to one another but *not* complements will appear altered in hue. Chevreul's studies showed that red next to orange appeared as a purplish-red next to a yellowish-orange. Furthermore, through his investigations he discovered that white, black, and gray also affected the hues adjacent to them, making them appear deeper, lighter, and richer respectively. Chevreul's accurate scientific findings regarding color relationships greatly influenced critics and through them the decoration of houses in the 1870s and 1880s.[24]

Technological developments in paint manufacturing and the first definitive statements on color theory contributed to the distinct color palette of the 1870 to 1890 period. Ready-mixed paints produced controlled colors in a variety of values from light to dark and enabled householders to choose from *tertiary colors* (those formed by mixing a secondary color with its adjacent primary) such as citrine, olive, and russet to create the complex paint schemes based on Chevreul's laws of color harmony. One of these laws, "Harmonies of Analogous Colors," pertained to closely related values of the same hue *or* identical values of two hues adjacent on the color wheel, while another, "Harmonies of Contrasts," governed widely separated values of the same hue, *or* complementary colors (which are, of course, two entirely separate hues), *or* widely separated values of two adjacent hues. Although these distinctions may appear to us as distressingly complex, writers of the period generally grasped and followed them. Furthermore, an understanding of nineteenth-century rules of color harmony renders color use during the last quarter of the nineteenth century intelligible and its use in restoration less arbitrary.[25]

For example, Eastlake recommended using one dominant hue in each room with other colors subordinate to it. His examples included a room in

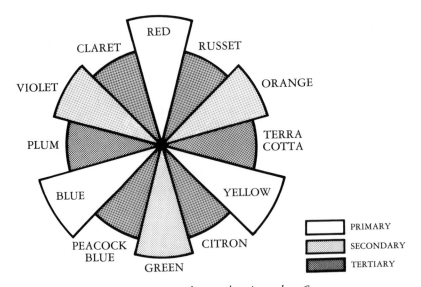

*A color wheel depicting primary, secondary, and tertiary colors. Complementary or contrasting colors are those opposite one another on the wheel (e.g., red-green and orange-blue). Analogous colors are those next to one another on the wheel (e.g., yellow-citron-green). (Drawing by Richard A. Votta)*

which the colors were variations in value and hue from green to blue and another in variations from Venetian red to brown. Both schemes are examples of Chevreul's "Harmonies of Contrasts," since both schemes involve widely separated values of two adjacent hues, blue and green in one and red to dark russet in the other. Church also followed Chevreul's theories in *How to Furnish a Home*. She ruled that rooms should never contain colors of equal intensity, even if complementary, and she recommended, for instance, a pale, dull sea green with a rich crimson or India red rather than fully saturated red and green. This suggestion followed Chevreul's "Harmonies of Contrasts" concerning different values of complementary colors. Miller identified schemes of "harmony" or "contrast" in *Interior Decoration*. A room painted in reds ranging in value from Venetian or India red to light red and salmon followed "harmony" while another painted in olive green or peacock blue with light red and salmon was in "contrast." The contrast was less strong if using olive green, a complement to red. Miller warned that "decorators who feel timid about colour, and who are conscious that an eye for colour is not their strong point, had better confine themselves to those effects which experience has shown us to be good, or else seek refuge in harmonies of colour; for where a room is decorated in tones of one colour it is not a very difficult matter to produce a leasing effect." Even this advice was based on Chevreul's laws of harmony and took advantage of the availability of predictable tertiary colors produced by new paint technology.[11]

## COLORS BY ROOMS

Design critics of the 1870 to 1890 period, providing a wealth of color schemes, took into consideration the kind of room, its aspect (meaning the direction it faced and the amount of light it received), the height, size, and shape of the space, plus the purposes for which the room would be used.[27] All the critics relied upon Chevreul's color theories and most used tertiary colors or some hue mixed with black or white.

### The Hall

During the 1870s, most critics agreed that the entry hall should use subdued hues arranged in a tripartite division of the walls. (See Plate 14.) Eastlake argued for painted walls, since he felt that wallpaper was too fragile to take normal hallway abuse. If the space was sunny, he recommended Pompeiian red; if dark, delicate green or warm gray. Williams and Jones drew a similar distinction, suggesting browns or darker grays in well-lighted halls and warm pomegranate, delicate green, or soft gray in dim ones. Ella Rodman Church also recommended pale greens or browns but suggested walls finished with paper and paint. One of her examples employed dado paper with a dull red ground patterned in black, topped with walls painted buff, green, or gray.[28]

By the mid-1880s, critics urged readers to use more vibrant colors in the entry hall. *House Painting and Decorating* proposed three schemes in 1886. For a dark hall it suggested papering in "low yellow tones" with woodwork in cherry and a frieze paper with an olive ground and figures of dull blue, olives, and gold. A second combination used walls painted in old gold or terra cotta with old oak woodwork; the ceiling was a lighter value of the wall and set off by a frieze containing a Pompeiian red ground with designs in olive, red, and yellow. The floor was stained deep olive. The third scheme, for a sunny hall in a cottage, employed olive-green walls with old oak woodwork, a frieze of dull purples, tans, and sunny greens on a plum-colored ground, and a floor stained mahogany or deep olive green.[29]

Shoppell detailed similarly lively schemes in *Modern Houses, Beautiful Homes* to replace the "invariable Sienna marble paper" popular as a finish in the entry hall and main staircase since the early decades of the nineteenth century. He recommended the following color combinations used in conjunction with a three-to-five-foot-high dado finished in paint or paper:

| WALLS | DADO/WOODWORK |
|---|---|
| yellow or buff | chocolate or olive green or dark blue toned with black |
| pale salmon | dark bronze-green |
| pale sage-green | dark sage-green or dull blue-green or olive-brown or India red |
| turquoise blue | chocolate or maroon[30] |

Brunner and Tryon suggested similar schemes for entry halls in *Interior Decoration,* although they also introduced a higher, two-part wall scheme with a paneled wainscot, perhaps six or seven feet up the walls with the remainder of the wall treated as a frieze. Two of their schemes used woodwork stained mahogany. One had walls painted and stippled in light red of approximately the same hue as the mahogany, the ceiling painted in yellow with red lines around the perimeter, and the frieze an "irregular design" in yellow. The other scheme employed greater contrasts with walls of yellow patterned in light brown or bronze, the latter carried onto the ceiling about eighteen inches and ending with painted moldings or bands in "strong colors"; the ceiling was painted a lighter value than the walls and left plain.[31]

PLATE 1. Family Group (1840), by Frederick R. Spencer, pictures the interior of a prosperous middle-class home. The red-and-green color scheme involving the walls, carpet, curtains, and upholstery is an example of the "harmony by contrast" favored by critics during the first half of the nineteenth century. Also typical is the lack of a separate border on the wall-to-wall carpeting and the grained finish of the woodwork. (The Brooklyn Museum, New York City)

PLATE 2. Paint microanalysis disclosed twelve different hues or values originally used in the double parlors of the Campbell-Whittlesey House built in 1835–1836 in Rochester, New York, which have been restored. The ceiling is two shades of blue, the walls warm gray, the woodwork shades of gray highlighted a straw color, and the panels beside the doors lilac with bronzed anthemia. (The Landmark Society of Western New York, Rochester; photograph by Adele E. Shepard)

PLATE 3. *The furnishings now in the dining room of the Vail House, built c. 1820 in Morristown, New Jersey, reflect its sometime use as a study. The floor now striped in drab and fawn reproduces the original painting uncovered in a corner of the room. The woodwork is grained and the cornice has been striped in several colors as Loudon suggested in* An Encyclopedia of Cottage, Farm, and Villa Architecture and Furniture *(1833). (Historic Speedwell, Morristown, New Jersey; photograph by Louis Meehan)*

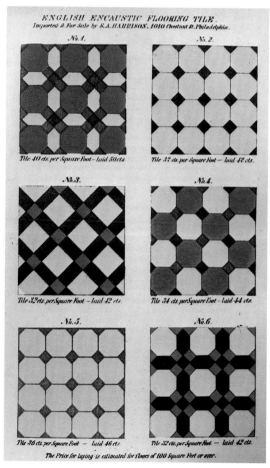

PLATE 4. *The six tile patterns illustrated in Samuel Sloan,* Homestead Architecture, *were manufactured in England and sold by S. A. Harrison, Philadelphia, and probably other companies as well. While Americans called these "encaustic" tiles, the English termed them "geometrics" to distinguish them from the patterned tiles they labeled "encaustic." Virtually identical tiles in the same red, black, blue, and buff colors are being reproduced in England today. (The Athenaeum of Philadelphia)*

PLATE 5. (above) *The distinctive stripes of the carpet in the sitting room of the Towne House, Sturbridge Village, identify it as a Venetian. The colors of surviving examples suggest that contrasting hues were very popular. (Old Sturbridge Village; photograph by Henry E. Peach)*

PLATE 6. (left) *It's Too Tight (1837), by Christian Mayr, depicts a fairly humble middle-class interior with a buff-and-green ingrain carpet laid wall to wall. The woodwork is painted white and the door grained. (Frank S. Schwarz and Son Gallery, Philadelphia)*

PLATE 7. Curiosity *(1833), by Christian Mayr, shows the hall of a well-to-do family whose daughters are curious about a visitor in the parlor. In a treatment fairly common during the first three-quarters of the nineteenth century, the woodwork is white, the door is grained. The red-and-green color scheme shows the "harmony by contrast" recommended by most critics. The carpeting, containing both Neoclassical and Rococo motifs, has so many colors it was either hand-knotted or an early, imported tapestry-weave. (Frank S. Schwarz and Son Gallery, Philadelphia)*

PLATE 8. *The parlor of the Vail House in Morristown, New Jersey, has been restored to c. 1840. The carpet remnant closely resembles the one illustrated in Plate 7. The arrangement of furniture, with a pier table between the windows topped by a looking glass to reflect the light from the girandoles and the center table with a solar lamp, is exactly what one would expect in a Grecian-style interior of that period. Venetian blinds painted green are the only window covering. (Historic Speedwell, Morristown, New Jersey; photograph by Louis Meehan)*

PLATE 9. *The decorative panels on the walls and ceiling of the double parlors of Acorn Hall, built in 1853 in Morristown, New Jersey, are remarkable survivors. The panels are much like designs recommended by Calvert Vaux in Villas and Cottages. The carpeting is imported English tapestry Wilton with a center seam and separate borders. (The Morris County Historical Society; photograph by Louis Meehan)*

PLATE 10. *The parlor of the Ebenezer Maxwell Mansion, built in 1859, has been restored following prosperous middle-class tastes. The carpeting and wallpaper are reproductions based on nineteenth-century examples; the window treatment was adapted from* Godey's Lady's Book. *A solar lamp occupies the center table beneath a gasolier. (The Ebenezer Maxwell Mansion, Inc., Germantown, Philadelphia, Pennsylvania; photograph by Louis Meehan)*

PLATES 11 AND 12. *The parlor and sitting room of the John Bohlen House at 238 Walnut Street, Philadelphia, watercolors painted by Edmond Darch Lewis (1835–1910) in 1857. The variety of colors in the parlor and the use of different materials as curtains and upholstery are typical of the midcentury interior. The sitting room, however, is rather plain, with roller blinds at the windows and old-fashioned carpeting on the floor. (The Historical Society of Pennsylvania)*

PLATE 13. *A ceiling design employing wallpapers illustrated in the 1885 catalogue of M. H. Birge & Sons, Buffalo, New York. The "old gold," Pompeiian-red, and peacock-blue colors of this set are typical of the tertiary colors popular at the time. (The Athenaeum of Philadelphia)*

PLATE 14. *This design for a stairway, "A Study in Neutral Greens & Marone," was illustrated in* Colour Studies *(1892). However, the abstracted patterns and the colors were popular years earlier. (The Athenaeum of Philadelphia)*

PLATE 15. A "morning room," or lady's parlor, designed by Louis C. Tiffany and illustrated in Woman's Handiwork in Modern Homes, by Constance Cary Harrison. The curtains have panels, emulating the tripartite division of walls, and hang below the stained-glass window. While the dado and woodwork are dark, the frieze, cornice, and ceiling decorations are light, increasing the appearance of height in the room. (The Athenaeum of Philadelphia)

PLATE 16. A dining room drawn by Walter Crane and illustrated in The House Beautiful (1881) by Clarence Cook. The setting contains all the trappings of the Aesthetic Movement: the Japanese fans and ginger jars, the eighteenth-century cupboards, convex mirror, and tea service, the Oriental rug, and a chair possibly designed by William Morris. The "old gold," terracotta, and teal-blue colors were extremely popular during the period. (The Athenaeum of Philadelphia)

PLATE 17. *These four wallpaper patterns in styles and colors favored by the critics of the 1870s and 1880s were illustrated in* Colour Studies. *Each motif is highly abstract and colored in tertiary hues, including olive green, terra cotta, old gold, and peacock blue.* (The Athenaeum of Philadelphia)

PLATE 18. *The restored library in the Mark Twain House, originally decorated by Louis C. Tiffany and Company, exemplifies high-style Aesthetic taste in America. (Mark Twain Memorial, Hartford, Connecticut)*

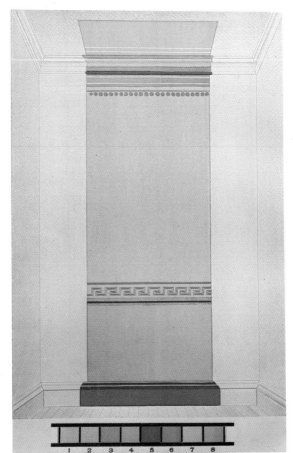

PLATE 19. *These two suggestions for wall treatments appeared in the February and April 1887 issues of* House Painting and Decorating. *They suggest how varied the approaches to interior decoration were becoming by the last decade of the nineteenth century. The terra-cotta wall, complete with painted dado, is less high style than the yellow wall topped with a stenciled frieze.* (The Athenaeum of Philadelphia)

PLATE 20. *This dining room was illustrated in A. S. Jennings,* Wallpapers and Wall Coverings, *published in 1903. The dado paper, entitled "Crown Hanging," was hand-printed in America by the Robert Graves Company, New York. While some of the accessories are Colonial American, the overall effect is one suitable for a Craftsman interior.* (The Athenaeum of Philadelphia)

PLATE 21. *The four plates illustrated by* Walter Pearce *in* Painting and Decorating *(London, 1898) represent polychromatic, complementary, monochromatic, and analogous color schemes, all recommended at the end of the nineteenth century. (The Athenaeum of Philadelphia)*

## HEAVY INLAID LINOLEUMS
### These color photos represent samples one-half yard square

**Pattern No. 201**  (Lot 5-2001)  
6 ft. wide.  Price **$2.50** a yard.

**Pattern No. 203**  (Lot 7-2001)  
6 ft. wide.  Price **$2.50** a yard.

**Pattern No. 205**  (Lot 13-2009)  
6 ft. wide.  Price **$2.50** a yard.

## HARDWOOD FLOOR EFFECTS For fitting around Rugs

**Pattern No. 600 N, Wood Grain**  
36 in. wide.  Price **65c** a yard.

**Pattern No. 400 N, Wood Grain**  
36 in. wide.  Price **65c** a yard.

**Pattern No. 845, Plank Oilcloth**  
36 in. wide.  Price **30c** a yard.

## PRINTED LINOLEUMS, HEAVY
### These Linoleums are not made less than 6 feet wide

**Pattern No. 622, Printed**  (Lot 1-8304)  
6 ft. wide.  Price **$1.20** a yard.

**Pattern No. 624, Printed**  (Lot 7-8280)  
6 ft. wide.  Price **$1.20** a yard.  
12 ft. wide.  Price **$2.80** a yard.

**Pattern No. 627, Printed**  (Lot 1-8390)  
6 ft. wide.  Price **$1.20** a yard.  
12 ft. wide.  Price **$2.80** a yard.

## FLOOR OILCLOTH
### Made in 36, 54 and 72 inch widths.  30 running yards to a roll

**No. 647, Floor Oilcloth**  
36 in. **35c**  54 in. **52c**  72 in. **70c**

**No. 630, Floor Oilcloth**  
36 in. **35c**  54 in. **52c**  72 in. **70c**

**No. 625, Floor Oilcloth**  
36 in. **35c**  54 in. **52c**  72 in. **70c**

PLATE 22. *Examples of oilcloths and linoleums illustrated in the 1906 catalogue of John H. Pray & Sons, Boston. Prices ranged from thirty to seventy cents a square yard. Patterns imitated encaustic tiles, wood planks, ingrain carpets, and decorative tiles. (The Athenaeum of Philadelphia)*

PLATE 23. *Encaustic tile patterns of the type familiar through most of the nineteenth century continued to be produced into the twentieth century. These illustrations are from the 1900 catalogue of Maw & Company Limited. (The Athenaeum of Philadelphia)*

PLATE 24. *The parlor of the James Whitcomb Riley House in Indianapolis, Indiana, restored in a fashion appropriate to the end of the nineteenth century. While it exemplifies no single traditional style, it is exactly the sort of ambiguous revival scheme that so many American households favored. (James Whitcomb Riley Memorial Association)*

## Parlor and Sitting Room

During the 1870 to 1890 period, critics writing for a middle-class audience argued it was unnecessary to have formal rooms designed to impress visitors (drawing rooms or parlors) as well as informal rooms for the everyday use of the family (second parlors or sitting rooms). Williams and Jones explained that although houses of the wealthy contained drawing rooms (actually "reception" rooms) and parlors (used by the family or guests on an extended visit), most middle-class American homes contained only one room devoted to both uses or, at best, a double parlor of which the family used one half while the other was reserved for visitors. Clarence Cook condemned formal parlors as "ceremonial deserts" and discussed only "living-rooms," one of the first uses of that term. Cook reasoned, "these chapters are not written for rich people's reading, and as none but rich people can afford to have a room in their houses set apart for the pleasures of idleness, nothing would be gained by talking about such rooms . . . ; happily, the notion that such a room is absolutely necessary to every respectable family is no longer so prevalent, nor held so binding as it once was."[32] Sarah Josepha Hale, "editress" of *Godey's Lady's Book,* had argued against these distinctions since midcentury.

A few authorities did maintain the distinction; for example, Harriet Prescott Spofford considered the drawing room separate from the sitting room. Spofford described the sitting room as a boudoir where a lady could receive friends of either sex; consequently, she was free to decorate it to suit her whims, even—if so inclined—as the interior of a wigwam. (See Plate 15.) Upstairs boudoirs were rare in America. Spofford reported they had been supplanted by family sitting rooms, which contained knickknacks too personal or insufficiently fine for the parlor. Drawing-room/parlor colors, according to Spofford, should be soft, gay, and delicate, matching the room's "more feminine character"—colors such as "peach blooms," "tender blues," "ethereal greens," and "gold-colored satins." However, she speculated that "everyone . . . in choosing the colors of the drawing-room will suit some special fancy or some necessity of complexion—a family of pale and sallow people not being able to have a great amount of green about them, for example, and a very rosy lady being quite unwise to surround herself with ruddier colors." Whatever the choice, Spofford urged readers to employ tertiary colors, *never* primary colors, which she labeled "crude." Her readers were also urged to follow the tripartite wall division.[33]

Williams and Jones preferred rich tints of blue, drab, gray, or pale rose— a somewhat old-fashioned choice of colors popular throughout the nineteenth century—although they favored the modern tripartite wall treatment, insisting that even if "the walls may be rough and the ceilings low," a dado and frieze would "give the appearance of height"—fashionable if incorrect advice.[34]

Several writers, when suggesting appropriate colors, took into consideration when the room would be most used—if only in the evenings, they recommended colors that reflected artificial light instead of absorbing it. Cook observed that white, carnation, sea-water green, golden yellow, and dandelion gold—the last almost too bright during the day—had a "very rich and exhilarating effect" at night. Constance Cary Harrison urged readers to select wallpapers that reflected light. Her suggestions included a French-style paper representing antique damask with an ivory ground and ivory design with gold "threads," used in conjunction with a pale-blue ceiling "sprinkled" with gold and black moldings picked out in gold. Metallic designs such as bronze or copper or pale-olive paper with an India red frieze or rust and silver on a neutral ground were among her other suggestions.[35]

The family's art collection might also determine parlor colors. Writers suggested that the best prints or watercolors hang in the parlor while oil paintings occupy the hall or dining room. Church's solution to color placement with regard to pictures was that "color may be concentrated in the dado and frieze, leaving the middle space, against which pictures are placed, of some neutral tint" such as French pearl-gray, warm stone-color, pale buff or lemon-yellow, delicate green, and the faintest pink like the "lining of some lovely sea-shells." A scheme for a room in faint pink included a dark-green dado with narrow gilt panels and a frieze of butterflies and flowers. Church also recommended pale-lemon-yellow or apricot-yellow walls with black woodwork. These suggestions did not exclude wallpapers, however, for "in speaking of the color of a room it is not meant that the walls must be of one single tint, but reference is made to the predominating hue, which exists even when pattern and coloring are complex."[36]

The amount of natural light a room received also influenced color choice, according to *House Painting and Decorating*. For example, in the scheme for a small reception room with good light and a high ceiling, the walls were covered in a paper using two values of warm gray approaching ashes of rose, the ceiling was a faint yellow, the frieze a ten-inch-wide flocked paper in India red bordered on either side with a three-inch paper containing gold, gray, and India red, and the woodwork painted the darkest gray in the paper. In the winter, the floor of this room was carpeted in the same dark gray with red, yellow, and olive in the design. In the summer, olive-colored matting, covered with Chinese cotton rugs in dull purple and ecru, were used. A second scheme for a "lightish" parlor suggested walls papered in two shades of dull blue with a Renaissance pattern in gold outline, a frieze of plain, flocked paper in dull red edged with gold and darker blue borders, and all the woodwork stained cherry. A sunny cottage sitting room might use a wallpaper with a dull-blue ground and a pattern the same hue as the cherry woodwork, a gray-blue ceiling, a frieze paper with an "old red" ground patterned in olives, dull yellows, old pinks, and touches of gold, and the floor stained mahogany. The picture rail beneath the frieze could be either cherry or dull gold.[37]

Sunny rooms offered greater variety of color schemes than dark rooms, according to *House Painting and Decorating,* and consequently the magazine concentrated on them almost exclusively. For example, a parlor on the south side of the house, with a peacock-blue carpet, olive-green window shades, and bronze-green woodwork, could have lemon-yellow or old-gold walls, a lighter tint of that color for the ceiling, and a frieze in either bronze-green flocked paper or dull peacock blue, again depending upon the wall color. For a darker treatment, the room would use the same floor, woodwork, and window coverings with bronze-green walls, a pale-yellow ceiling, and a frieze in deep-lemon-yellow flocked paper. A woman building a home in Hepzibah, Georgia, a summer retreat near Augusta, requested suggestions for interior colors from *House Painting and Decorating.* In response, the magazine recommended terra cotta for the parlor walls, Tuscan red for the dado, gray for the ceiling, dark-brown stain on the woodwork, and patterns stenciled in "suitable primary colors" on the "centre-pieces, borders, corner-pieces and dados." The magazine warned that "it should always be borne in mind that the coloring of a room should not only harmonize with the upholstery and furniture, but should act as a foil does to a picture—as a background for the appointments of the apartment."[38]

R. W. Shoppell suggested that parlor schemes provide "a pleasing contrast of color" to those in the dining room; his rationale was that these rooms were often adjacent and used during the same social occasion. Consequently, he offered the following pairs of colors in *Modern Houses, Beautiful Homes,* suggesting that one color be used for the wall and the other color for the dado, with the colors reversed in the adjoining room:

| DRAWING-ROOM | DINING ROOM |
| --- | --- |
| gray blue to turquoise or pale sage green | dull red |
| salmon pink or pale apricot yellow or turquoise or Nile blue | dark olive or sage |
| lemon-yellow or citrine | dull peacock blue |
| pale blues | chocolate or fine browns[39] |

*Dining Room*

Shoppell's suggestion that colors appropriate for the parlor were equally appropriate for the dining room reflected the most fashionable taste of the period and marked an end to what Fred Miller belittled as that "stage of ignorance when dining-rooms were decorated red, studies brown, and drawing-rooms white and gold." Shoppell's advice also confirms the changing uses of rooms in middle-class households by the last quarter of the nineteenth century. Thirty years earlier, most families of modest means used the same room as dining and sitting room. By the 1870s, however, many middle-class families used the dining room only for taking meals. Harriet Prescott Spofford observed that because the family met in the dining room three times a day, the room should have a look of "solid comfort" and its colors should be "substantial," not faded; as Brunner and Tryon pointed out, one could not have a good dinner in "a cheerless room." Art, too, was a consideration. "Good engravings and paintings of fruit and flowers are suitable for a dining-room, but representations of dead game are not very agreeable subjects," wrote Ella Rodman Church, thus marking an end to a midcentury fashion popular with those who could afford it, of subjecting hapless diners to oil paintings of freshly slaughtered game and gasping fish or carvings of wooden rabbits and quail hung in clusters on the panels of sideboard doors. Debunking another fashion that had been popular among the upper classes, she added, "neither does one enjoy being stared out of countenance, while eating, by one's ancestors or those of other people, although the dining-room is generally considered the proper place for family portraits." Church argued that oil portraits belonged in the hall or library, not the parlor or dining room. This was a point she contested with Eastlake, who, writing fourteen years earlier for a design-conscious audience, had recommended portraits, along with other oil paintings, specifically for dining rooms.[40]

The tripartite wall division was especially popular in dining rooms. Walls of a single color marked people of "uncertain" taste, according to Spofford. Her recommendations included bluish slaty gray outlined in dull India red with a carpet of royal purple, or the same carpet with citrine-colored walls. One could also use a wallpaper of pale azure with a delicate lemon-colored pattern and a carpet in peacock blue. With red walls, a Turkish carpet in crimson and deep blue was best. In all cases, the carpet and walls contrasted in full, rich colors (not pastels) and the curtains carried the color of the carpet onto the walls.[41]

Changes in American dining customs affected the decoration of dining rooms. Instead of sitting down to the principal meal at midday, many families had dinner at night. This significant shift was especially noticeable among urban populations whose places of employment were distant from their places of residence and whose fixed work hours did not permit leisurely meals at noon. The traditional dark and somber dining room was no longer appropriate, according to Clarence Cook, since dark colors absorb light and most of his readers ate their principal meal by artificial light. (See Plate 16.) He recommended rich, sober but cheerful colors that appeared attractive at all times of the day; for example, black walnut wainscoting topped by a pale-lemon-yellow paper with figures in dark green and red, a ceiling papered in two shades of blue-gray, and a three-inch cornice painted red and black with a half-inch gold molding beneath it. In the absence of wainscoting, Cook recommended painting the baseboard and chair rail dead black, using distemper paint in brown for the dado and Venetian red for the walls.[42]

Ella Rodman Church suggested several schemes for dining rooms. One, using walls of the palest green with thin red and blue stripes outlining the woodwork, was adapted from *Rural Homes* (1851) by Gervase Wheeler. Another employed a crimson dado and frieze with light-yellow paper covered in blue-and-black designs for the remainder of the wall. Moldings painted dark, cool green separated each section while other woodwork in the room was painted either black with moldings of the same green or green with moldings in crimson. A third scheme used a light-olive-green frieze, a wainscoting of maroon and gold or black and gold, and a field of sage-green wallpaper or paint. A crimson molding or paper was placed at the cornice height, while the picture and chair rails were either crimson, green, or black as was the remaining woodwork.[43]

*House Painting and Decorating* recommended terra cotta, yellow, or olive schemes for dining rooms. In a dark dining room having only one window, the suggestion was a paper in low tones of yellow and a frieze with an olive ground and figures in dull blues, olive, and gold. One might also employ paper in two shades of "Indian pink" (pinkish terra cotta) with a frieze paper patterned in "a bold old pink floral design" against a maroon ground. Dining rooms with golden oak woodwork successfully used olive greens.[44]

Shoppell observed that dining-room colors must accord with the artwork as well as with the wood of the furniture. For example, sage-green, olive-green, or dull-red walls all supplied good backgrounds for oil paintings. For rooms with mahogany or walnut furniture, sage, olive green, and dull gray-blues were good, whereas furniture of oak or ebonized pieces were effective with reds and crimsons. Shoppell described one dining room with oak furniture in some detail. The walls *appeared* olive-toned, although they were actually papered with a design of oranges and leaves on a dull, slate-blue ground giving the appearance of olive. The dado was a plain flocked paper in deep crimson, almost ruby, run horizontally around the room to avoid seams. The top of the dado was painted in a broad black line with a gold stripe. The carpet in a red, blue, green, and orange Turkish design appeared almost "rose-purple" when seen from a distance, and the chairs were upholstered in bronze-green leather. A far more subdued dining room contained a vellum-colored frieze with a stenciled pattern, walls in golden-brown paper with an indistinct, overall pattern, and the woodwork simply varnished pine with painted decorations in the panels of the doors and shutters.[45]

### Library

Most interior decoration sources during the 1870 to 1890 period considered a library integral to a refined household, agreeing with Holly that "it is not too much to say that every man owes it to himself, no less than to his family, to provide in his home a place where he may gather his dear ones for counsel and instruction."[46]

Spofford proposed placing libraries on the north or northwest sides of houses to receive ample natural light through large windows while avoiding bright sunlight. Over high dadoes, she recommended deep purples and violets or deep shades of emerald green. Moorish designs were appropriate if the space was also a gentleman's smoking room; finishes included fabrics and wallpapers patterned in rich red and blue with gold and silver, providing a background for parrots in gilt cages, latticework, a guitar, and "foreign-looking" plants.[47]

Williams and Jones's design in their "ultimate" library called for plain or embossed leather paper on the walls in brown, stone, dark-green, crimson, or dull-red colors. Rich velvet or cheaper striped woolen rep in "Indian tints" made appropriate upholstery and curtain materials.[48]

*House Painting and Decorating* preferred a red scheme that consisted of wallpaper with an Italian Renaissance design executed in two medium shades of Pompeiian red and topped with a "rich" frieze such as "a handsome hand-finished processional . . . showing classic figures, or an Italian Renaissance border showing garlands, masques, etc." on a deep-red ground. A golden-olive ceiling, bronze picture rail, and woodwork a "golden shade of old oak" completed the scheme.[49]

Brunner and Tryon favored wooden panels forming a coffered ceiling—some households used pressed tin to achieve this look—or paper or stamped leather for a lighter effect. The important point, they warned, was that "loud, startling color, glaring decoration, or coarse grotesque carving, are wholly out of place in a library."[50]

### Bedrooms

Bedroom color schemes were generally determined by the direction the room faced, yet critics offered a remarkable diversity of colors from which to choose. Spofford proposed light tints for south-facing rooms—she specifically named gray-green and sea blue—and dark values for north-facing rooms such as violets, deep blues, and reds. She theorized that dark hues absorbed heat while light hues did not, thus reasoning that dark hues would "warm" a cool, north-facing room and lighter values "cool" a warm, south-facing one. Church generally agreed with Spofford regarding south-facing rooms, but for those facing north, she preferred "delicate pink," "pale green," or "dainty buff," choices distinctly different from Spofford's. *House Painting and Decorating* concurred that "blue is too cold a color for a north room unless it is to be used entirely as a summer room and you desire it to be as cold-looking as possible," and suggested medium shades of "old pink" (terra cotta) for the walls, a lighter tint of the same color for the ceiling, light bronze-brown for the woodwork and frieze, the latter with a design in rosy purple, old pink, and olive. The magazine noted that an eastern exposure was also "cool" and suggested walls in sea green, a maroon or deep-green frieze, and a ceiling in pinkish-yellow. For a warm, south-facing bedroom, the trade journal preferred walls papered in two values of medium golden olive, a soft-yellow-pink ceiling, an olive-green frieze, and oak woodwork. The architects Brunner and Tryon simply commented that southern exposures did best with blues and grays and all others with reds and yellows.[51]

Most writers agreed with Williams and Jones that bedrooms should be "quiet and subdued, . . . the reverse of conspicuous and obtrusive, while a sense of warm, cozy comfort in Winter, and cool refreshing daintiness in Summer should pervade the whole from carpet to ceiling, and from wall to window." They urged wallpapers with "traceries of soft, contrasted hues" such as cream, amber, fawn, rose, or blue in patterns of passionflowers, honeysuckle, wild roses, blackberries, crow's-foot, oak leaves and acorns, geometrics, and patterns imitating French chintz. Shoppell urged colors that appeared cool and clean. He suggested finishing the cornice, ceiling, and walls in values of the same hue while the doors and woodwork were picked out in "corresponding" tones. Borders in harmony or contrast with the overall scheme were appropriate if the ceiling was fairly high. *House Painting and Decorating* devised a similar scheme using walls papered in two shades of drab on which the pattern was outlined in gold, the ceiling finished in a light-drab floral-figured paper "powdered" in gold, the frieze done in deep drab with flowers in red, yellow, and green, and the woodwork painted the darkest drab from the wallpaper.[52]

## WALLPAPERS

We have seen that a few critics throughout the nineteenth century favored flat, two-dimensional designs for wallpapers and carpeting, but consumers had blithely ignored theory in favor of more "realistic" three-dimensional designs. The Centennial presented its nearly ten million visitors an opportunity to see products based on the "reform" styling favored by Eastlake, including Jeffrey & Co.'s display of wallpapers designed by William Morris and Walter Crane. Christopher Dresser, an English designer and trained botanist who had worked with Owen Jones, visited the fair en route to Japan where he intended to pursue Japanese design. However, by the time he left, he had reached an agreement with the Philadelphia firm of Wilson and Fenimore to patent and produce thirteen of his wallpaper designs the following year.[53]

In addition to English designs, exhibits of lesser-known and more exotic nations such as Turkey and Japan caught the public imagination. The Japanese government spent $600,000 on its exhibitions at the fair, the largest amount of any participating country. Americans were bewitched by the exotic designs from these heretofore little-known areas of the world and responded by purchasing nearly all the Japanese products exhibited at the fair.[54]

Most critics were wildly enthusiastic about the new wallpaper designs, which shared three characteristics prescribed by Eastlake. First, the patterns appeared flat and lacked any dimensionality or realistic shading. Second, the patterns were generally smaller in scale than those of the preceding periods. Third, the designs employed secondary or tertiary hues with little use of primary colors.

Eastlake informed readers of *Hints on Household Taste* that wallpapers were, after carpets, the most poorly designed furnishings in the home. "Common sense points to the fact, that as a wall represents the flat surface of a solid material which forms part of the construction of a house, it should be decorated after a manner which will belie neither its flatness nor solidity." Therefore, Eastlake encouraged readers to avoid "all shaded ornament and patterns, which by their arrangement of colour give an appearance of relief" and use instead those "treated in a conventional manner—i.e. drawn in outline, and filled in with flat colour . . . but without attempt at pictorial gradation." Eastlake echoed Christopher Dresser, who earlier had written in *The Art of Decorative Design* (1862) that "walls should at all times be flat; and the very appearance of rotundity should be avoided. . . ."[55] American authors supported these sentiments.

The public acceptance of the "reform" critics' belief that decoration should take into account the *reality* of both the materials used and the surfaces decorated marked a turning away from French designs in favor of English ones in the years immediately following the Centennial Exhibition. In 1881, Clarence Cook summed up America's acceptance of the new taste. "It may be said," he wrote, "that France makes no account of one of the prime articles in the creed of modern English and American schools of Decorative Art, that natural representation of flowers and fruits, and for that matter, imitations of all sorts, should be sedulously avoided. The French permit themselves full liberty in the matter, imitate anything and everything they can force into the service of decoration, and when they feel like it, paint flowers and fruits on wall-papers . . . as to deceive the very elect. We Americans," he continued somewhat wistfully, "being I suppose at the very root more akin to the English than to the French, have blindly accepted the English dictum in this matter, and look upon wall-papers with any but set conventional patterns and sombre colors, as vulgar. . . . 'Tis as much as a man's reputation for good taste is worth, to confess that he likes to see a pretty flowered paper on a bed-room wall; and one can hardly estimate the courage it would take to own that one liked an old-fashioned landscape-paper in a hall-way or in a dining-room."[56]

In place of the large, realistically colored, and natural-appearing representations of flora or fauna that French wallpaper companies did so well, the English critics substituted "conventional" (meaning nonrepresentational) patterns that they deemed appropriate designs for walls. These new designs fell into three general groups with some overlap occurring between the groups.

First, critics preferred strongly geometric patterns employing round, square, diamond, or polygonal shapes laid out in diaper or half-drop patterns of the sort discussed by Christopher Dresser in *The Art of Decorative Design*. As to the scale of the designs, most American critics agreed with Eastlake that for "ordinary-sized" rooms the patterns should not exceed five or six inches in any direction and in "Bedrooms, &c., much less will suffice" because "nothing dwarfs the size of rooms so much as large-patterned papers."[57]

Also approved were papers depicting natural objects, such as flowers, foliage, and birds in a highly stylized ("conventional") manner. (See Plate 17.) William Morris's designs were among the most critically acclaimed. Eastlake praised his designs and urged readers to purchase papers from

*Eastlake favored "conventional" designs, meaning abstract ones, over realistic ones. This wallpaper, illustrated in the 1877 edition of* Hints on Household Taste, *which he adapted from an Italian pattern hundreds of years old, embodies his beliefs. Both floral and animal motifs are abstract and only two colors were used, thus eliminating any possibility of naturalistic shading. The pattern is a "half-drop": the design repeats stepwise rather than in a straight line. (The Athenaeum of Philadelphia)*

Morris, Marshall, & Co., of Bloomsbury. This reference is one of the earliest in America to William Morris, a leader of the British Arts and Crafts Movement. Morris designed his first wallpaper in 1862 and ultimately produced forty-one wallpapers and five ceiling papers—not including variations in color available for each design, nor the patterns on which he collaborated with others. In 1873, Bumstead and Company of Boston became the American agent for Morris's papers, although other firms later stocked them. For instance, the John Jacob Glessners of Chicago and their architect, Henry Hobson Richardson, bought Morris's designs at Marshall Field and Company for their South Prairie Avenue house completed in 1887. By that date American manufacturers also offered papers in the Morris style at about one-third the cost of the originals.[58]

A third style popular during the period were wallpapers with Japanese motifs. Tiffany, Dresser, Christian Herter, Walter Crane, and other well-known designers produced some extraordinary "Japanesque" designs during the 1870s and 1880s. Late in the period, however, manufacturers also produced hackneyed, Japanese-inspired wallpapers using a formula relying on the asymmetrical placement of common motifs such as fans, vases, and kimono-clad figures.[59]

Naturally, consumers continued to purchase wallpapers in styles other than those approved by critics, and critics continued to rail against their use. Williams and Jones complained in *Beautiful Homes* that striped papers resembled posts marching around the perimeter of a room and made hanging

*Japanesque designs created by Fred Miller and illustrated in* Interior Decoration. *While the birds and carp might have been too realistic for some critics' taste, the narrow borders were suitably abstracted. (The Athenaeum of Philadelphia)*

*A study in the Cambridge, Massachusetts, home of Henry Wadsworth Longfellow, photographed in 1899. Charles, the poet's elder son, had lived in Japan from 1871 to 1874. When he returned, he decorated this room with wallpaper and fans he had purchased during his stay. (National Park Service, Longfellow National Historic Site)*

pictures difficult. They also disliked designs in which the individual portions of the repeat were so widely separated that even subtle colors appeared to contrast. Shoppell complained "a favorite wall-paper lately has been a white or gray, plain or watered ground, with a stamped and gilded bunch of flowers, or a huge 'fleur-de-lis' at regular intervals, the bunches of flowers presenting no better effect than might have been got with a splash of liquid gold from a brush, directed on the most rudimentary geometric plan. A picture hanging on such a wall generally cuts into three or four of these gilded nosegays." And *House Painting and Decorating* urged readers to avoid a pattern having "a look of motion" because "nothing is more distressing to the eyesight than to be in a room where the pattern of the paper seems always crawling like a mass of worms."[60]

Now that machines could print wallpapers in up to twenty colors at a time, critics began to stress subtlety. Good designs relied on a blending of colors, explained Constance Cary Harrison, so that "the general effect of the paper is rich, low-toned, and neutral, and yet has a glowing color-bloom." She added, "American taste, hitherto inclining toward heavy color and intense gilding, as still seen in some restaurants and concert-halls, has during the last two years taken a long stride forward in the matter of paperings."[61]

Writers on the period discussed the notion of "color-bloom," or the overall effect of colors when placed together and viewed at a distance. Williams and Jones told their readers, "in a well finished room we shall always upon investigation, find the entire scheme of decoration possesses a character, a relation as it were one thing to another. The background and groundwork of the whole represented by paper and carpet are subservient to the furniture and decorations." (See Plate 18.) For that reason, they encouraged householders to select wallpapers containing secondary and tertiary colors—such as those mentioned in the preceding sections of this chapter—with only small amounts of primary colors. Eastlake proposed that "where two shades of the same colour are employed, and quietness of effect is especially desired, the overlaid tint should be but very little darker than the ground; and if drawings, &c., are to be hung upon it, the pattern should be hardly discernible from a little distance." Eastlake permitted just "a spot of gold" if desired but other critics were less certain. Shoppell thought "gold is of doubtful service in enhancing the effect of a paper, especially if the design be good. It is, moreover, expensive, and the Dutch metal often used in its place is apt to turn black." In addition to gold, papers employed silver and bronze.[62]

Critics also took account of the relatively brighter light of gas and kerosene, warning readers to consider the effect of all light sources on wallpapers. Fred Miller found it "advisable always to look at a paper by gaslight as well as by daylight, for there are some papers which look well by sunlight but are ineffective by artificial light; greens and yellows are very deceptive, the former looking dull and gloomy by gaslight, and the latter pale and monotonous. Reds are the safest colours, as they do not materially change in effect; blues and blue-greens are also tolerably safe, although they are apt to look very much darker by gaslight than by daylight."[63]

Americans became major consumers of wallpapers during the last quarter of the nineteenth century. *House Painting and Decorating* reported twenty-nine wallpaper manufacturers in America in 1885; all but three belonged to the American Wallpaper Association. In 1884 alone, the twenty-six member firms sold over 31 million rolls of wallpaper, not including hand-printed papers, varying in price from ten cents to $50 a roll. If a householder desired wallpaper, there was almost certainly an affordable product available.[64]

# FLOORS

Although John Claudius Loudon described parquet in 1833 as "lately fashionable" for English villas, and a few midcentury American architects recommended hardwood floors, the demand for wall-to-wall carpeting remained strong well into the fourth quarter of the nineteenth century. However, the popularity of Eastlake's ideas signaled the beginning of a new aesthetic in all areas of household design, including floors. Eastlake maintained that Oriental carpets laid over wooden floors formed an aesthetically superior floor because of the "conventional treatment" of the carpet design. Eastlake also valued the slight irregularities that exhibited the weavers' skill—an argument strongly supported by William Morris. Orientals were also less wasteful than wall-to-wall carpeting that could never "suit another [room] without further alterations," and hid the floor "contrary to the first principles of decorative art, which require that the nature of construction . . . should always be revealed. . . ."[65]

American writers concurred. Cook admonished readers, "the advantage of a hard-wood floor, or of a common floor covered with wood-carpeting, is so great on the score of health and labor-saving, that it would seem as if only the prejudice that comes from old associations could long keep up the fashion of carpets." The author of the article "Sanitary Decoration in the Home," which appeared in *House Painting and Decorating,* stressed the salutary value of wooden floors, because the "street soil carried into the house on our shoes, the internal soot and dust, and the soft matters that are occasionally dropped about, such as particles of food" are "very liable to putrefy when subjected to damp and warmth." He urged householders to lay "good hardwood polished parquet." The critics' preference for hardwood floors combined with exotic carpets from "the lands of the Orient," heralded a new fashion for floor coverings in the last quarter of the nineteenth century.[66]

## WOOD FLOORS

American households could not adopt hardwood floors and area rugs overnight because most houses built earlier in the century had softwood floors. Critics offered solutions: painting the floor, laying a "wood carpet" over it, or replacing it with parquet. Eastlake preferred parquet, which he assured readers was "much in vogue" in English country houses. Because laying parquet could be quite expensive, he suggested using ornate "parquetry floor borders" two or three feet wide around the perimeter of the room, with a carpet in the middle. *Hints on Household Taste* illustrated four borders from A. J. Arrowsmith of Bond Street, London. American critics approved

*Parquetry floor borders illustrated in the 1877 edition of* Hints on Household Taste. *(The Athenaeum of Philadelphia)*

of this solution, while suggesting that halls use parquet as the only floor covering.[67]

Other American critics, including Ella Rodman Church, recommended "wood carpeting" to reduce costs yet achieve the effect of parquet. This material was thinner than parquet—being composed of strips of hardwood, about one-fourth inch thick, glued to a heavy muslin backing—and could be installed over the original flooring. According to the catalogue of the John W. Boughton Company of Philadelphia, the New York architect E. C. Hussey originated the product, which could also be used as wainscoting. The Decorative Wood Carpet Company of Warren, Illinois, carried over fifty patterns during the 1880s, in addition to wainscoting and floor medallions; they assured prospective buyers the product would outlast five oilcloths or ten Brussels carpets. Depending upon the design, borders ranged in price from eight to eighty-five cents a linear foot and entire floors from eighty-five cents to $1.75 a linear yard, making "wood carpeting" competitive with ingrain and Brussels. Critics recommended it for all rooms that might otherwise use parquet, as well as for kitchens, where tight joints and hardwood made maintenance easier.[68]

Wood carpeting made attractive, parquetlike surfaces affordable. According to the Boughton Company, manufacturer of wood carpets and parquet floors, "the common remark, 'that a bare floor is so cheerless,' comes wholly from the impression given by an ordinary pine floor with its unsightly cracks. . . ." Nevertheless, a great many earlier houses retained their soft-

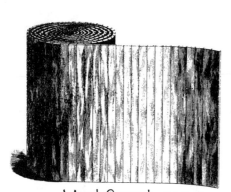

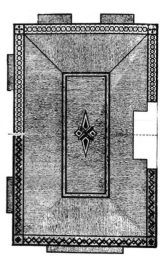

Left: *A roll of "wood carpet" illustrated in the 1890 catalogue of S. C. Johnson, Racine, Wisconsin. Naturally, much fancier designs were available, as the border* (center) *and entire floor* (right) *pictured in the c. 1885 catalogue of the John W. Boughton Company, Philadelphia, suggest.* (The Athenaeum of Philadelphia)

wood floors and some architects continued to specify them. For those households, critics had suggestions for decorative treatment. Once the floor was cleaned, the cracks puttied, and the surface smoothed, Williams and Jones recommended stenciling in two or three stains to resemble inlaid woods. A less ambitious approach involved staining the floor uniformly in dark brown with a little red, followed by a coat of shellac. A third alternative was to paint the floor. Spofford advised painting a decorative border on bedroom floors and placing a carpet in the center to "keep the place comfortable to the feet." Ready-mixed-paint companies began to market products expressly for floors. The Glidden Varnish Company of Cleveland, Ohio, marketed "Jap-a-lac," a combination varnish and stain available in twelve colors for floors, mopboards (baseboards), and wainscoting in bathrooms, kitchens, laundries, and toilet rooms. H. W. Johns M'f'g Co. of Boston, New York, and Philadelphia produced a line of six colors—silver gray, lead, light yellow, dark yellow, terra cotta, and maroon—which it assured customers would "dry within fifteen hours with a firm, hard gloss." Since a gallon cost only $1.45 to $1.60 and covered nearly four hundred square feet, paint remained a bargain floor covering.[69]

*The variety of center pieces and corner blocks illustrated in the c. 1880 catalogue of the Decorative Wood Carpet Company, Warren, Illinois, enabled one to purchase the appearance of a custom floor. (The Athenaeum of Philadelphia)*

## TILE FLOORS

Downing was probably the first American architectural critic to recommend encaustic tiles for floors; others quickly followed, including Gervase Wheeler, Calvert Vaux, and Samuel Sloan. Eastlake insisted these tiles were "the best mode of treating a hall-floor, whether in town or country . . . for beauty of effect, durability, and cheapness." He added, "To Messrs. Minton, I believe, we are indebted for the earliest revival of this ancient art in modern times." Some critics favored tiles that recalled ancient styles. "It is a pretty idea," wrote Williams and Jones, "to imitate the old Roman fashion, and introduce some motto or legend upon the pavement . . . thus following the lead of Minton, and others who copy the designs of the tiles of Herculaneum and Pompeii, and other ancient cities. Some of the designs and legends are peculiarly appropriate," they urged, "as for instance that of the chained dog, with the motto 'Cave canem,' and the cheery word of welcome 'Salve.'" While Eastlake illustrated examples from Maw & Company Ltd. in gold, terra cotta, brown, and black, his American editor remarked that "Neapolitan tiles . . . are cheaper than English tiles, and if of the best quality are very durable. Their patterns are chiefly taken from the ancient mosaic pavements of Herculaneum and Pompeii." He concluded that vestibules were "the true place for a mosaic pavement or pavement of encaustic tiles, while a parquet floor is better fitted for the floor of the stairhall, especially in a cold climate like that of New England."[70]

While Minton paving tiles were used in the United States Capitol and elsewhere, importing these tiles was expensive. To meet the rising demand for tiles, many domestic manufactories opened during the 1870s and 1880s, including American Encaustic Tile, United States Encaustic Tile, Low Art Tile, Trent Tile, and others. Critics recommended their use on hearths, around chimney openings, and in vestibules as floors and wainscoting in conservatories, porches, kitchens, laundries, and bathrooms. Shoppell praised halls laid in encaustic tiles as "an occasional relief from the hot carpeted rooms."[71]

## OILCLOTHS AND LINOLEUM

Oilcloth, linoleum, and kamptulicon (made from cork) also continued to offer "relief" from carpeting and were generally less expensive than encaustic tiles. Eastlake advocated oilcloths for halls and passages. However, he condemned those oilcloths imitating marble or parquet as "thoroughly false in principle," while exhorting readers to select those simple, "geometrical diaper" patterns in "two tints, or—better still—two shades of the same tint (which should not be a postitive [primary] colour)." Nor should there be any "attempt to indicate relief or raised ornament in the pattern."[72]

In America, most critics favored oilcloth after parquet or encaustic tiles as the best possible floor covering for vestibules and the floor of stair halls. Like Eastlake, some critics deprecated the tendency to design oilcloths to mimic patterns common to other materials. "There is room yet, in spite of the variety of patterns in floor-cloths, for some improvement," wrote Shoppell. "The favorite tile patterns are frequently very happy combinations of color, and have a pleasing effect. The imitation will, however, grow wearisome soon, and what are wanted are designs peculiar to floor-cloth itself, and not a pretentious imitation of something costlier." He warned, "too many colors should be avoided, as also too small and scattered a pattern. Greater breadth of effect is obtained by a moderate uniformity of color, such as chocolate and buff, Indian red and buff." Shoppell discouraged following earlier nineteenth-century tastes because "the once much-used black and white marble floor cloths are too gray and gloomy to suit the advanced love of color among us, however they might have satisfied a previous generation."[73]

Writers considered linoleum appropriate for stair halls and possibly for other rooms. Church believed it warmer than oilcloth with a more pleasant texture, as long-wearing as the best English oilcloth, but less expensive and with better designs. (One might contest her argument regarding price; E. F. Denning & Co. of New York advertised oilcloths from fifty cents to $1.15 a square yard compared to linoleum at ninety cents and $1.) Church was not enthusiastic about linoleum in kitchens because it was "quickly injured by grease," and the 1890 catalogue of the Glidden Varnish Company suggested repairing worn linoleum with Jap-a-lac. Despite these drawbacks, photographic evidence suggests widespread use of linoleum in halls and kitchens during the last quarter of the nineteenth century. One critic suggested placing linoleum with a parquet design around the edges of a dining-room floor with a carpet in the center.[74]

Households might have employed two other floor coverings: kamptulicon and paper carpets. Kamptulicon, a mixture of India rubber and cork developed by Elijah Galloway in 1844, was quite costly. Like linoleum, installation involved gluing the material to the floor. Shoppell, one of the few critics to mention it, described it as a "soft, warm floorcovering made of cork and India-rubber" and recommended its use around the perimeter of bedrooms with carpets in the center of the floor. Paper carpet was mentioned occasionally throughout the nineteenth century; by the 1870s, paper floor coverings appeared in various forms. Spofford directed householders to make their own, first layering the floor with newspapers, then covering with a coating of thick flour paste, and ending with a layer of wallpaper in a "decided" pattern. The whole was then sized with glue and covered with a common varnish. Williams and Jones preferred a different technique: coarse muslin was stretched and tacked into place and thoroughly wet with a thin paste; then lengths of wallpaper in a checked or mosaic pattern were applied, and when dry, the whole was varnished with two coats of shellac followed by two coats of copal varnish. They assured readers that if the finish coats were periodically reapplied, the "fake oilcloth" would last for years. One can only wonder if these suggestions were actually followed.[75]

## MATTING

Grass and hemp mattings remained popular during the 1870s and 1880s as the least expensive floor coverings, ranging in price from fifteen to fifty cents a yard. "Domestic straw matting" was the most expensive variety and, according to E. F. Denning & Co., a new item. "It is a very superior article," stated their catalogue, "manufactured in this country from imported straw, is seamless throughout and very fine and even, lying perfectly smooth on the floor, and possessing the advantage of having cotton for the chain, instead of straw, as in the China mattings." Installation was an additional eight cents a linear yard.[76]

Matting most often appeared in bedrooms where critics opposed wall-to-wall carpeting for reasons of hygiene. Since few houses had fine hardwood or parquet on the second floor, matting served as a good alternative in those areas of light use. For year-round country use and for city houses during

*Grass matting and small rugs remained a common floor treatment, particularly for bedrooms, throughout the nineteenth century. The bedroom of Susy, Mark Twain's daughter, was recently restored in that manner. The myriad objects on the walls are also typical of the later decades of the nineteenth century. (The Mark Twain Memorial, Hartford, Connecticut)*

the summer, matting often was the only floor covering in bedrooms. Rugs might be laid over the matting during the winter. Although mattings in "tempting patterns, worked in dark colors" were marketed, critics disapproved of them because "the dye does not penetrate the fibre deeply and the surface soon assumes a worn-out or rusty appearance." To make the light, straw-colored mattings interesting, Church suggested a border in "plain woolen stuff of a color to harmonize with the wall and furniture covering."[77]

Critics occasionally recommended China or Canton matting for use in vestibules or stair halls. Williams and Jones preferred checkered matting in crimson or deep brown and white for vestibules, warning readers to lay it with "white metal tacks" to avoid the rust stains of iron tacks. A fancier treatment might be used in imposing stair halls; Church suggested bordering the matting with flannel or felt in a color harmonizing with others in the hall. No writers recommended matting on stairs and many admitted it was not the best choice for vestibules because it held dust and dirt and was fragile. Its major advantage was price.[78]

Occasionally, a household used matting in more formal rooms. Shoppell praised matting for its "refreshing coolness" in hot weather and for having a "bright and clean appearance." He added that it could be used to advantage in a parlor containing a piano, because "musical sounds strike clearer and sharper than in a room carpeted all over." He suggested that "where parquetry is too expensive," a good plan "is to cover the floor all over with India matting . . . and afterward spread foreign rugs and mats about here and there."[79]

## DRUGGET

By the fourth quarter of the nineteenth century, few critics mentioned drugget; interestingly, most who did were women who prescribed it solely for the dining room. "Coarsely woven flannel stamped in a brilliant pattern" or burlap painted to resemble a Turkey carpet were frequent suggestions. Earlier in the century, druggets were used to protect better carpeting in dining rooms; by the 1870s, a drugget might be the only floor covering, placed over parquet or stained and varnished floorboards. If heavy enough, the drugget was simply laid on the floor, although lighter ones were fastened to metal hooks imbedded in the floor expressly for that purpose.[80]

## CARPETING

Ironically, by the time most of the carpetmaking in America had become mechanized, thus producing easily affordable goods, Eastlake and his followers urged householders to eschew wall-to-wall carpeting. To support the new aesthetic, the critics claimed that it offered hygienic benefits while saving expense. Ella Rodman Church agreed with most reformers:

> Very few carpets are properly used; they are stretched into every possible corner, so that not an inch of space shall be left uncovered, and places are notched out for the various recesses, until the expensive fabric is utterly spoiled for any other room than the one to which it is fitted. It is not handsome arranged in this way, being far more picturesque as a large square, or oblong rug, showing all around it a yard or so of dark polished floor. A bordering of inlaid wood-work is very pretty, and not much more expensive than first-class Brussels carpet. Such a floor covering has a sort of old-time and Eastern look about it, and may be taken up and shaken with comparative ease—a few nails along the edges keeping it in place when down.[81]

Because previous styles of interior decoration had placed a premium on wall-to-wall carpeting and most houses contained unattractive wood floors, this new fashion was neither universally nor immediately accepted. As a compromise, critics suggested that if householders preferred fully carpeted floors, they should use wall-to-wall carpets with coordinating borders sewn onto them, "thus preserving still to some degree remembrance of its rug-like character." Williams and Jones assured readers that borders were "now so universally used, and add greatly to the elegance of a carpet, that we advise their use whenever practicable." This technique, often mistakenly attributed today to all nineteenth-century carpeting, actually became common during the 1870s.[82]

Consequently, writers advanced two methods of carpeting floors during the fourth quarter of the nineteenth century. The preferred method called for a large carpet to be placed in the center of the floor, exposing parquet, wood carpeting, good hardwood, or matting around the perimeter of the room. Critics directed that the carpet should never be so large that heavy pieces of furniture stood on it, nor so small that several carpets were needed, creating a "patchy" appearance and a safety hazard. The alternative, offered grudgingly by the critics, was wall-to-wall carpeting finished with a wide border simulating the effect described above. Borders were prescribed for every carpet intended to cover the floor completely, whether the costliest Axminster or the cheapest ingrain.[83]

Householders could select from a wide range of carpet types to satisfy either design choice. Eastlake advocated "true" Orientals because they illustrated the *worker's* skill rather than the *machine's* ability to produce highly regular patterns. American writers such as Clarence Cook suggested a Turkish, Persian, or Smyrna carpet as the best, "even if it strain our purse a little, for a good rug will last a lifetime." Furthermore, the Orientals were so thickly woven and comfortable that "after much using a good Eastern rug, walking on the best body Brussels is like walking on the wooden floor. . . ."[84]

Despite these exhortations, most Americans purchased machine-made carpeting produced in America, where improvements in carpet weaving occurred throughout the nineteenth century. The production of Axminster carpeting, made by hand since 1755 on large looms by weavers who tied each knot separately in the manner of Oriental carpets, was finally mechanized between 1867 and 1877 by Alexander Smith and Halcyon Skinner. The finished product imitated the hand-knotted carpet but was constructed in an entirely different manner. Nonetheless, Axminsters remained the most expensive domestically produced carpets of the period, selling for $2.50 to $3 a yard, although increased production eventually reduced the cost to about $1.75 a yard.[85]

Brussels, Wiltons, and moquettes comprised a second group of pile carpets less expensive than Axminsters but generally similar in appearance (although the pile of Brussels carpets was looped, rather than cut; see Chapter 2). By the 1880s, a "body Brussels"—in which the colors were woven to form the pattern—cost about ninety cents a yard, while a "tapestry Brussels"—in which specific areas of the continuous strand of face yarn were dyed to form the pattern—cost about half that. Body Brussels were "a universal sort of carpet, not too rich for the poor, not too poor for the rich," Harriet Prescott Spofford assured her readers; she believed there were "no prettier carpets than the Brussels, although others may be more luxurious to the foot . . . with the proper padding they may be made equally luxurious, and more durable than any." Wiltons remained more expensive than body Brussels, costing $2.25 to $4 a yard in the 1870s. "Moquette" is a term that originally described a type of hand-knotted carpet made in France in the eighteenth century; by the 1870s it signified an American machine-made carpet similar to a machine-made Axminster. Moquettes cost about $1.50 a yard during the period 1870 to 1880. Spofford warned that "Moquettes are finer and thinner" than Axminsters and "less enduring; nor can they, after being soiled, be clipped and shorn off again, and come out freshly as good as new, as the Turkey can."[86]

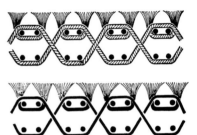

*Cross sections of* (top) *Axminster and* (bottom) *moquette weaves show they were virtually identical. These examples were illustrated in* A Century of Carpet and Rug Making in America *and in* Carpet Manufacturer. *(The Athenaeum of Philadelphia)*

Ingrain, Venetian, and list—three flat-pile carpets discussed in Chapter 1—remained popular during the 1870s and 1880s, although the earlier distinctions between two- and three-ply ingrains had generally faded. While Spofford observed that "the two-ply ingrain is within the means of almost everybody," and the "three-ply, which is much heavier, wears still longer . . . [and] is about as serviceable as a Brussels," most writers and, indeed, many stores, distinguished between ingrains by the quality of the yarn (the amount of wool) rather than the weave. Cotton ingrains cost twenty-five cents a yard, while woolen ones might be $1 to $1.25. Williams and Jones advocated ingrains for "the cottage *orné* in the suburbs of the city, *or in the 'flats' of the same,* and to our young housekeeper as well," and with prices so low ingrains "afford even 'the million,' an opportunity to cover their floors tastefully." Church, addressing a more affluent audience, advised ingrains for servants' rooms.[87]

As to the other flat-pile carpets, Spofford identified Venetian as "nearly as old a carpet as any we have; its pattern is in simple stripes, the woollen warp woven over woof of coarse linen strands." Most critics included Venetian in any discussion of floor coverings, but Ella Rodman Church recommended it only for the stairs leading to the third floor and servants' rooms. Rag and list carpets, like Venetians, were relegated to areas of hard use, such as halls and kitchens, or spaces of little importance, such as servants' rooms, in the middle-class urban households of the 1880s.[88]

*Carpet Designs*

The critics of the 1850 to 1870 period offered clear advice to householders regarding carpet patterns. Eastlake strongly preferred the designs of Oriental carpets and condemned any "pattern . . . shaded in imitation of natural objects, [which] becomes an absurdity when we remember that if it were really what it pretends to be, no one would walk on it with comfort." His American editor added, "how can a peaceful citizen, clad in a dressing-gown, and with a long pipe in his mouth, be expected to walk over such a dangerous wilderness, which would be better suited to an inhabitant of the tropics?" Other critics echoed these sentiments: no matter what the manufacturing process, designs should be "conventional" and the colors subdued, like those in Oriental carpets. Eastlake cautioned his readers to evaluate the terms used by shopkeepers when describing their wares. "Handsome" was certain to be showy, generally ponderous, and almost always filled with superfluous ornament. "Elegant" referred to anything curved in form. "Graceful" meant fragile and generally was attached to any design giving a false impression of its actual purpose. Eastlake urged his readers to select any carpet characterized merely as "neat," for it was certain to be a simple, good design free of ostentatious ornamentation.[89]

These were not new ideas, merely newly accepted. Earlier, even when the demand for "dazzling surfaces of flowers to be walked over and trodden under foot" was at its peak, some critics had favored "mosaic" patterns and

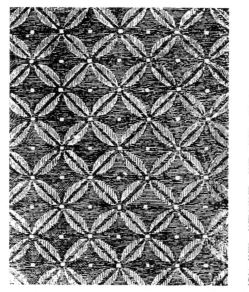

*Eastlake included these two carpet patterns in* Hints on Household Taste *(1877 edition) as examples of designs appropriately "conventional" for households unable to afford Oriental carpets. (The Athenaeum of Philadelphia)*

derided those patterns containing realistic foliage or architectural elements. However, Oriental patterns and "conventional" designs became popular only during the last quarter of the century. Williams and Jones reflected the change, happily reporting in 1878, "To go into a Carpet store to-day is to wander over the lands of the Orient, not as in the days past to walk upon baskets and vases of flowers, and vegetation of every conceivable form; but upon imitations of ancient tiles, and floors of inlaid rare soft wood, porphyry and quiet somber stones upon designs of quaint and curious character, that lead the mind back to ancient days."[90]

In addition to a preference for "conventional" designs, critics reminded their audience that a carpet would be seen from all parts of a room and the pattern should, consequently, have *radiating symmetry,* extending equally in all directions. This suggestion was drawn directly from Christopher Dresser, who used plant motifs to illustrate his theory in *The Art of Decorative Design.* Along with designs originating in the center and radiating outward, as in some Oriental carpets, critics also advocated small designs laid in a diaper pattern.[91] The designs of Christopher Dresser and William Morris, whose work followed these precepts, were frequently praised by critics.

Critics also offered advice regarding carpet colors. Writers of the 1870s and 1880s condemned the vibrant colors of the 1850s and 1860s. Carpet should serve as "the main body tint from which the rest of the room works up in lighter tints." Since carpets should appear neutral, critics recommended backgrounds of tertiary colors and patterns of secondary colors—little or no white or primary colors should be in evidence. They maintained that the overall color of the carpet, its "bloom" when seen from a distance, should contrast with the colors of the walls.[92]

*Christopher Dresser, a trained botanist, included these designs in* The Principles of Decorative Design *(London, 1875) to show how nature may be adapted to create the "conventional" (abstract) designs favored by Eastlake and his followers. (The Athenaeum of Philadelphia)*

### Carpet Use

In front halls with parquet or wood carpeting, a rug small enough to be easily cleaned could be laid; wall-to-wall carpeting was *never* to be used there. Stairways constructed of good hardwood did not require carpeting, but most critics suggested a runner of Brussels or Axminster for the main staircase. If carpeting was used, they recommended purchasing enough to allow a small surplus to be folded under the first riser, thus allowing the carpet to be shifted as the surface wore. In a narrow hall, the overall color of the carpet might be the same as the walls and similar to the wood of the floor, so as not to call particular attention to itself.[93]

Naturally, the best carpets covered floors in parlors and sitting rooms. An issue addressed by critics was whether to treat the floor in each room of a double parlor identically. Cook argued that nature did not seek absolute symmetry, therefore double parlors need not be identical, although the

*Few houses contain only one style. Phil-Ellena, built in Philadelphia in the middle of the nineteenth century, was photographed during the last decades of the century. The marbleized and ashlar-scored walls of the entry hall and the floor painted to resemble tiles or parquet all date to the first years of the house. The Oriental rugs, however, follow popular taste at the time the photograph was taken. (Library Company of Philadelphia)*

designs should "balance" one another. In any case, according to Church, "a pronounced carpet, however beautiful in itself it may be, is, under all circumstances, destructive to harmonious furnishing.[94]

Williams and Jones suggested, as an added touch, that families with dogs or cats add a rug just for the pet in the sitting room, "in order to prevent the soil that of necessity comes from constant use of cushion, sofa-corner or even the rugs belonging to the room." They recommended quilted scarlet flannel, lined in oilcloth, and fringed in wool for this purpose.[95]

Dining rooms employed rugs—not carpeting—because rugs were easier to keep clean. For similar reasons of hygiene, design critics generally opposed fully carpeted bedroom floors: "Wholly carpeted bedrooms are simply an abomination," stated *House Painting and Decorating*. Small carpets placed beside the bed and near the dressing table were recommended because they were easily cleaned and could be taken up to allow the floor to be swept each day. Nonetheless, many households that could afford wall-to-wall carpeting in the bedrooms apparently preferred its warmth to "a few oases of mats in a desert of cold, polished wood." Ella Rodman Church, who favored wooden floors or matting in bedrooms, remarked that "when money is not scarce, and the principles of hygiene are a sealed book, the housekeeper hugs her carpet to her heart and will not give it up." In such cases, "let it be a soft gray . . . of the smallest possible pattern, either with or without a border."[96]

# WINDOWS
As in other areas of household decoration, critics of the 1870s and 1880s followed Eastlake's prescription for simpler window coverings. His designs, which he believed emulated Gothic styling, employed an entirely new vocabulary of fabrics and colors. Gothic taste also sparked the use of stained glass in domestic settings—a fashion that continued into the twentieth century. As might be expected, not all householders subscribed to the new fashions set by the reformers. Some preferred the more ornately composed designs based on traditional, generally French, taste. Others made do with less expensive, often old-fashioned, window coverings. The modern homeowner or curator will have to determine the path most appropriate for the particular house.

## WOODEN BLINDS AND SHUTTERS

Exterior paneled and louvered shutter blinds were now painted to contrast with the body color of the house, rather than the nearly universal green or stone colors of the past. Interior shutters with movable louvers—sometimes called "rolling slats"—were stained or painted to coordinate with the color scheme of the room. In a great many houses, the interior shutters were designed to fold neatly into recesses in the window casing when not in use.[97] Interior wooden blinds provided privacy and protection from sunlight, making them especially useful during the summer months. Marion Harland's description in "Mrs. Prime's House" in *Godey's Lady's Book* is quite vivid: "It was a close August morning; oppressing even at seven o'clock, the breakfast hour. . . . The front and back doors were closed; the windows up stairs and down also, sashes and blinds. . . . In the breakfast room the shutters were bowed slightly, admitting sufficient light to enable the family group to see one another's faces, and what was upon the table."[98]

## WIRE SCREENS

American homes continued to use blinds of gauze or wire of the type Loudon had described in 1833 and Wheeler had recommended in 1851 "to exclude those flying torments." Some, of course, were homemade, of the type illustrated in paintings and engravings and described by writers throughout the nineteenth century. Williams and Jones illustrated a pair made of Indian

*A close look reveals the same sort of netting used as "bug bars" to screen a porch (above) in Concord, Massachusetts, about 1865 as in the windows of a summer cottage (opposite) in Madison, Wisconsin, in July 1894. (The Society for the Preservation of New England Antiquities, Boston, Massachusetts; and the State Historical Society of Wisconsin, Conover Collection, Frederick Conover, photographer)*

gauze painted with flowers and birds, bound with silk ribbon, and threaded top and bottom onto steel rods hooked to the window molding. Another type of blind described as "especially useful and appropriate to the dining-room" was made of coarse curtain net embellished with crochet done in black cotton. "Such screens," promised Williams and Jones, "are exceedingly elegant, and give a beautiful finish to a window, besides frequently shutting out unpleasant views."[99]

By the 1880s, however, American factories produced wire window screens expressly to exclude insects. J. W. Boughton, a Philadelphia manufacturer of wood carpeting, advertised that his factories were, "during the early Summer, devoted to the manufacture of Window and Door Screens, to protect dwellings, offices, &c., from the *destructive and disgusting annoyances of FLIES and MOSQUITOES.*" Although Shoppell labeled all wire blinds "dismally ugly," the product was wildly successful. Homeowners could purchase custom-fitted frames made of walnut, oak, ash, or poplar that slid on tongued stops, while tenants could purchase adjustable blinds to accommodate a variety of

*These homemade Indian gauze screens with flowers and birds were illustrated, complete with painting directions, in Henry T. Williams and Mrs. C. S. Jones,* Beautiful Homes. *(The Athenaeum of Philadelphia)*

**Comfort! Economy! Luxury!**

**WIRE WINDOW SCREENS**

AND

**MOSQUITO BARS.**

WITH A LANDSCAPE SCREEN.

*The landscape on this painted wire screen from the c. 1880 catalogue of Howard & Morse, New York, bears a striking resemblance to a screen on the Morrill Homestead in Strafford, Vermont, pictured earlier. (The Athenaeum of Philadelphia)*

windows. Boughton's custom screens cost twenty to thirty-five cents a square foot; adjustable screens cost from fifty cents to $1.40 each.[100]

The wire mesh was painted for protection against rust in either a plain color—black, green, or drab being the most common—or decoratively, as Loudon and Webster had suggested fifty years earlier. The Boughton catalogue described the latter as a "landscape screen . . . elegant and necessary for privacy." Marion Harland sarcastically described a pair of "wire blinds of finest net" inside the lower sashes of the windows in the dining room of "Mrs. Prime's House" painted with landscapes "in the ingenious second mourning style which does not permit the designs to be inspected from without. The subject upon one is a shipwreck, the other a church yard by moonlight." Most catalogues illustrated designs of less melancholy subjects. For commercial establishments, dealers would letter the screens in colors or gold.[101]

Cotton or wire-mesh blinds were not always effective, however. Elizabeth Custer, wife of General George Armstrong Custer, recorded a summer spent

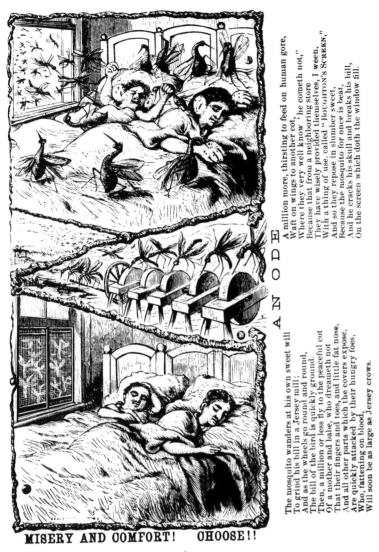

AN ODE

A million more, thirsting to feed on human gore,
Waft on wings to another cot,
Where they very well know "he cometh not,"
Because that from a neighboring store
They have wisely provided themselves, I ween,
With a thing of use, called "BOUGHTON'S SCREEN,"
And so they repose in slumber sweet,
Because the mosquito for once is beat,
And he cracks his skull and breaks his bill,
On the screen which doth the window fill.

The mosquito wanders at his own sweet will
To grind his bill in a Jersey mill;
And as the wheels go round and round,
The bill of the bird is quickly ground.
Then, a million or less fly to the peaceful cot
Of a mother and babe, who dreameth not
That their fingers and toes, and little fat nose,
And all other parts which the covers expose,
Are quickly attacked by their hungry foes,
Who, fattening on blood,
Will soon be as large as Jersey crows.

**MISERY AND COMFORT!    CHOOSE!!**

*"An Ode" to the mosquito accompanied this advertisement in the c. 1885 catalogue of the John W. Boughton Company, Philadelphia, but the pictures say it all. (The Athenaeum of Philadelphia)*

at Fort Lincoln, in the Black Hills of Dakota Territory, during the early 1870s: "We fought in succession five varieties of mosquitoes; the last that came were the most vicious. They were so small they slid easily through the ordinary [bug] bar, and we had to put an inside layer of tarlatan on doors and windows." Even with double protection, she added, "We did not venture to light a lamp in the evening, and at five o'clock the netting was let down over the beds, and doors and windows closed. When it came time to retire, we removed our garments in another room, and grew skillful in making sudden sallies into the sleeping-room and quick plunges under the bar."[102]

## WINDOW SHADES

Window blinds, commonly known as "roller shades," formed an integral part of most window treatments, especially on windows without interior louvered shutter blinds. "It is as unpleasant to have the full glare of sunlight streaming through an apartment, as to be annoyed by prying eyes, or suffer the feeling of fear at imagining some outside spectator gazing into our apartments during the evening hours," wrote Williams and Jones in 1878. They urged readers to purchase ready-made shades or make their own using patent spring rollers "so readily adjusted that any lady may manage to fix all her windows without troubling anyone."[103]

Critics described three types of shades. One was generally made of Holland, a fine linen, and came in a variety of colors; the 1885 catalogue from Stern Bro's of New York listed white, ecru, sage, brown, blue, and cardinal. While householders might select colors to fit the scheme of the room, critics preferred white, buff, or gray to avoid tinting the light entering the room. Harrison explained that window shades in red Holland, for instance, suggested "a descent into the Inferno at every afternoon tea." The material

Left: *A decorative window shade was part of the window treatment illustrated in the March 1875 issue of* Godey's Lady's Book. Right: *R. W. Shoppell included an example in* Modern Houses, Beautiful Homes, *but by the arrangement of cords it would appear the "shade" would draw from side to side rather than roll up. (The Athenaeum of Philadelphia)*

could be embellished with fringe at the hem or even stitches in outline work, such as those illustrated in *Godey's Lady's Book* in March 1875. Whatever the choice, the shades should be "uniform in material and color throughout the front of the house, at least, for nothing so mars the beauty of a 'front' than windows showing, even at a distance, all the colors of the rainbow, or even two or three of them."[104]

Transparent shades were the second possibility, particularly for windows lacking views. Williams and Jones recommended decorating architect's or artist's tracing cloth, which produced a mellow light like that through ground-glass lampshades, with transfer work of diaphanie or vitromania, two popular craft items during the nineteenth century. Designs might include those "from the Medieval and Renaissance period, with its gorgeously robed knights, musicians, saints and madonnas, to the lovely landscapes and Oriental groups, or domestic scenes of our own more modern times." Eastlake omitted window shades in *Hints on Household Taste* but denounced "potchimanie, diaphanie, and other modern drawing-room pursuits . . . in vogue with young ladies," as "utterly opposed to sound principles of taste."[105]

A third type of shade, made of oilcloth in white or colors, was opaque. Some retailers advertised these shades with marbleizing or graining or with borders. Williams and Jones believed plain silver or gold bands with small ornamental scrolls in the corners were the "most genteel" and urged buyers to avoid "the gaudy, many-colored 'horrors,' that are offered in shops," which are "better fitted for a saloon than a private dwelling, and should never be admitted into the tasteful homes."[106]

## ORNAMENTAL GLASS WINDOWS

A rekindled interest in Gothic design resulted in an increased use of stained glass in homes during the fourth quarter of the nineteenth century. It was especially favored for stairways, vestibule doors, and side-wall dining-room windows in city apartments without a view. When the cost of stained glass was prohibitive, diaphanie and vitromania were sometimes substituted. Appropriate subjects for dining-room windows included flowers, fruits, or traditional designs such as "Departure for the Chase," "The Seasons," or "The Twelve Months." Simpler windows, composed of alternating panes of white ground glass with red, for example, were always correct.[107]

In addition to diaphanie and vitromania, there were other methods of achieving the effect of stained glass without the high costs. Books and magazines offered a variety of handicraft suggestions. One could transfer decalcomania designs (much like modern decals); one could paint on glass using transparent colors; or one could make an "epiphanie" by cutting a design into heavy cardboard and filling the spaces with colored cellophane or tissue paper. Less expensive and less time-consuming was to imitate etched glass by pouncing a putty bag all over the window glass and, once the putty dried, varnishing it. By using this technique over a stencil, one created the illusion of etched and clear glass. A similar effect was obtained by applying lace to the glass and varnishing over it.[108]

## CURTAINS

In accord with the principles of the reform movement in design, Charles Eastlake ruled that curtains should be simple and functional, and, like wall and floor coverings, should serve as background to a room's contents. He condemned ornate treatments as "burlesques" of what curtains should be and denounced current fashions for their "ugliness and inconvenience." Believing medieval curtains hung at windows and doors "to exclude cold and draughts" to be superior devices, he described them as "suspended by little rings, which slipped easily over a stout metal rod—perhaps an inch or an inch and a half in diameter. Of course, between such a rod (stretched across the top of the window) and the ceiling, a small space must always intervene; and, therefore, to prevent the chance of wind blowing through in this direction, a boxing of wood became necessary, in front of which a plain valance was hung, sometimes cut into a vandyke-shaped pattern at its lower edge, but generally unplaited. As for the curtains themselves, when not in use they hung straight down on either side, of a sufficient length to touch, but not sweep the ground."[109]

Eastlake grumbled that in modern practice, "the useful and convenient little rod had grown into a huge lumbering pole as thick as a man's arm," and

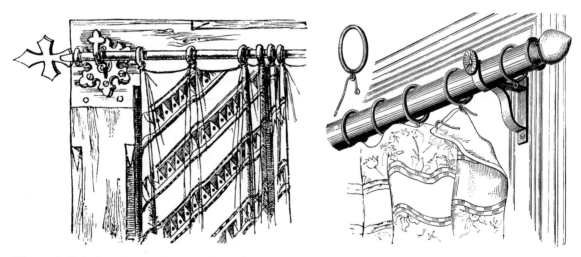

*These methods for hanging curtains appeared in* (left) *Eastlake,* Hints on Household Taste, *and* (right) *Cook,* The House Beautiful. *Neither curtain is gathered at the top by pinch pleats. (The Athenaeum of Philadelphia)*

"in place of the little finials which used to be fixed at each end of the rod to prevent the rings from slipping off, our modern upholsterer had substituted gigantic fuchsias, or other flowers, made of brass, gilt, bronze, and even china, sprawling downwards in a design of execrable taste. . . ." As for gilt cornices, Eastlake found them to be "contemptible in design" and too often made of thin, sharp-edged metal, "liable to cut and fray the curtain."[110]

In America, householders concerned with fashion adopted the new, simplified window treatments espoused by the reformers. Eastlake's pronouncements actually differed little from those of Loudon, Webster and Parkes, or Downing during the 1830s and 1840s. They had recommended panels of fabric hung from rings on a rod, which might be topped with a valance of flat or pleated material as described in Chapter 1. Like the earlier curtains, the reform styles required a minimum of material, just enough to cover the window when closed. Almon Varney, author of *Our Homes and Their Adornments*, advised that two lengths of fabric, each thirty inches wide, were sufficient for most windows. These panels were not generally pleated at the top, but hooked to rings; the weight of the fabric and the flannel interlining improved "the set of heavy textures," forming them naturally into folds. The hardware was generally brass or wood. The diameter of the pole varied, depending upon whether it was visible or covered with a valance; if visible, the pole was large enough to look as if it could hold the heavy curtains, even if a smaller size was structurally adequate. Curtain poles required judicious selection, however, for critics warned that "singular fancies have been perpetrated in the matter of . . . pole-ends, but the strange hallucination that bunches of tin grapes are the natural product of a rigid brass pole, has by this time, we hope, been exploded." Retail catalogues listed poles in 1½- to two-inch diameters made of brass, walnut, ash, ebony, and cherry. And while cornices were, in the estimation of many, no longer correct, they too were offered in walnut, ebony, ash, gilt, and hammered brass—suggesting that previous fashions coexisted with the new.[11]

The new style of curtain differed from earlier nineteenth-century styles in several respects. In earlier periods, curtains were looped back during the day; consequently, curtain panels were cut longer than the actual distance from rod to floor so that even when drawn up and back the fabric would just reach the floor, and when closed at night, the excess fabric would "puddle." By the 1870s, however, reform critics disapproved of looping back curtains during the day and labeled excess fabric trailing on the floor as "vulgar."[112] Instead, curtain panels just touched the floor and might be slightly pulled back with cords and tassels, depending upon the style of the room. Eastlake, and other reformers, opposed tiebacks for rooms in the Gothic style; a room finished in Renaissance or Louis XVI, however, generally included curtains tied back with cords and tassels.

The height from which curtains were hung also depended upon the style of furnishing used in the room. During the 1830s and 1840s, most poles were attached to the molding at the top of the window. By 1870, rooms furnished in the Gothic style continued that practice with an ornate frieze occupying the space above. However, Renaissance and Louis XIV styles generally placed cornices and lambrequins next to the ornate molding occupying the top of the room in place of a frieze. Whatever the style, window treatments never covered the frieze or molding, since "its unbroken line is one of its chief charms."[113]

By the 1870s and 1880s, the use of a lambrequin—as most writers of the period identified a valance—depended upon the room's style of furnishing. Eastlake recommended them to exclude drafts. Favoring the Gothic style, he suggested an unpleated panel of fabric (which might be cut into a pattern at the hem) suspended from a boxing at the top of the window; anything more was inappropriate. However, styles such as Renaissance and Louis XIV required more elaborate lambrequins, including the loops, festoons, fringes,

*A "vandyke" lambrequin of the type Eastlake recommended. It is doubtful, however, if he would have approved the rest of the curtains. Illustrated in Williams and Jones,* Beautiful Homes. *(The Athenaeum of Philadelphia)*

*While Eastlake and his followers exhorted their audiences to employ simple curtains in their homes, magazines such as* Godey's Lady's Book *blithely continued to illustrate ornate styles such as this one, which was later reprinted (without acknowledgment) by Williams and Jones in* Beautiful Homes. *(The Athenaeum of Philadelphia)*

cords, and tassels so favored during the preceding decades. *Godey's Lady's Book* virtually ignored Eastlake's reform notions and continued to illustrate the ornate styles it purported to have introduced to America during the 1850s. And while claiming to follow Eastlake's theories of design, Williams and Jones handily copied in their own work the same designs illustrated in the *Lady's Book* several years earlier![114]

Reformers' beliefs in the simplicity of the overall design did not preclude rich trimmings. Eastlake echoed Pugin in maintaining that because fringes evolved from the practice of tying off the cut ends of fabric to prevent further unraveling, all fringe was to be *the same color* as the fabric it trimmed. Most critics, however, advocated curtains and lambrequins on which the fringe was a *contrasting color,* to match something else in the room, such as the upholstery. Even critics who generally disapproved of trimmings—claiming, for instance, that "the grandiose bullion fringes with wooden pendants, encased in twisted yellow silk, are generally abominable"—sometimes admitted that if "worked in quiet colors harmonizing with the curtains, and kept to some very simple outline, may look exceedingly well, and by no means barbaric."[115]

The amount of trimming and embroidery involved in a window treatment depended generally upon the style being emulated. Eastlake's Gothic designs were theoretically simple, but in reality they required embellishment to achieve the proper effect. Fabrics such as wool rep or plain damask might be embroidered with silk along both the sides and hem or in wide bands running parallel to the floor. Velvets or heavy woolens were considered judicious choices for a Gothic interior and might be embroidered with heraldic devices, unicorns, peacocks, tigers, roses, religious images, or Byzantine emblems. For rooms with a more Oriental flavor, critics suggested Japanese designs including swallows, cranes, and grasses, imitating designs by Marshall, Morris & Company of London.[116]

Whatever the motifs, colorful bands could be introduced to create an overall effect. Most critics prescribed *horizontal* rather than vertical bands for two reasons. First, the designs would not be lost when the curtains were drawn back. Second, cross-bands—as writers called them—echoed the new, three-part wall division by using a different fabric for each area: for example, plush (velvet) for the dado, bands of embroidery for the rail, and wool or plush of a different color for the wall. In addition, each large area of solid color could be embroidered or the entire curtain panel could be banded with five-inch-wide strips of velvet placed every eighteen inches.[117]

Such extensive use of embroidery and banding worked best in rooms where Gothic, Japanesque, or Moorish designs dominated, because the fabrics used there, including velvets, plushes, plain wools or damasks, silks, serges and baize, and camel's-hair cloths as well as blankets, were somewhat plain.[118] While embroidery was also used on Renaissance or Louis XIV

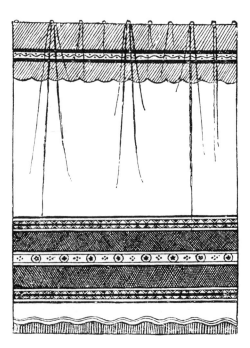

*Curtains showing "cross banding"* (right) *and the "dado effect"* (opposite), *illustrated in Eastlake,* Hints on Household Taste, *and Holly,* Modern Dwellings. *(The Athenaeum of Philadelphia)*

curtains, the more ornately conceived lambrequins made up in patterned fabrics such as damasks or brocades required little additional adornment.

Formal rooms employed the richest fabrics and most ornate designs. The curtain materials corresponded in richness to the upholstery fabrics in these rooms, including velvets, stamped plushes, wools, tapestries, damasks, reps, and satins. In contrast with the practice in earlier decades, a variety of colors and fabrics was used within each room. Plainer upholstery fabric was embellished, like the window curtains, with bands of contrasting color.

Lighter curtains and roller blinds were used in addition to heavy panels and lambrequins. Eastlake preferred Swiss lace made of heavy cotton thread for glass curtains and derided the midcentury styles of muslin curtain "on which semi-naturalistic foliage and nondescript ornament is allowed to meander after an extravagant and meaningless fashion." Lace curtains varied considerably in price; a pair of Nottingham lace curtains in four-yard lengths cost $1 to $6 depending upon the design, while Brussels lace curtains might cost $35 to $100 a pair. Whatever the material, critics agreed with Eastlake that the designs should differ from "those of former days, when our fathers and mothers thought there could be nothing more beautiful than the representation upon their window drapery of immense tropical jungles of leafage, ferns and palms, mixed with roses, tulips and lilies of the valley." Most writers recommended plain muslin in white, cream, or colors (costing from sixty cents to $4 a yard), which could either be edged in lace or have panels of lace inserted. For an even less expensive curtain, the homeowner might use cheesecloth edged in lace or common dairy strainer cloth bordered with drawnwork and knotted fringe along the sides.[119]

Whatever the material chosen, most critics agreed that sheer curtains generally were not attractive by themselves. In the summer a room might employ only lace curtains and a lace lambrequin, but other seasons required a more substantial treatment. If cost was a consideration, then lace curtains with a lambrequin longer on the sides than in the middle was acceptable, according to Spofford. Silk lambrequins over lace curtains created a light, airy effect, and were appropriate substitutes in parlors for more expensive curtains.[120]

## PORTIERES

The portiere, or doorway curtain, reached nearly universal popularity during the last quarter of the century. Doorway curtains had appeared in a few French sources at midcentury, and *Godey's Lady's Book* had proposed their use to prevent drafts and soil from passing under closed doors, but portieres rarely appeared before the 1870s. Once in vogue, portieres remained in use for a half century.

Nineteenth-century writers seemed uncertain as to the origin of portieres. Spofford linked them to "Medieval usage" when, she claimed, curtains played "an important part in the style, screening recesses and dividing rooms." Harrison suggested an earlier origin, believing "there is something thoroughly Eastern in the conception of a portiere" because the first use was in the Tabernacle in Jerusalem. Whatever the origin, critics commended portieres for their graceful folds, appearance of hospitality, and for providing another opportunity to display needlework skills.[121]

Generally, portieres hung at the doorways of public rooms, such as the parlor, library, and dining room. They also appeared between double parlors, even in conjunction with sliding doors. They were less often used at bedroom doors. A few critics argued that "the portiere is preferred by many to any door at all" and urged readers to "discard their doors to the 'shady side' of the lumber-room or . . . dispose of them to some lover of doors." In most locations a portiere was visible from both sides; consequently, each side was finished and embellished to correspond in color and style with the room or hall. The work rarely repeated the curtains at the windows, however, or

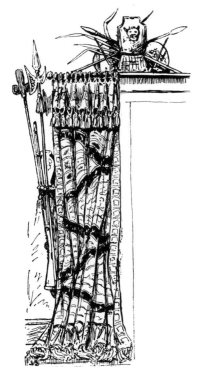

*Portieres illustrated by Eastlake's American followers:* Cook, House Beautiful *(left),* Spofford, Art Decoration Applied to Furniture *(top), and* Harrison, Woman's Handiwork in Modern Homes *(far left).* The additional trim at the top of Harrison's design was known as a "Queen's valance." *(The Athenaeum of Philadelphia)*

one lost "a great opportunity for telling colors." In addition to the fabrics recommended for windows, portieres were also made from more exotic goods such as striped India shawls, kilim, Turkish or ingrain carpets, or strips of old silk dresses sewn together and woven into panels.[122]

Most reform critics argued that portieres should be functional, meaning that the panels should be hung using the same rods, rings, and pins suitable for window curtains, so that the panels could be opened and closed. A few even suggested that portieres should never be tied back with cords and tassels, although a great many contemporary illustrations show them tied back and with panels arranged in such a way as to be immobile. The hem of a portiere should just touch the floor—anything more was "vulgar"—and they should not be so full as to "lose" the designs worked on them.[123]

## INCIDENTAL DRAPERIES

As may quickly be seen in contemporary photographs, more surfaces than merely windows and doors were draped during the 1870s and 1880s. In new houses of the period, fireplace mantels surmounted by several tiers of wooden shelves stained or painted to match the other woodwork needed only to be accessorized with plates, Japanese fans, Indian ginger jars, and the like. But critics disparaged the marble mantels of earlier nineteenth-century houses as "cold" and "unsuggestive." Their solution was a drapery of lambrequin hanging six to ten inches down from the mantel. Felting,

*Critics offered suggestions to owners of houses built before the fourth quarter of the nineteenth century and thus lacking ornate mantels. With an illustration entitled "Another Way of Dealing with the Commonplace," Clarence Cook recommended an embroidered lambrequin hanging from the mantel and shelves above it to update a midcentury coal-burning fireplace. (The Athenaeum of Philadelphia)*

*The parlor of the Ramsey House in St. Paul, Minnesota, photographed in 1884, illustrates the way earlier furniture styles might be made to blend with the aesthetic interior recommended by critics. (Lovell Photo, Minnesota Historical Society)*

flannel, velvet, plush, serge, and satin were some of the fabric choices and all could be further embellished with decorative edging and embroidery. A few writers suggested that curtains be hung *beneath* the mantel shelf as well, covering the grate when not in use, a set of "mini-portieres" that took the place of the earlier fireboards.[124]

Tables and pianos supplied two other locations for the display of fabric and embroidery skill. Velvet, felt, wool cloth, and satin were common materials for table covers to be used over marble-topped tables, which Ella Rodman Church labeled "parlor tombstones." The same fabrics appeared as scarves atop pianos; one critic suggested, "when, as is customary for the accommodation of singers, the upright piano is turned to face the room, a square, flat hanging, of a size to cover the fluted silk at the back, may be made of Turk satin, sateen, serge, plush or linen, and embroidered, the ends fringed or trimmed with antique lace."[125] From a twentieth-century perspective, a needlework frenzy seemingly overran the public rooms of the middle-class house during the 1870s and 1880s, resulting in "throws" for sofas, cushions, pillows, and antimacassars for chairs and sofas; wall pockets to hold letters, magazines, and newspapers; and assorted other draperies—in short, scarcely an inch was left unembellished.

The colors of all these fabrics "corresponded" to those on the walls, ceiling, and floor, but were never identical; nor were they allowed to dominate the room. Cook cautioned readers that "if the tone of the room be accented anywhere, it should be by something small,—a vase, a cushion, a bit of tapestry,—not by any large piece of furniture, nor by any large space of wall or drapery." Window curtains should "gently contrast" with the walls, and portieres should blend with both, while not repeating either in color, design, or material. All these surfaces might contrast or harmonize, but they followed the rules of color harmony and they took into account the popular preference for tertiary colors—such as peacock blue, gold and russet browns, sage greens, and dull brick-reds—as did the embroidery and trimmings used in the room. Although the number of colors used within a room might appear impossibly large by modern standards, the use of complementary and adjacent hues of varying values created a unified, distinctly nongarish effect when thoughtfully planned and executed.[126]

## BEDROOM HANGINGS

Bedrooms generally employed plainer fabrics and less ornamentation, in part as a response to health and hygiene concerns. Critics continued to favor washable cotton—such as chintz, dimity, cretonne, muslin, and plain or dotted Swiss—which had been promoted by writers throughout the nineteenth century. Bedrooms, of all the rooms in the house, required sunlight and fresh air every day, stressed Clarence Cook, and no fabric should be used that would be injured by such a regimen.[127]

The half-tester bedstead now found favor with critics because its curtains, while "picturesque," did not hinder ventilation around the sleeper. Generally, the same fabric curtained both bed and windows in simple panels. Eastlake advocated curtains in bedrooms hemmed two or three inches above the floor so they did not interfere with the sweeping of the room. He insisted that curtains disposed "in heavy and artificial folds, such as one sees depicted sometimes at one corner of a theatrical drop-scene . . . is one out of many instances which might be quoted to illustrate the perversion of modern taste in such matters." The curtains of a half-tester required twenty yards of fabric, such as chintz, and twenty-eight yards of a colored lining (based on fabrics twenty-five inches wide).[128]

Oddly, no critic mentioned the use of mosquito netting for beds, as was

By the fourth quarter of the nineteenth century, critics recommended simple bedsteads with little curtaining. The iron bedstead with canopy (left) *appeared in Eastlake,* Hints on Household Taste; *the wooden bedstead* (below) *was illustrated in Cook,* The House Beautiful. *(The Athenaeum of Philadelphia)*

used in Elizabeth Custer's Black Hills residence, although there were a variety of canopies, nets, and fixtures of commercial manufacture. Some of these contrivances resembled umbrellas hung from the ceiling, and others opened to a rectangular shape to drape French and half-tester bedsteads. Catalogues also included netting in gauze or lace bobinet available in a variety of colors including white, pink, blue, brown, drab, green, and yellow. A gauze net for a large bed cost about $3, while the same in bobinet cost $8.[129]

Most American critics preferred that the toilet tables in bedrooms be draped, an issue on which they were in disagreement with Eastlake, who found the draperies inconvenient, hard to maintain, and representing "a milliner's notion of the 'pretty.' " Williams and Jones, however, judged that "a toilet-table is one of those tasteful additions to a lady's bed-chamber or

*This recently restored half-tester bedstead once occupied a bridal chamber in the Palmer House in Chicago, as seen* (opposite) *in the engraving from* The Palmer House Illustrated (1876). *Rebuilt following the Great Fire in 1871, the hotel was a wealth of revival styles. (Courtesy of the Chicago Historical Society)*

dressing-room, which is, perhaps, more characteristic than any other portion of the furniture." They suggested dimity for the top, and cretonne, Swiss, or lace over colored, glazed muslin for the skirt. Even Spofford, a disciple of Eastlake, dissented on this issue, suggesting "muslin curtains, suspended from a pretty ornament close beneath the ceiling, falling and parting over the toilet-table . . . have been in use for hundreds of years" because "they save the glass from dust and specks, and are drawn before it, according to ancient usage, on occasion of a death in the family."[130]

As for colors and patterns, most critics suggested using the same fabrics on beds and at windows. If the walls and floors were patterned, the fabric should be plain, and vice versa. For example, Eastlake recommended dimity trimmed with braid colored in contrast to the other surfaces in the room. If the walls were painted a plain, light color, then patterned chintz, cretonne, or printed cotton were good choices that also hid soil.[131] In general, bedroom fabrics were lighter in weight and paler in color than those found in formal rooms.

Naturally, all these strictures varied according to individual situations. For example, in 1872–1873, Elizabeth Wood Kane traveled through Utah Territory with her husband, Thomas, and two of their children. The family visited Mormon homes in cities all along the frontier. South of Salt Lake City the family reached the town of Scipio, which Mrs. Kane described as "the poorest and newest of the settlements we stopped at." Nevertheless, her description

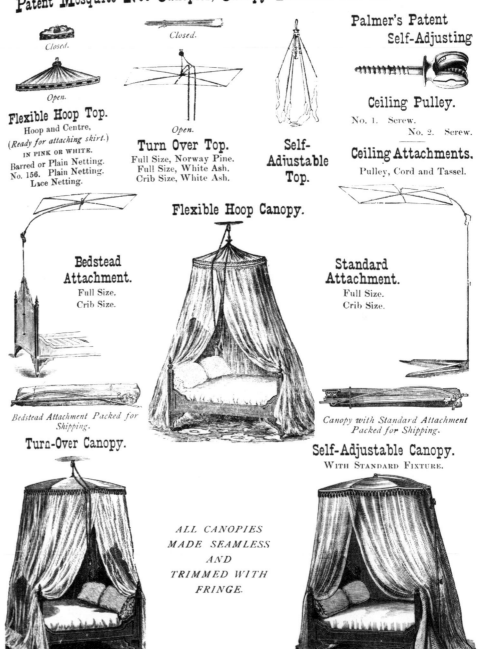

**Patent Mosquito Net Canopies, Canopy Fixtures and Attachments.**

*Closed.*

*Open.*

**Flexible Hoop Top.**
Hoop and Centre,
*(Ready for attaching skirt.)*
IN PINK OR WHITE.
Barred or Plain Netting.
No. 156.   Plain Netting.
Lace Netting.

*Closed.*

*Open.*

**Turn Over Top.**
Full Size, Norway Pine.
Full Size, White Ash.
Crib Size, White Ash.

**Self-Adjustable Top.**

**Palmer's Patent Self-Adjusting**

**Ceiling Pulley.**
No. 1.  Screw.
No. 2.  Screw.

**Ceiling Attachments.**
Pulley, Cord and Tassel.

**Flexible Hoop Canopy.**

**Bedstead Attachment.**
Full Size.
Crib Size.

**Standard Attachment.**
Full Size.
Crib Size.

*Bedstead Attachment Packed for Shipping.*

*Canopy with Standard Attachment Packed for Shipping.*

**Turn-Over Canopy.**

**Self-Adjustable Canopy.**
WITH STANDARD FIXTURE.

*ALL CANOPIES MADE SEAMLESS AND TRIMMED WITH FRINGE.*

Although some manufacturers advertised window screens, a good many others continued to manufacture traditional "bug bars," in the form of netted canopies. Quite a variety were illustrated in the 1886 catalogue of Frank A. Hall, New York. (The Athenaeum of Philadelphia)

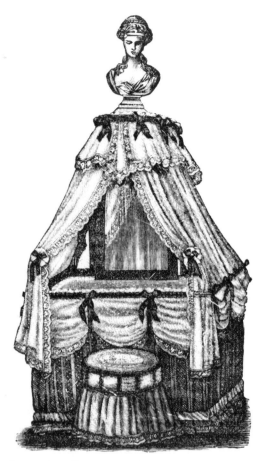

*These toilette tables graphically illustrate the differences between the reform and traditional styles. Eastlake recommended a dresser with a mirror and simple scarf (left), while Williams and Jones devised a fully curtained "novelty" in* Beautiful Homes. *(The Athenaeum of Philadelphia)*

of conditions in a one-room cabin illustrates how diligently families attempted to maintain the vestiges of civilization. "There was a substantial bedstead in one corner," she wrote, "and curtains of old-fashioned chintz were tacked from the ceiling around it as if it had been a four-poster, and a neat patchwork counterpane covered the soft feather-bed. A good rag-carpet was on the floor; clean white curtains hung at the windows; and clean white covers, edged with knitted lace, covered the various bracket shelves that supported the housewife's Bible, Book of Mormon, work-basket, looking-glass, and a few simple ornaments." In addition, "two or three pretty good colored prints hung on the walls" and "there was a mahogany bureau, a washstand, a rocking-chair, and half a dozen wooden ones, with a large chest on which the owner's name was painted."[132] One can only wonder how many of these pieces had been made locally, which had made the trip by wagon, and which, if any, might have been "imported" by the transcontinental railroad.

# 4

# THE 1890 TO 1900 PERIOD

During the last decade of the nineteenth century the population of the United States increased by thirteen million, with a quarter of that growth attributable to immigration. Utah was admitted to the Union in 1896 as the forty-fifth state—once its legislators officially agreed to abandon polygamy. Cities attracted natives and immigrants alike; by 1900, nearly 40 percent of Americans were classified as urban. Thirty-seven cities boasted populations larger than 100,000, and the number of inhabitants in four of those cities exceeded a million. Horse-drawn and electric trolleys found competition in newly developed elevated trains and subway systems with speeds averaging twenty miles an hour. A worker might live ten miles from the downtown area and still reach work within half an hour, the length of time most commuters considered acceptable. These fixed transportation networks encouraged urban growth in prescribed directions.

The internal-combustion engine was not yet a force to be reckoned with, but the bicycle was. In 1878, Colonel Albert Pope founded the first American factory to produce these vehicles in Hartford, Connecticut. While early production was limited, seventy thousand workers produced over a million bicycles valued at $22 million by 1900. Agitation for better roads by the League of American Wheelmen persuaded Congress in 1893 to appropriate $10,000 to study improved road-building techniques—at that time there were only two hundred miles of hard-surfaced roads in the United States. After 1900, automobile manufacturers joined the "wheelmen" in their demands.[1]

Outside of cities, nearly thirty thousand miles of railroad track were laid between 1890 and 1900. The railroads continued to play the major role in the transmission of information as well as in the movement of raw materials and finished products. In 1893, two Minnesotans, Richard Sears and A. C.

*The stair hall and inglenook of "The 1890 House" in Cortland, New York. ("The 1890 House" Museum and Center for Victorian Arts, Cortland, New York; photograph by Dede Hatch)*

Roebuck, founded a company in competition with Montgomery Ward. The catalogues and merchandise of both firms reached into areas of the country never before tapped and aided in "homogenizing" the American home.

While it was possible to telephone Chicago from New York City in 1892, there were only about 1.5 million telephones in the United States by 1900 and most were interurban hookups. The postal service was far more influential in the lives of most Americans. Postal reform during the period substantially reduced the cost of sending first-class mail, so that by 1885 a one-ounce letter could be mailed anywhere in the United States for two cents (a charge that remained in effect until 1932 with the exception of the war years, 1917–1919). Postcards cost a penny. By 1890, the number of post offices had quadrupled from 104 in 1880 to 454.[2]

These urban post offices provided *free delivery*, and the number of carriers increased during the succeeding decades. There was no rural mail delivery until 1896, when the government conducted the first tentative experiments with Rural Free Delivery from three West Virginia towns. Within a year, the system spread to twenty-nine states and by 1899 encompassed forty states and one territory. Rural carriers also collected mail along their routes. They earned $300 a year and supplied their own transportation. The exact route followed by a carrier often depended upon the condition of the roads. The carriers of rural mail soon joined other lobbyists for improved roads.[3]

*Godey's Lady's Book*, founded in Philadelphia in 1830 and the quintessential arbiter of taste for several generations of American women, ceased publication in 1898. So did Peterson's *Ladies' National Magazine* and Arthur's *Home Magazine*. The demise of these periodicals was little noticed since others had begun to replace them, including *The Ladies' Home Journal* (1883), *The Ladies' Home Companion* (1886), *Vogue* (begun for wealthy New York women in 1892), *House Beautiful* (1896), and *McCall's Magazine* (1897). *House and Garden* (1901) soon joined the competition. Suggestions for home decorating in these new and ever more widely available magazines urged readers to adopt simpler, less cluttered interiors, following the philosophy—if not the recognizable style—of Eastlake and his fellow reformers.

During the last decade of the nineteenth century, no single critic dominated as had Downing and Eastlake in earlier decades. Eastlake's reform philosophy still prevailed, but critics applied the philosophy to a variety of styles. "Some people want their houses pure white throughout, while others have them painted dark as possible," observed a housepainter in 1893, "and some peculiar combinations of color are often selected, but we never dare object, or we might lose the job."[4] The words of this craftsman suggest the variety of apparently conflicting styles available in the final decade of the nineteenth century. What critics there were in the 1890s appeared to favor divergent styles—such as the various revival styles and the Craftsman style.

Householders were left to find their own way out of the thicket, often missing the point that a reform interior was not so much a single style as it was a philosophy of decoration; divergent styles might represent a similar quest for simple, good design.

The two styles most associated with reform philosophy were both seen at the Centennial Exhibition held in Philadelphia in 1876. Chapter 3 showed how the ideas of Eastlake and his followers formed the basis for the Arts and Crafts Movement (later the Craftsman style) in America. A second style found at the Exhibition caught the fancy of many of the ten million fairgoers, and would become known as the Colonial Revival. Fairgoers visited the New England log-house kitchen furnished with what became icons of the style: a walk-in fireplace, candlesticks, spinning wheel, and cradle.[5] In the decades following 1876, Americans began in earnest to furnish their homes in the Craftsman and Colonial Revival styles according to reform principles of decoration that favored simplification over excess, honesty over fakery, and handcrafted objects over mass-produced ones.

Clarence Cook, an American critic whose work favored Charles Eastlake and the designs of the British Arts and Crafts Movement, predicted five years after the fair in his book *The House Beautiful* (1881): "A change is coming over the spirit of our time, which has its origin partly ... in the memorial epoch through which we are passing, but which is also a proof that our taste is getting a root in a healthier and more native soil. All this resuscitation of 'old furniture' and revival of old simplicity ... is in reality much more sensible than it seems to be to those who look upon it as only another phase of the 'centennial' mania." Throughout the rest of the century, the nostalgia grew. *House Beautiful* assumed in 1899, "The fact that colonial designs in furniture, especially, are among the most restful, graceful, and artistic yet produced, makes it probable that the liking for them is genuine and lasting." The praise for the past was not unconditional, however; *House and Garden* warned readers against such fads as the "brass warming-pans with which some persons incomprehensibly decorate their parlor walls" and cautioned, "our ancestors put good material and skilled cabinet-making into some of the ugliest articles that ever disfigured a drawing-room." Edith Wharton and Ogden Codman, Jr., authors of *The Decoration of Houses* (1897), agreed, condemning "that cheap originality which finds expression in putting things to uses for which they were not intended."[6]

Besides the Colonial Revival, some critics favored other traditional (revival) styles of furnishing such as Louis XV, Louis XVI, and Empire. While *Household News* and *House Beautiful* occasionally printed articles on the French styles, the source most immediately responsible for the French Revival was *The Decoration of Houses*, in which Wharton and Codman illustrated sixteenth-, seventeenth-, and eighteenth-century European interiors. Directing their book at wealthy Americans, the authors attributed "the vulgarity of current decoration" to "the indifference of the wealthy to architectural fitness," which they hoped to remedy.[7]

In 1893, an article in *House Painting and Decorating* predicted a return of the French-inspired Rococo style popular in mid-nineteenth-century America. The writer reasoned that if tertiary colors were the prevailing schemes for interior decoration during "the period of aesthetic dress, dominated by Oscar Wilde and his followers," then "now that crinoline is said to be once more coming into sway, it is not at all unlikely that the decorative styles of thirty or forty years ago will again come into play." The author was partially correct; Rococo-style furnishings did reappear at the turn of the century, although crinolines did not.[8]

Furnishings in the various revival styles were readily available well into the first decades of the twentieth century; American manufacturers produced furnishings and finishes for middle-class purchasers in styles identified as Colonial, Louis, and Empire. *House Beautiful* warned, however, that "modern imitators have a curious habit of combining in one table, for example, all the decorative motives which the original designers would have spread over half a dozen different objects, and the result is most appalling in its ugliness."[9]

Although both the traditional and Craftsman styles claimed to favor reform simplicity, many critics who favored Craftsman styles condemned the traditional styles. *House Beautiful*, which favored Craftsman furnishings, acidly reviewed *The Decoration of Houses*: "were the influence of the book to be generally accepted . . . it is safe to say the progress of good decorative art would be set back not less than thirty years, on a level with the days directly after the [Civil] war. The book is especially dangerous as it hides in the soundest precepts insidious advice and execrable taste. It is hoped that its price will soon deter many from buying it, who might be misled." Wharton and Codman's sin had been to illustrate and praise interiors well beyond the means of the average householder. Wharton and Codman also objected to the tendency among late nineteenth-century critics to pronounce moral judgments on questions of design. They suggested that architecture and decoration were to be seen, not sermonized; "nothing can be more fallacious," they had written in *The Decoration of Houses*, "than to measure the architect's action by an ethical standard."[10]

*House Beautiful* praised the simple lines and honest design of the Craftsman style, "not only because, other things being equal, the simpler the design, the better it wears upon our eyes, and the less likely it is to grow out of fashion, but principally because only the simple forms of decorative art can be cheaply made, and thus be of service to the greatest number." The same magazine hailed the new Craftsman style as "the extreme protest of modern artistry against finicky and false construction."[11]

While critics argued the relative merits of Craftsman over revival styles, the purchasing public became increasingly muddled. Individual homeowners failed to grasp or little cared for the tenets of reform held in common by all the critics, regardless of the particular style they espoused. Lacking this understanding as well as any firm leadership, many homeowners pursued personal aesthetic whims and arrived at a style that can only be called a hybrid, in which Japanese fans, Moorish "cozy corners," spinning wheels, peacock feathers, Morris chairs, French draperies, and small rugs atop wall-to-wall carpeting formed a decorative pastiche without a decorative philosophy. Critics bemoaned the confusion and occasionally advised, "if you set out to have your house designed in a distinctive style, keep consistently and persistently to that style. We question the taste that demands a Louis XIV reception room, a Japanese hall, a Moresque library, and *fin de siècle* bedroom."[12] Yet many houses of the 1890s were so arranged—and not merely the houses of the middle class. Mrs. Potter Palmer created just such an interior in Chicago along fashionable North Lake Shore Drive. And it is this hodgepodge of decoration, so common to interiors at the end of the nineteenth century, that ultimately prompted many twentieth-century critics to condemn *all* Victorian interior decoration.

While Americans decorated their interiors, perhaps paying too little attention to the critics' philosophy of simplicity and too much to the various styles they espoused, other issues demanded attention. The Panic of 1893–1894 saw widespread unemployment and the march on Washington of Coxey's Army; prosperity did not fully return until 1897. The following year, America flexed its muscles in a brief, one-sided war against Spain, marking the emergence of a new colonial power. Women urged their causes of equal education, opportunities for work, and the right to vote with increasing stridency. In one of the best-known, if little understood, acts of the time, a plainly dressed, middle-aged woman entered a saloon in Wichita, Kansas, on a December morning in 1900. Armed with a stout cane, an iron rod, and several large rocks, Carry Nation destroyed a painting of the naked Cleopatra and all the bottled liquor, as well as the calm of the early morning drinkers. The women's fight for temperance clamored for national attention.

Amid this economic, political, and social turmoil, Victoria, Queen of England and Empress of India, died quietly on January 22, 1901. The woman who had given her name to an era had spent the last forty years of her reign a widow trying to govern her life and those of her subjects as she thought her husband would have wished, thus epitomizing the ideal wife of the nineteenth century. With her support, Albert had orchestrated the 1851 Crystal Palace Exhibition in London, generating a flurry of other exhibitions in France, England, and America, and raising a furor among the British creative community. This resulted in the rise of a variety of design schools, leading to the reform philosophy, which in its myriad forms remained influential at the end of the nineteenth century.

# WALLS AND CEILINGS During the last decade of the nineteenth century, the treatment of walls, ceilings, and woodwork depended upon homeowners' preference for traditional (revival) or Craftsman styles, as well as their understanding of the call for simpler interiors.

Wall treatments of late-nineteenth-century houses were simpler than those of the preceding decades. Gone was the tripartite division—a room might employ wainscoting or a frieze but rarely both. As early as 1886, the design-conscious might have read, "the ubiquitous dado has seen its day in certain apartments; in halls and dining-rooms it still holds its own, but fashion has decreed that in drawing-rooms and bedrooms it is to be known no more for the present." Even Wharton and Codman, who advocated a thirty-inch-high dado as the base of any well-designed room, admitted that in America most dadoes were too high (or the ceilings too low) to be attractive. As a rule,

*A dining room illustrated in the c. 1890 catalogue of B. A. Cook & Company, Fitchburg, Massachusetts, showing the use of wainscoting below a plate rail. By the last decade of the nineteenth century, wainscoting could still be found in entry halls, dining rooms, and libraries, but rarely in other rooms. (The Athenaeum of Philadelphia)*

wainscoting appeared only in the hall, dining room, or library.[13]

Finishes for walls included paint (oil-based and calcimine were the most common), paper, fabric, and embossed materials such as Lincrusta-Walton, anaglypta, and Tynecastle tapestry, all of which had been available in preceding decades. The designs and use of these materials depended upon the style of the house; a French-revival interior required treatments quite different from a Craftsman, and a hybrid interior might draw from both. (See Plate 19.)

For traditional interiors, Wharton and Codman relied on European precedents, and advocated fresco painting, paneling, and tapestry hangings. But these finishes were affordable only by the wealthy; middle-class households used wallpapers and less expensive fabrics such as chintz to emulate the better finishes. The National Wall Paper Company chose five of its member firms as exhibitors in a Louis XVI- and Empire-inspired pavilion at the Columbian Exposition, held in Chicago in 1893. Against the cream and gold background of the five display rooms, visitors saw papers inspired by the French Empire styles, stripes, florals, and Renaissance "tapestry" papers.[14]

Many rooms finished in such traditional schemes employed wall and frieze

*Montage of the exhibit of H. Bartholomae & Company at the Columbian Exposition in Chicago, 1893, which typified the revival styles shown by the other American wallpaper manufacturers. This illustration and others appeared in an article in the July 1893 issue of* House Painting and Decorating. *(The Athenaeum of Philadelphia)*

papers without wainscoting. Popular papers for the walls included those composed of one-inch-wide stripes of two shades of the same hue; these papers were also available in more ornate designs with Empire wreaths, ribbons, or flowers between the stripes. Papers imitating the designs of old tapestries, and flocked papers printed in one color (which created the effect of two values of one color because of the way in which the surface reflected light), were used in public rooms. Empire designs also employed classical wreaths or damask patterns. Floral papers imitating chintz or cretonne were available with matching fabrics. The florals were popular for bedrooms as well as sitting rooms if the furniture was delicate in scale.[15]

Frieze papers varied in width from five to thirty inches. (Kayser and Allman, a Philadelphia company, offered twenty frieze-paper patterns in the thirty-inch size in 1893, along with narrower ones.) The simplest wall scheme involved painting or papering the walls a single color topped with a patterned frieze paper just below the ceiling molding. Frieze papers often echoed the pattern of a matching wallpaper and frequently were printed on the same colored grounds as the wallpapers—a decided shift from the previous period. A householder could choose from several combinations of pattern and color. For example, a patterned paper might be combined with a frieze of the same ground but without a pattern. Or one could choose a frieze paper containing a ground blended of several colors resembling the *irisé* or "rainbow" effect popular earlier in the nineteenth century, over which was printed a pattern complementing that of the wallpaper. Thus, a wallpaper of four-inch-wide stripes of steel blue, alternating flat and satin finish, was capped by a frieze in which the ground shifted from steel blue through red to dull mustard-yellow, the whole printed with a series of festoons of naturalistic roses. Yet another treatment used the same patterns but reversed the colors; the ground and pattern colors on the wallpaper becoming the pattern and ground colors of the frieze paper.[16]

Another popular type of frieze paper overlapped the edge of the wallpaper and came in a variety of styles, including Romanesque, Louis XV, Louis XVI, and Empire. One author described such a paper produced by H. Bartholomae & Company: "The frieze, of a magnificent rococo motive, invades the field of the wall with a bold display of scrollage with great freedom of effect, and smaller detached rococo motives echo the frieze at regular intervals over the wall. The combination, lacking the formal lines that separate the old-time frieze from the wall, is entirely satisfactory." Frieze papers were used into the twentieth century, but gradually lost popularity as ceiling colors were carried over the cove molding and down to the picture rail.[17]

In Craftsman interiors, distinctly different wallpapers were applied. (See Plate 20.) Papers printed with realistic displays of foliage or classical motifs

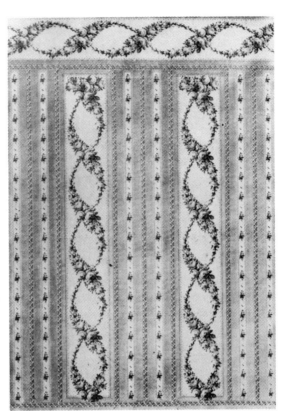

*Examples of revival styles in wallpapers during the last decade of the nineteenth century, illustrated in A. S. Jennings,* Wallpapers and Wall Coverings. *Top left: This paper was considered suitable for hall or parlor; the coordinating frieze paper is printed on a "rainbow" type ground. Top right: "Marie Antoinette" paper. Left: An "Empire Treatment" deemed suitable for dining room or hall. (The Athenaeum of Philadelphia)*

were avoided; instead, wallpapers with more geometric, abstracted patterns were used. Frieze papers might appear in the rooms of Craftsman houses lacking wainscoting; above wainscoting, however, a single paper without a frieze was more likely. While American wallpaper manufacturers displayed mainly traditional designs at the Columbian Exposition, English firms exhibited Arts and Crafts patterns. The English firm of Messrs. Jeffrey & Co. drew positive comments for the superb work of their designers, including Walter Crane, Lewis F. Day, and C. A. Voysey. Their papers and those of William Woollams & Co. were marketed and praised in America for their flat, nonrealistic ("conventional") patterns, although critics cautioned householders to use them judiciously. *House Beautiful* warned against using such papers floor to ceiling since "the boldness of the design renders them practically unfit for the ordinary living room." However, when applied with restraint, the magazine went on to explain, these papers could achieve great effect: "A large hall with a high dark wainscot takes on additional beauty from such a paper when used above the woodwork." In addition, "the Morris designs are in reality pictures themselves . . . any attempt to hang other pictures on them results in a most confusing effect."[18]

A great many reform interiors used plain papered walls. Critics praised solid-colored papers such as cartridge, ingrain (also known as "felt"), and grounds. Cartridge papers were thick, stiff, and generally printed in only one color. Ingrain papers were manufactured from dyed pulp, producing slight variations in color caused by the texture. Grounds were papers printed in one color without the addition of a design. "No one need fear to use a good plain papered wall 'because it is not the fashion,'" announced *House Painting and Decorating*. "He or she will be in the most excellent company, for a plain wall is unquestionably the best background possible."[19]

By the end of the decade, plain papers lost some of the market to burlaps and canvases, which offered texture and the possibility of decorative stenciling. These fabrics could be used in their natural states or, once applied to the walls, could be sized and painted; it was important to paint or stencil with fairly thin colors so no texture was lost. Denims in red, blue, and gray and imported grass cloths became popular wall treatments by the end of the century.[20]

Hybrid interiors offered some of the most "unusual" design schemes. A room might be labeled an "East India Room," with walls and ceiling covered in matting and bamboo strips, and a frieze in India silk, or a "Japanese Room," with Japanese paper and gilded grilles over plain paper for wainscoting and frieze. Yet another scheme, described as "artistic," utilized matting for a dado, burlap above it with Manila rope to cover the seams, and a frieze of interlocking festoons also of Manila rope. Finally there was the room papered in greenish-gray felt paper and a frieze of birch bark "with festoons of trailing Florida moss"—the writer described the effect as "decidedly unconventional."[21]

Decorated ceilings, especially wallpapered ones, remained popular into the twentieth century. Critics and manufacturers advocated placing on the ceiling borders matching the wall frieze, giving the room a "higher and nobler appearance." Arthur Seymour Jennings suggested in *Wallpapers and Wall Coverings* (1903) that these borders, consisting of several lines of color in addition to the patterns, should occupy about one-sixth of the total width and length of the ceiling. This treatment spread color and pattern onto the ceiling instead of confining them to the edges of the room. *House Decoration*, a handbook first published by Cassell and Company in 1894, included diagrams recommending specific layouts for ceiling designs involving the entire surface, not merely the perimeter. Another critic condemned plain ceilings presenting only "gaunt nakedness to dominate over luxurious walls and gaily clad floors," and suggested their origins were the "stern severity of the pseudo-Grecian phase" that "cast its gloom" during the early decades of the nineteenth century.[22]

Not all critics approved of these ornately decorated ceilings, and by the middle of the 1890s, those who supported the philosophy of simplification urged a return to simpler ceilings and friezes. *Household News* warned readers in 1894, "a bold and brilliant ceiling, either in frescoing or of paper, is enough to drive one mad, besides destroying the unity of color." The mag-

 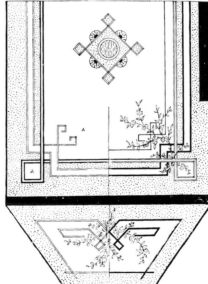

*Some critics continued to suggest complex patterns for ceilings, such as these two, illustrated in A. S. Jennings,* Wallpapers and Wall Coverings. *Both ceilings utilized various wallpapers; the one on the right was specifically recommended for a bedroom with a bay window. (The Athenaeum of Philadelphia)*

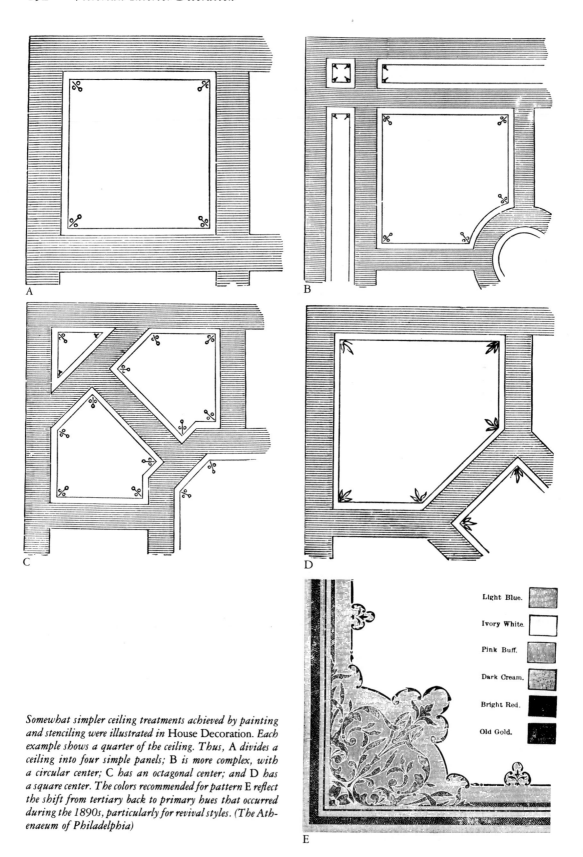

Somewhat simpler ceiling treatments achieved by painting and stenciling were illustrated in House Decoration. *Each example shows a quarter of the ceiling. Thus, A divides a ceiling into four simple panels; B is more complex, with a circular center; C has an octagonal center; and D has a square center. The colors recommended for pattern E reflect the shift from tertiary back to primary hues that occurred during the 1890s, particularly for revival styles. (The Athenaeum of Philadelphia)*

Light Blue.

Ivory White.

Pink Buff.

Dark Cream.

Bright Red.

Old Gold.

A

B

C

D

E

*This parlor in New York State generally accords with the reform philosophy; the walls, ceiling, window, and portiere designs are quite simple. The mantel drapery and Oriental touches are vestiges of the Aesthetic Movement. (The Athenaeum of Philadelphia)*

azine preferred simple ceiling papers or even plain, painted ceilings over the "pyrotechnic effects that, united with obtrusive walls and gaudy furniture, were enough to send the best balanced persons, unfortunate enough to occupy such a room, into an insane asylum." Wharton and Codman condemned plaster ornaments resembling "attenuated laurel-wreaths" and "puny attributes taken from Sheraton cabinets and Adam mantel-pieces" as well as the "vulgar papers" used on many ceilings. In the average room, they insisted, "a plain plaster ceiling with well-designed cornice is preferable to any device for producing showy effects at small cost."[23]

Following the philosophy of simplicity, two new ceiling treatments appeared at the end of the century. In one treatment, ceiling paper with an unobtrusive pattern was employed; sometimes the paper was even carried down the wall to the picture molding, a distance of six inches to three feet, depending upon the height of the ceiling. The junction between the wall and ceiling was either bridged by a cornice, left plain, or connected by a cove. In the second treatment, the ceiling was painted in a tint that blended with the wallpaper. With this approach, a single wallpaper covered the wall from ceiling to baseboard. A picture rail was either placed at the top of the wall or over the paper about twelve inches from the ceiling. In either case, the same paper continued to the ceiling.[24]

## WOODWORK

The treatment of woodwork during this period reflected the reform philosophy of simplification. Until the 1870s, grained woodwork had been the preferred finish, followed by woodwork painted a hue generally the same as the walls but darker. Eastlake and the reformers of the Arts and Crafts Movement disapproved of "dishonest" grained finishes and advocated staining and varnishing hardwoods or painting softwoods in tertiary colors that contrasted with the walls. By the 1890s, the reform philosophy wholly condemned the fakery of grained woodwork. Critics favoring the Craftsman interior recommended stained and varnished woodwork, particularly for rooms on the first floor of the house. Critics favoring revival styles urged painted woodwork, particularly for French and Colonial interiors. Natural wood might be suitable for dining rooms or halls, often furnished in different styles, but never in the drawing rooms or bedrooms; "white woodwork with a highly-polished surface is gaining in public favor," *House Painting and Decorating* assured its audience. The same magazine, favoring the revival styles, alerted readers that the time was past "when varnish alone was considered to convey a title of respectability and when painted interior woodwork was supposed to be a sure indication of poverty and social inferiority, for now even the richest and most favored socially dare to paint their woodwork, if it suits them best to do so." Exponents of both Craftsman and revival styles accepted painted woodwork in bedrooms, kitchens, and bathrooms for its sanitary qualities.[25]

Picture rails could be placed next to the ceiling molding or below the frieze, if the room had one. While larger pictures still hung from exposed cords, smaller ones often hung from screws hidden behind them on the wall, the latter marking the beginning of modern picture-hanging technique.[26]

## COLORS

By 1890, primary and secondary colors began to replace tertiary hues. Critics agreed that color schemes might successfully combine either contrasting or analogous colors; they even occasionally showed a monochromatic scheme. (See Plate 21.) Schemes employing contrasting colors, such as red and green, had been popular throughout the nineteenth century, while analogous schemes gained in popularity only during the last quarter of the century.

Critics often suggested analogous schemes during the 1890s. In a letter to the editor of *House Painting and Decorating*, printed under the title "Color and the Associations," the writer recommended using six hues, beginning with grayish-blue and ending with greenish-blue, for decorating a single room. Walter Pearce used creamy yellows through medium russets to illustrate an analogous scheme in *Painting and Decorating* (1898). These schemes reflected the reform philosophy that held that the fewer the colors used in a single room, the better. According to Wharton and Codman, "each room should speak with but one voice: it should contain one color, which at once and unmistakably asserts its predominance." As an example, they recommended that all the fabrics in a room be one color (as was popular during the first half of the nineteenth century) and the walls neutral ivory or gray.[27]

The scheme of a room might also be based on contrasting ("complementary") colors. Often, critics recommended that one of the hues be used for both floor and window coverings. Most writers agreed that the contrast of intense, pure chroma produced "crude, garish, and unbalanced pairs." Consequently they favored schemes not directly opposite one another on the color wheel, judging pure red with pure green unacceptable but pure red with greenish-blue pleasing. In 1897, Oliver Coleman astutely observed in *House Beautiful* that fear was what caused most people to reject intense primary hues in favor of pastels and secondary colors. "Like a man who realizes he has not an acute and accurate ear for music, and hence in singing murmurs softly to himself, so most of us in dealing with the various combinations of reds and blues and yellows murmur in tints for fear a sudden pause may find us shouting off the key and in another tune. This is, no doubt, why buff is almost always used for yellow, why green is sage, and crimson but a mawkish pink."[28]

The growing use of "open planning," in which all rooms on the first floor of a house might open onto the hall or one another, led experts to suggest that the color schemes for each room should be chosen with the other rooms taken into consideration. For example, *House Beautiful* responded to a reader's request regarding her first-floor rooms with the suggestion that the hall have India-red walls and ceilings, woodwork stained dark, and a dark-red rug; that the dining room have tapestry paper in green and red, a red ceiling, woodwork stained green, a green rug, and re curtains; that the parlor be in "old blue" with a French floral paper above the picture rail and on the ceiling a paper containing red, green, and blue.[29]

Room use was another consideration. Halls required low, quiet tones; parlors were light and cheerful (and were never executed in "hot colors" such as salmon or terra cotta); dining rooms were "full-toned, rich, juicy"; libraries "thoughtful and sober"; and bedrooms should be "cleanly, airy, and cheerful." Identifying colors by weight, Pearce described "heavy" colors as low-toned tertiaries, mineral and earthy greens, white, and, by association, stone, slate, bronze, and copper colors, all suitable for halls, dining rooms, and libraries. "Light" colors included pure tints, fawn, sky grays and sky blues, silver, gold, and foliage greens, all good for parlors and bedrooms.[30]

Successful color placement meant utilizing the darkest hues for the floor and, possibly, the woodwork, while the walls, frieze (if present), and ceiling were progressively lighter. *Household News* advised the following combinations for wall and frieze in 1895:

| WALL | FRIEZE |
|------|--------|
| robin's egg blue | dull yellow |
| pale olive | warm salmon |
| golden brown | blue |
| claret | buff |
| French gray | vermilion |
| olive | orange |
| pale lilac | lemon yellow |
| blue | warm fawn |
| apple green | warm tan |
| chocolate | pea green[31] |

Stained and varnished woodwork was also taken into consideration when a room's scheme was chosen. Mahogany blended well with deep blue or orange-yellow but never with red. Other recommendations included: maple with old pink or gray; walnut with golden yellow; chestnut with reddish-brown or tan; and light oak with gray-blue or pale olive.[32]

# FLOORS

## WOOD FLOORS

The Wood-Mosaic Company of Rochester, New York, offered the following advice, not without some bias, in its 1898 catalogue under the heading, "How to Treat a Soft Pine Floor": "If very bad use it for kindling wood. Most soft pine floors are very bad. If in fair condition cover it with thin parquetry or wood carpet. Or, if it must be scrubbed and mopped like a barroom or a butcher's stall, cover it with linoleum or oil cloth. In this case don't cover with parquetry. Don't cast pearls before swine. Or it may be painted. Paint adheres well to pine. Don't cover it with a dusty, dirty, disease disseminating carpet."[33]

During the 1890s, the style of the interiors and the amount of disposable

income determined how owners might treat their floors. Wharton and Codman of course preferred marble or parquet; however, few middle-class
American households could afford to follow that advice. Instead they often
purchased "wood carpeting," or a thin, three-eighths-inch parquet—both far
less expensive than seven-eighths-inch tongue-and-grooved parquet. In 1894
an article in *Household News* reported, "wood carpeting is more and more
coming into vogue, as housekeepers understand its advantages in the matter
of cleanliness and beauty." The writer added, "this manner of finish was first
brought about by the use of rectangular carpets, so that a handsome decorative border was a necessity." Both revival and Craftsman interiors utilized
wood carpeting available at $1.50 to $18 a yard to cover the entire floor,
particularly in the public rooms of the house; few owners placed the material
in bedrooms where it would rarely be seen by guests. Wood carpeting could
be laid over existing softwood floors in older houses using wire finishing
nails that were driven in, set, and their holes filled to match the wood.
Modern owners have discovered to their regret that if such a floor has been
sanded too often or too enthusiastically in the intervening years, the surface
layers of putty and wood might be removed, causing the nail heads to reappear. This problem rarely occurs with tongue-and-groove parquet, which
was thicker and installed by being blind-nailed (that is, slant-nailed through
the tongue); however, its greater cost prevented most middle-class households from using it.[34]

Another treatment for softwood floors was to disguise them with paint.
Heath & Milligan Mfg. Co. of Chicago advertised "Creolite," a ready-mixed
paint for interior floors. In its catalogue it offered a few suggestions regarding
use, since "rugs are everywhere growing in favor" because they are "stylish
and more healthful than they ever were when attached to the floor." Since
"hardwood floors are expensive and might well be called a luxury . . . it is
rapidly becoming the style to paint floors, especially to paint a deep border
and spread a rug in the center. This produces the desired effect of a hardwood
floor at a minimum expenditure." Heath & Milligan advertised that "no

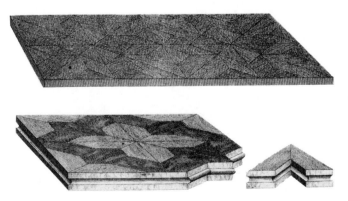

*The 1890 catalogue of the S. C. Johnson Com-
pany, Racine, Wisconsin, contained two grades of
parquetry, one ⅜ inch thick, with glued edges,
and the other ⅞ inch thick, with tongue-and-
grooved joints. The thicker version was a superior
product; prices for it were available only upon
request, suggesting the company sold a great deal
more of the cheaper material. (The Athenaeum of
Philadelphia)*

room can be made more artistic at less expense than to paint the floor border of one color and the baseboards of the same fundamental color in another shade," which "can be done to match the draperies and rug." Creolite was available in ten colors, cost $1.35 a gallon, and, according to the manufacturer, dried overnight.[35]

## TILES, OILCLOTH, AND LINOLEUM

Tiles, oilcloth, and linoleum all continued to be produced during the last decade of the century. A glance at most catalogues of household furnishings, however, will reveal that oilcloth was rapidly losing to other products as a popular floor finish. While W. & J. Sloane of New York sold oilcloths manufactured by the R. H. & B. C. Reeve Company of Camden, New Jersey, and Wharton and Codman mentioned oilcloths in *The Decoration of Houses*, linoleum became the flooring choice for those able to afford it. Sears, Roebuck and Company carried both oilcloth and linoleum in its 1897 catalogue, describing the latter as "very like oil cloth except that there is ground cork in its composition, which makes it much heavier, more durable; also, very much softer to walk on."[36] (See Plate 22.)

Linoleum patterns at the turn of the century imitated wooden floors or ceramic tiles—either encaustic patterns or more contemporary geometric shapes. Most of the designs included in the catalogue of John H. Pray & Sons, Boston, for example, came in six-foot widths and varied in price from $1 to $2.50 a yard. Patterns imitating wooden planks and advertised "for fitting around rugs" came in three-foot widths and cost thirty to sixty-five cents a yard. (The oilcloths sold by the same company were available in three-, 4½-, and six-foot widths priced between twenty-five and seventy cents, making them about half the price of linoleum.)[37]

Encaustic tiles remained on the market, and manufacturers added to their lines more complex patterns and tiles of various sizes and glazes. The 1884 catalogue of the French company Boch Frères contained patterns imitating mosaic floors based on those found at Pompeii and Herculaneum. In addition to these patterns, manufacturers also produced various shapes and sizes of unpatterned tiles in black or white glazes that could be laid to form patterns and borders. These simple tiles were very popular for bathroom walls and floors.[38] (See Plate 23.)

## MATTING

Homeowners had two types of grass matting to choose between: Chinese matting made entirely of grasses, or the more flexible Japanese matting, woven of grass weft and cotton warp. Either type could be purchased in

*Tile patterns illustrated in the 1900 catalogue of Maw & Company Limited, Shropshire, England. The company continued to market traditional encaustic tile patterns* (left), *along with newer styles* (center, right). *(The Athenaeum of Philadelphia)*

plain or patterned styles of various colors. *Household News* judged Japanese matting, retailing from fifty cents to $1 a yard, a superior product and advocated purchasing the plain, natural-colored variety for its durability and reversibility. Wharton and Codman also suggested grass matting for the floor of a lady's morning room. Most writers, however, relegated this material to bedrooms or the parlors of country houses. In either case, it might be tacked to the floor over a padding of newspapers and partially covered with rugs, depending upon the season. Occasionally other materials, such as denim, were used in the same manner.[39]

## CARPETING

Nothing is better than polished hardwood floors "covered with luxuriant rugs of rich Oriental patterns," purred *House Painting and Decorating* in 1893, and other critics agreed.[40] But those homeowners without hardwood floors or the money to purchase a true Oriental substituted other floor coverings.

Machine-woven Axminsters, Wiltons, and Brussels, ranging from $1 to $3 a yard, were used wall to wall or to imitate Oriental rugs. Naturally, carpeting choice depended in part upon cost; American Axminsters and Wiltons averaged double the price of body Brussels. Venetian carpeting, long heralded as economical and particularly useful for stairs, remained in production, although critics rarely mentioned it by the 1890s. Tapestry Brussels lost favor with critics espousing reform who warned, "it is better

## JAPANESE STRAW MATTINGS
### Cotton warp, 40 yards to the roll, 36 inches wide

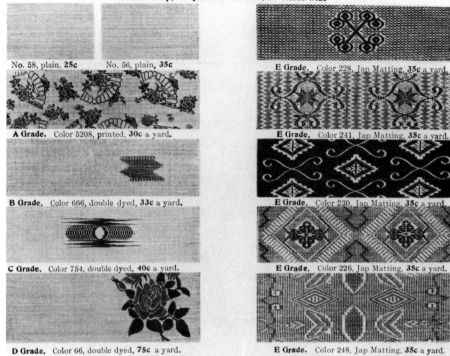

No. 58, plain, **25c**    No. 56, plain, **35c**

**A Grade.**  Color 5208, printed, **30c** a yard.

**B Grade.**  Color 666, double dyed, **33c** a yard.

**C Grade.**  Color 754, double dyed, **40c** a yard.

**D Grade.**  Color 66, double dyed, **75c** a yard.

**E Grade.**  Color 228, Jap Matting, **35c** a yard.

**E Grade.**  Color 241, Jap Matting, **35c** a yard.

**E Grade.**  Color 230, Jap Matting, **35c** a yard.

**E Grade.**  Color 226, Jap Matting, **35c** a yard.

**E Grade.**  Color 248, Jap Matting, **35c** a yard.

The color numbers indicate the combination of colors and about the style of patterns that can be furnished in each grade.  When ordering give the number under each sample wanted and about that style and color will be sent.

## CHINA STRAW MATTINGS  40 yards to the roll, 36 in. wide

The color number indicates the combinations of colors and about the style of patterns in each grade.  When ordering give the number under each sample wanted, and about the style and color will be sent.

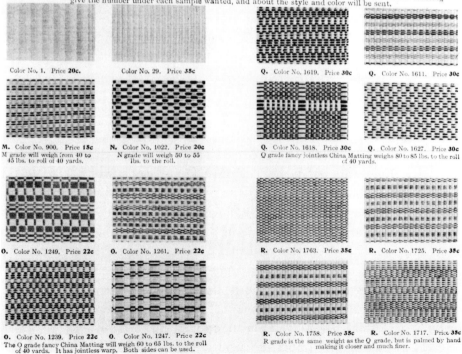

Color No. 1.  Price **20c**.

Color No. 29.  Price **35c**

**Q.**  Color No. 1619.  Price **30c**

**Q.**  Color No. 1611.  Price **30c**

**M.**  Color No. 900.  Price **15c**
M grade will weigh from 40 to 45 lbs. to roll of 40 yards.

**N.**  Color No. 1022.  Price **20c**
N grade will weigh 50 to 55 lbs. to the roll.

**Q.**  Color No. 1618.  Price **30c**

**Q.**  Color No. 1627.  Price **30c**
Q grade fancy jointless China Matting weighs 80 to 85 lbs. to the roll of 40 yards.

**O.**  Color No. 1249.  Price **22c**

**O.**  Color No. 1261.  Price **22c**

**R.**  Color No. 1763.  Price **35c**

**R.**  Color No. 1725.  Price **35c**

**O.**  Color No. 1239.  Price **22c**

**O.**  Color No. 1247.  Price **22c**

The O grade fancy China Matting will weigh 60 to 65 lbs. to the roll of 40 yards.  It has jointless warp.  Both sides can be used.

**R.**  Color No. 1758.  Price **35c**

**R.**  Color No. 1717.  Price **35c**

R grade is the same weight as the Q grade, but is palmed by hand making it closer and much finer.

*The 1906 catalogue of John H. Pray & Sons, Boston, contained a variety of patterns in Japanese matting (top), which had cotton warp, and Chinese matting (bottom), which was entirely of grass. Prices ranged between fifteen and seventy-five cents a yard. (The Athenaeum of Philadelphia)*

**LENOX AXMINSTER CARPETS**
Width of Carpet 27 in.   Width of Border 22 in.

Pattern No. 1712.   Price $1.50 a yard.

Pattern No. 1714.   Price $1.50 a yard.

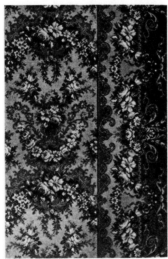

Pattern No. 1713.   Price $1.50 a yard.

Pattern No. 1715.   Price $1.50 a yard.

*Machine-made Axminster carpets woven in twenty-seven-inch widths with twenty-two-inch-wide matching borders were illustrated in the 1906 catalogue of John H. Pray & Sons, Boston. The prices were $1.50 a linear yard, and the patterns suitable for Craftsman or revival styles. (The Athenaeum of Philadelphia)*

to live on a bare floor than to purchase a tapestry Brussels." Their production ceased in the twentieth century.[41]

Ingrain carpeting, the single most common floor covering throughout the nineteenth century, also began to decline in popularity, although American looms continued to weave it until the 1930s. When writers of the 1890s mentioned "ingrain," they generally meant the two-ply weave, since the higher price of the more durable three-ply had led to its replacement by inexpensive Brussels carpeting in many houses. Two-ply ingrain, costing twenty-five to seventy cents a square yard, remained in modest households, country houses, and bedrooms.[42]

Notwithstanding the popularity of hardwood floors and area rugs in the last decade of the nineteenth century, many households retained wall-to-wall carpeting. Wharton and Codman instructed readers, "in houses with deal [pine] floors, where nailed-down carpets are used in all the rooms, a restful effect is produced by covering the whole of each story with the same carpet, the door-sills being removed so that the carpet may extend from one room to another." They especially favored this treatment for small houses where it "will be found much less fatiguing to the eye than the usual manner of covering the floor of each room with carpets differing in color and design."[43] This suggestion, like the one given earlier regarding color selection for rooms opening onto one another, probably resulted from increasingly open plans, particularly on the first floor of houses.

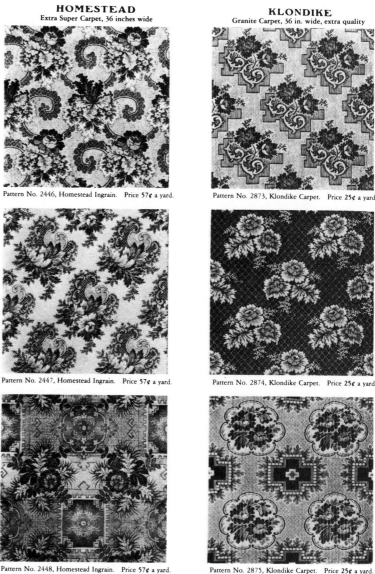

HOMESTEAD
Extra Super Carpet, 36 inches wide

KLONDIKE
Granite Carpet, 36 in. wide, extra quality

Pattern No. 2446, Homestead Ingrain.    Price 57¢ a yard.

Pattern No. 2873, Klondike Carpet.    Price 25¢ a yard.

Pattern No. 2447, Homestead Ingrain.    Price 57¢ a yard.

Pattern No. 2874, Klondike Carpet.    Price 25¢ a yard.

Pattern No. 2448, Homestead Ingrain.    Price 57¢ a yard.

Pattern No. 2875, Klondike Carpet.    Price 25¢ a yard.

*Ingrain carpets illustrated in the 1906 catalogue of John H. Pray & Sons, Boston. These patterns came in thirty-six-inch widths and were priced between twenty-five and fifty-seven cents a yard. (The Athenaeum of Philadelphia)*

During the 1890s, the best carpets (aside from Orientals) had the simplest patterns. Critics opposed multicolored bunches of flowers or figures on a brightly colored ground in favor of simple geometric patterns of one hue on a ground of a slightly darker value of the same hue. Furthermore, critics endorsed the new fashion of placing patterns on walls or floors but not both in the same room—this was a distinct shift from earlier styles. Perhaps in response, carpet manufacturers began to produce a new item called "filling," meaning a solid-colored carpet, often a Brussels. Filling might be used as the only floor covering, particularly in rooms with patterned walls, or laid as a base for smaller rugs scattered about the room following the approved fashion. Since the seams of a plain, solidly colored carpet were much more obvious than those with overall patterns, manufacturers adopted "broad looms" by the beginning of the twentieth century; these could produce goods in twelve-, fifteen-, and eighteen-foot widths.[44]

In another development of the last decade of the nineteenth century, H. Bartholomae & Company, manufacturers of wallpaper, contracted with two other American companies to produce fabrics and carpeting designed to match their wallpapers. The results were exhibited at the Columbian Exposition; *House Painting and Decorating* reported, "we do not know of any other wallpaper firm making a specialty of their designs in this manner." The same journal predicted that "this scheme of having all under the control of one manufacturer cannot fail to result in a decided advance in interior decoration."[45]

For both revival and Craftsman interiors, small rugs atop hardwood floors remained the most fashionable approach during the last decade of the nineteenth century. Critics praised the style, not merely for its correctness regarding the reform aesthetic. One writer advocated leaving a space between the carpet and the wall or else "the sportive moth will multiply in clover, and there the dust will keep him snug and warm." Bad enough in a parlor, critics warned that "of all places in the world where dust and debris ought never to be allowed to accumulate, the [bed]chamber is that place. A weekly freshening of these floor coverings is an absolute necessity."[46] We must remember that efficient electric vacuum cleaners were twentieth-century innovations. Until then, carpets were swept or beaten, and the larger the carpet, the more difficult—and infrequent—the task.

There were several types of rugs homeowners could choose among when selecting small rugs to place on their hardwood floors. In addition to true Oriental carpets, homeowners could purchase machine-made carpets woven in designs imitating those from Turkey, Persia, or India. They might also braid rags and stitch them into oval or circular rugs. *House Beautiful* suggested Navajo blankets—which appear in many of the Craftsman interiors of the 1890s—as wall or floor coverings. Animal skins were another popular choice.

*Henry T. Williams and Mrs. C. S. Jones recommended animal-skin rugs in* Beautiful Homes *(1878). The rugs were still in style when this photograph of the sitting room of the William H. Cannon home in Madison, Wisconsin, was taken c. 1897. Notice, too, the footstool in the parlor that balances rather precariously on a rack of antlers. (State Historical Society of Wisconsin; photograph by Annie Schildhauer)*

*Household News* listed a variety, including leopard skins for $25 to $50 and tiger skins (with heads) for $100 to $200. It is the rare photograph of an 1890s middle-class interior that has no animal skin as an accent rug. According to Williams and Jones, useful rugs might be made from game animals, sheep or lamb skins, or "even small and (dare we term them so?) common skins, such as rabbit, squirrel, opossum, raccoon . . . even the domestic . . . pussy may be made into a thing of use and beauty."[47] The hybrid interior—reflecting a clear misunderstanding of the reform philosophy— often placed an assortment of these rugs atop wall-to-wall carpeting.

Whatever the floor covering, most critics suggested it be the darkest color in the room, providing a visual base for all the other furnishings. Wharton and Codman permitted the carpet to contrast with curtains and upholstery fabrics *if* the walls were paneled or painted in a neutral color, such as ivory or gray; for example, one might combine a dull-green or dark-blue carpet with crimson upholstery and hangings. However, if the walls were elaborately decorated or hung with many pictures, then the curtains, upholstery, and carpet should all be the same color without any pattern—the only permitted exception to this rule being an Oriental carpet.[48] Here, too, the hybrid interior ignored the rule of simplicity, for a showy display of pattern.

# WINDOWS

### WOODEN BLINDS AND SHUTTERS

In the well-designed house, according to Wharton and Codman, window curtains were unnecessary. But the poorly designed house, lacking interior shutters or attractive moldings around windows, must have its large expanses of plate glass covered. Wharton and Codman preferred solid-paneled interior shutters folding into recesses beside the windows—an interior from the Grand Trianon, Versailles, was used to illustrate the point!—combined with exterior shutters with wide, fixed slats to control light. This older arrangement was far superior, they assured their audience, to "the frail machine-made substitute now in general use."[49]

Most American houses in the late nineteenth century were, nonetheless, equipped with just such "frail substitutes"—machine-made interior shutters often with some louvered and some solid panels. Drapery-cutting books even offered suggestions for window curtains to use with these shutters. In his *Practical Handbook on Cutting Draperies* (1890), N. W. Jacobs recommended placing curtain poles on extension brackets "extending far enough into the room to clear the blind when folded at right angles with the window." He added, "this often spoils the effect of the drapery, and better results can

*Interior shutter blinds with louvers remained popular at the end of the century. The c. 1895 catalogue of the Willer Manufacturing Co. of Milwaukee, Wisconsin, illustrates a particularly popular type containing solid and louvered panels. (The Athenaeum of Philadelphia)*

be had by fastening the upper section of the blinds, or by taking them off altogether."[50]

## WINDOW SCREENS

Window screens, which had entered factory production at the beginning of the last quarter of the nineteenth century, became increasingly common. The Willer Manufacturing Company of Milwaukee, Wisconsin, informed householders that screens "are not, as many suppose, an expensive luxury, but in fact, a good paying investment, saving as much as their cost in a single season." The company manufactured screens for the bottom half of a window, the full sash, or for doors, in steel wire mesh, either plain or painted in black or bronze; they did not advertise the decoratively painted screens mentioned by earlier manufacturers. Despite the claims of advertisements, many houses continued to use netting—not factory-produced screens—at windows, as photographs from the 1890s attest. Even with screens, *Household News* reported in 1895, "one of the housewife's chief trials is the universal depravity in summer time of cockroaches, ants, and mosquitoes. Of course there are screens in all her windows, from attic to cellar but," the author despaired, "Jimmy and Jenny are forever flying in and out the wire doors, and a whole army of pests are watching to make a raid into the fort whenever occurs a chance." The only solution was to drive insects from the house each morning and tightly close the blinds.[51]

## WINDOW SHADES

A variety of cloth window shades was also available during the last decade of the nineteenth century. Spring-operated roller shades, much like those available today, gradually replaced the older pulley-operated systems. They were available in plain, striped, or patterned linen. An English critic suggested placing the pattern of decorative shades toward the glass; "when the light shines through it, the pattern will be seen very distinctly in the room, whereas the wrong side would look very bad from the street." In *Homes and Their Decoration* (1903), Lillie Hamilton French advocated window shades for privacy in urban houses, although she insisted all window shades must hang at the same height or the exterior of the house would appear sloppy.[52]

## CURTAINS

Many styles of curtains and draperies were available during the last decade of the nineteenth century, but critics deplored the difficulties of curtaining the windows of rooms in which each window was a different size and shape, a common architectural conceit of the time. "One's ingenuity is called into

## SHADE FRINGES.

No. 215. 3 inch; Linen.
Per dozen yards, $2.50.

No. 201. 3 inch; Linen.
Per dozen yards, $2 50.

## SHADE PULLS.

No. 1014. Silk, per gross, $4.50.

No. 5. Linen, per gross, $4.50.
ALL COLORS.

No. 1017. Silk, per gross, $4.50.

## DECORATED SHADES.

No. 236. Velvet only. No. 236 B. Gold only.
No. 188. Velvet and Gold.

No. 2298. Velvet only. No. 2298 B. Gold only.
No. 2299. Velvet and Gold.

No. 3306. Velvet only. No. 666. Gold only.
No. 3206. Velvet and Gold.

No. 717. Velvet only. No. 718. Gold only.
No. 3365. Velvet and Gold.

*The c. 1895 catalogue of the Jay C. Wemple Co., Chicago, Brooklyn, and New York City, gives some indication of the roller-shade patterns and embellishments available at the end of the nineteenth century. (The Athenaeum of Philadelphia)* service," remarked N. W. Jacobs in *Practical Handbook on Cutting Draperies*, about a room with a bay window as well as single windows of varied sizes. Furthermore, designs continued to reflect the differences between Craftsman and revival interiors throughout the last decade of the nineteenth century. Jacobs, a drapery maker, summarized the history: "There were more first-class drapery men in the trade a decade since than there are at the present time, a fact which is accounted for by reason of the change in style of drapery." He explained, "when the Eastlake and Queen Anne designs came into favor, almost any one could plan and cut the plain, straight valances and the long curtains. The experienced salesmen were . . . forced into other channels of life." Unfortunately, Jacobs continued, "when the French style of drapery came back, there were comparatively few men in the trade who could originate or adapt designs. . . ." (See Plate 24.) Jacobs was not the only drapery maker to bemoan the situation. F. A. Moreland, another draper to

**NOTTINGHAM LACE CURTAINS.**

No. 104 WHITE
3 yards by 40 inches
$0.75 per pair.

No. 105 WHITE
3 yards by 45 inches
$0.95 per pair.

No. 106 WHITE
3 yards by 45 inches
$0.95 per pair.

No. 107 WHITE
3 yards by 46 inches
$1.05 per pair.

*These Nottingham lace curtains in the 1906 catalogue of John H. Pray & Sons, Boston, were inexpensive window coverings priced from seventy-five cents to $1.05 a pair. Each panel was three yards in length and ranged in width from forty to forty-six inches. (The Athenaeum of Philadelphia)* publish a book in 1890—*Practical Decorative Upholstery*—recounted that "French drapery . . . fell into disfavor in the time of the Eastlake reform, but it has recovered its prestige to such an extent that in some cases it descends to actual slovenliness by overcrowding with material." He reminded readers that the object of curtaining windows "should be to decorate and not to encumber the spaces."[53]

Householders generally continued to use heavier materials over glass curtains at windows, particularly during the colder months of the year, but writers disagreed as to whether overcurtains should cover the window molding or not. Favoring a reduced amount of fabric at windows, *House Painting and Decorating* explained, "people no longer think that all the woodwork of the window must be covered up and hidden by heavy upholstery, so the architect is called upon to design daintily fashioned wooden trim and mouldings for his windows, and the painter is called upon to finish those in the highest style of his art." Yet other writers advised that windows appeared larger if the hardware was taken beyond the window frames. Edith Wharton and Ogden Codman supposed the decision rested on the beauty of the molding: "In the modern American house, where the trim is usually bad, and where there is often a dreary waste of wall-paper between the window and the ceiling, it is better to hang the curtains close under the cornice." With the critics in disagreement, it is not surprising that illustrations and photographs from the period depict both treatments.[54]

Of course, the plainest window treatment was simply sheer panels of fabric mounted on rods inside the window frame and hanging just to the sill, not to the floor, a treatment some writers praised as a substitute for window shades. Fabrics used in this manner included laces—such as Brussels, Swiss, Irish point, and Nottingham—and muslins, plain or dotted, in white or off-white. These simple panels of fabric were shirred onto brass or hardwood rods (only rarely were they hung from rings or pins). Sometimes a double hem was used at the top to create a ruffled heading. The panels hung free at the bottom or were attached to another brass rod. If two rods were used, the panels might be tied with ribbons in the center, creating a diamond-shaped opening, particularly recommended for windows in bedrooms and on doors. Homeowners might also use two pairs of sheer curtains set into the casing of a double-hung window or a single pair at the bottom sash—the latter known as "Morris" or half curtains. Morris curtains were particularly recommended if the upper part of the window had a panel of stained or leaded glass. Venetian curtains, called "Austrian shades" and made of sheer fabrics, also reappeared in design books.[55]

Another simple treatment was to hang panels of fabric from rings on a pole, possibly a traverse pole of the type discussed in Chapter 1. By the end of the century, fabrics were commonly woven in fairly wide widths, and more fullness was employed in making curtains. One draper counseled that

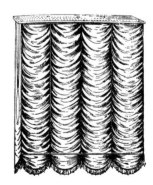

*This "Austrian shade" pictured by Frederick T. Hodgson in* The Practical Upholsterer *resembles "Venetian curtains" employed during the late eighteenth and early nineteenth century. (The Athenaeum of Philadelphia)*

*N. W. Jacobs illustrated four methods of arranging glass curtains in*
Practical Handbook on Cutting Draperies. *He identified* A *as full
panels;* B *as a diamond pattern;* C *as a pair of double-sash curtains;
and* D *as a half-sash curtain, also called a "Morris curtain." (The
Athenaeum of Philadelphia)*

two widths of fifty-inch goods were sufficient for the average window, providing the material was *pleated* and then attached to the rings—directions
that are quite different from those offered in preceding decades. Pleating
was often sewn at the top edge of the curtain, forming box pleats. Drapery
hooks were attached behind each pleat, low enough to bring the top of the
curtain close to the edge of the pole. The finished length of a curtain panel
depended upon whether the curtain was to traverse the window or not. A
curtain intended to be pulled across the window would clear the floor.
However, some designs reflected earlier styles, with stationary panels held
back with cords or looped over drapery knobs, in which case the panels
were several inches longer because they would be drawn up. Overcurtains
might reach the windowsill or the floor, although most critics conceded the
full length was better.[56]

*This illustration of a traverse pole in* Practical Decorative Upholstery, *by F. A. Moreland, suggests that little improvement in the device had occurred throughout the nineteenth century. (The Athenaeum of Philadelphia)*

In either case, a valance or drapery might appear above the curtains,
generally hanging from a brass pole or one of wood stained to match the
woodwork. A great many designs of the period echoed styles popular during the early years of the nineteenth century, such as simple panels topped
with valances including flat lambrequins, simple box pleats similar to "piped
valances," more ornate constructions employing pinch pleats, or novelties

*A rare illustration of a bay window pictures a valance with box pleats. F. A. Moreland described this treatment as "a plain and tasteful way of treating a bay window, and especially appropriate for a dining-room or library, though not in order for a room that is to be treated in the French style of decoration." (The Athenaeum of Philadelphia)*

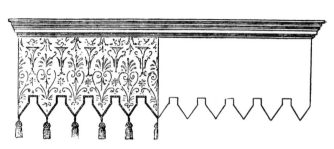

*A flat lambrequin pictured in* The Practical Up-holsterer *resembles the "geometric valances" pictured by Thomas King and the "vandyke" described by Charles L. Eastlake earlier in the century. (The Athenaeum of Philadelphia)*

*This pleated valance, illustrated by N. W. Jacobs, is similar to "piped valances" pictured by Thomas King and John Claudius Loudon. (The Athenaeum of Philadelphia)*

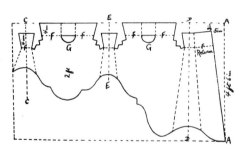

*Pinch pleats at the top of curtains entered the popular vocabulary of the drapery maker during the last decade of the nineteenth century. This valance and its complex cutting pattern were illustrated in* Practical Handbook on Cutting Draperies. *(The Athenaeum of Philadelphia)*

NO POLES,
NO RINGS,
NO PINS.

*This device illustrated in the c. 1900 catalogue of the Gobelin Company, Washington, D.C., created the illusion of pinch pleats without the complicated cutting and sewing. (The Athenaeum of Philadelphia)*

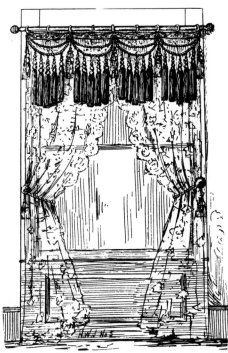

*A valance made entirely of fringe was illustrated in* Practical Handbook on Cutting Draperies. *(The Athenaeum of Philadelphia)*

composed of buttons or clasps attached directly to the cornice or window architrave. The simpler valances generally appeared in Craftsman interiors, while the more ornate ones were preferred for interiors evoking one of the revival styles. In lieu of fabric, one might also hang a "valance fringe" over the curtains, attaching it to the same rings as the curtains themselves.[57]

A more traditional approach—and therefore one popular in revival styles—was to hang a "French shawl drapery" at the top of the window. Identified by one draper as the most commonly used fashion of the time, a "French

*Three different versions of "French shawls," as some drapers called swags and cascades at the end of the nineteenth century. These designs, illustrated in* Practical Handbook on Cutting Draperies, *suggested using two different colors for the pair of "French shawls" in the illustration on the right. (The Athenaeum of Philadelphia)*

*In this "French shawl" arrangement, pictured in* Practical Handbook on Cutting Draperies, *the swag hung below a fringe valance, permitting light to enter the top of the window. The design was particularly useful in windows with stained-glass transoms. (The Athenaeum of Philadelphia)*

shawl" consisted of a swag over a pole with cascades on either side. In some designs, one or both cascades were lengthened, forming full-length curtain panels along the window. Another design created more ornate draperies using two swags in different colors. Even windows with stained-glass transoms—popular during this period—could use swags without hiding much of the glass. A rather narrow swag hanging at some distance from the pole with the space between filled with fringe, enabled one to enjoy draperies and decorative glass at the same window.[58]

For rooms receiving little sunlight but requiring curtained windows, critics proposed decorative grilles, placed at the top of the frame, with curtains below. Jacobs suggested that "screens [grilles] for the upper half of the sash take the place of stained glass," explaining, "the effect is better in some instances." Manufacturers and retailers, including Sears, Roebuck and Company, marketed grilles in a variety of styles through the first decade of the

*"Grilles" were used at windows and doorways beginning about 1890. They remained popular well into the twentieth century, as these patterns from the 1910 catalogue of Sears, Roebuck and Co. attest. (The Athenaeum of Philadelphia)*

twentieth century, and surviving photographs attest to their popularity in middle-class homes throughout the country.[59]

Fabric choice varied with each room. The richness of the fabric depended on the income of the household and the room in which the material hung; as a general rule, the best materials were reserved for public rooms. Parlors received damasks, tapestries, satins, and brocatelles in wool or silk; stamped velvets, velveteens, and corduroys; or less expensive materials such as cretonnes, velours, or Indian textiles. Dining rooms looked best in plushes (velvet), velours, satins, or tapestries. Generally, satins, damasks, brocades, brocatelles, and floral cretonnes were used in houses favoring revival styles, while velvets, plushes, corduroys, and plain weaves appeared in Craftsman-inspired interiors. When rich and heavy materials were used, they were interlined with flannel to protect them from the sun and to improve their "hang," a workroom technique employed throughout the century.[60]

*This window treatment with "French shawls" and two curtain panels suspended from a grille was illustrated in* Practical Handbook on Cutting Draperies. *(The Athenaeum of Philadelphia)*

## PORTIERES

Portieres, which reached the height of their popularity in America during the last decade of the nineteenth century, were done in styles similar to those used for windows. Not unexpectedly, Wharton and Codman belittled portieres by suggesting they were essential only when doors and doorways were poorly made; better construction would render them obsolete. Most critics, however, endorsed them. In the words of one, they provided a "patch of color or the softening of the hard lines of the wooden door-jamb," and appeared "less forbidding" than a closed door.[61] Portieres were hung at the entries to rooms without doors, as well as over sliding doors, and even appeared at doorways having hinged doors. Their use in parlors, dining rooms, and libraries was nearly universal.

The style of the portieres reflected the room's decoration. Critics favoring the Arts and Crafts Movement echoed Eastlake and recommended that portieres consist of panels hung from wooden or brass rings on a pole fitted within the doorjamb or placed at the spring of an arch in an open doorway. In cases where following these suggestions would place the pole higher than seven feet, six inches from the floor, thus making the portieres difficult to manipulate, writers offered several solutions: First, one could use a grooved pole containing cords and connected with a pulley system; second, the top of the door might be filled with grillework, with the pole beneath it at an acceptable height; third, the pole might be located at the proper height and the space above left empty; fourth, in a solution favored for revival interiors, the portieres could be made as festoons (see Chapter 1) and drawn by cords threaded through rings sewn onto the back of each panel. In all cases, each side of the portiere was finished to correspond with the room it faced. When

*Grilles were also used at doorways to hold portieres, as illustrated in* Practical Handbook on Cutting Draperies. *(The Athenaeum of Philadelphia)*

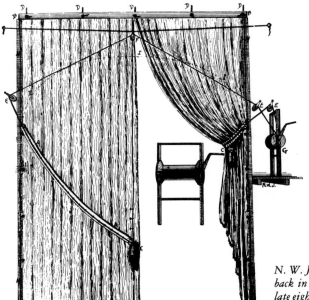

*N. W. Jacobs illustrated this portiere looped back in a manner much like festoons of the late eighteenth and early nineteenth century. (The Athenaeum of Philadelphia)*

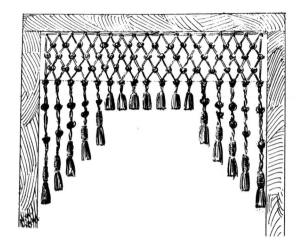

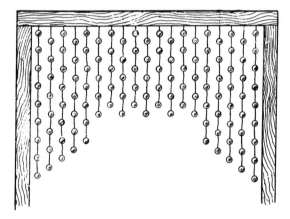

*Three unusual trimmings for doorways, using fringe and wooden balls, were pictured in* Practical Handbook on Cutting Draperies. *(The Athenaeum of Philadelphia)*

pleated—a common technique by the 1890s—the hooks were hidden within the pleats and between the two layers of material making up each face of the portiere. Rarely were portieres shirred onto poles because this would make it difficult to slide them to and fro.[62]

There were differences of opinion as to whether portieres and window curtains should be of the same fabric and color in a given room. Craftsman interiors generally employed the same fabric at windows and doorways, while interiors drawing on a revival style used different colors and materials. One critic chose to disregard the philosophy of simplicity altogether and advocated each door be treated separately in a single room, except in bedrooms, where all materials should be identical.[63]

Although portieres were supposed to fulfill a practical function, surviving photographs record the use of rather frivolous materials for them in many middle-class homes at the end of the century. Jacobs included portieres of netted cords in silk, worsted, or cotton, and companies such as Pray & Sons of Boston advertised similar portieres in a variety of colors well into the twentieth century. Curtains of bamboo or beads were also hung, although

## ROPE PORTIERES
### All Rope Portieres are 7¼ feet long but can be easily shortened

This Portiere extends from 3½ to 5¼ feet.  This Portiere extends from 4 to 7 feet.  This Portiere extends from 5 to 7½ feet.

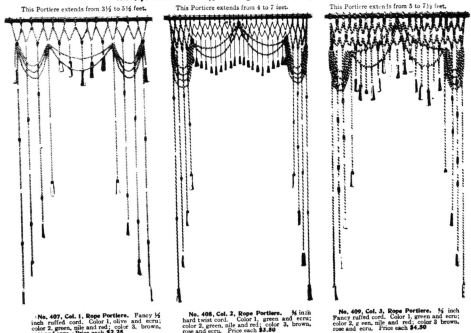

**No. 407, Col. 1, Rope Portiere.** Fancy ½ inch ruffed cord. Color 1, olive and ecru; color 2, green, nile and red; color 3, brown, rose and ecru. Price each **$2.25**

**No. 408, Col. 2, Rope Portiere.** ⅝ inch hard twist cord. Color 1, green and ecru; color 2, green, nile and red; color 3, brown, rose and ecru. Price each **$3.50**

**No. 409, Col. 3, Rope Portiere.** ⅝ inch Fancy ruffed cord. Color 1, green and ecru; color 2, green, nile and red; color 3 brown, rose and ecru. Price each **$4.50**

## ARTLOOM TAPESTRY CURTAINS

**No. 101, Col. 2, Red.** This curtain is woven with an overshot figure on a heavy ribbed ground, producing a bold effect. 46 inches wide by 102 inches long. Made in all the 8 colors described with No. 105, opposite page. Price per pair **$3.00**

**No. 103, Col. 1, Stripe.** French stripe curtains for either door, windows or cozy corner. Also frequently used for Couch Covers. 50 inches wide by 3 yards long. Made in 3 colors. Color 1, red and green color 5, green and olive. Price per pair **$4.50**

**No. 100, Col. 12, Red and Green.** An inexpensive hanging for window or doorway. It is low in price but not cheap in appearance. 40 inches wide by 102 inches long. Made in 6 different colors. Color 1, red; color 3, blue; color 4, brown; color 6, olive and rose; color 10, green; color 12, red and green. Price per pair **$2.50**

*The 1906 catalogue of John H. Pray & Sons, Boston, pictured rope portieres, and panels suitable for door and window curtains and sofa covers. The prices ranged from $2.25 to $4.50. (The Athenaeum of Philadelphia)*

*House Beautiful* complained in 1898, "if there be any practical or decorative use to which one may put portieres of beads or colored bamboo, it has never been discovered."[64]

## BED HANGINGS

In all but the wealthiest of houses, cotton materials, particularly chintzes or cretonnes, remained popular for bedroom use. *House Beautiful* recommended lining chintz or cretonne with cotton or China silk of contrasting color, another technique suggested earlier in the century. None of the late-nineteenth-century critics mentioned mosquito netting at beds, perhaps because window screens were considered superior. Furthermore, the critics rarely recommended that bedsteads be curtained. *Household News* reported in 1894 that bedstead canopies and draperies were merely handsome and grudgingly suggested, "If they must be used, then make a valance fifteen inches deep about the canopy, and loop the long hangings clear back to the head-post to admit air to the sleeper."[65]

*Techniques for curtaining half-tester and four-poster bedsteads, illustrated in* Practical Decorative Upholstery. *Compare these treatments with those employed earlier in the century. (The Athenaeum of Philadelphia)*

# GLOSSARY

ARCHITECTURAL PAPERS
Wallpapers printed to imitate
architectural elements such as
columns, arches, and balus-
trades.

ARCHITRAVE   The molded trim
above a door or window opening.

ASHLAR   A masonry wall built
of square- or rectangular-cut
stones; wallpaper or decorative
painting having the appearance
of cut stonework.

AXMINSTER   A cut-pile carpet
that was first woven by hand in
the eighteenth century to imitate Oriental carpets. Machines
capable of weaving Axminster
carpeting were developed in
America between 1867 and
1877.

BEAD   A simple decorative
molding with a semicircular
profile used in architectural elements such as cornices or the
frames of doors and windows
(also called "beading").

BRUSSELS   A durable looped-
pile carpet developed in Brussels c. 1710 and woven by
machine in America by the
mid-nineteenth century. The
various-colored yarns are woven
into the body of the carpet when
not part of the face pile (also
called "body Brussels").

CALCIMINE   A term used principally in America to describe a
paint made of tempera colors,
water, and sizing (sometimes
spelled "kalsomine" in the nineteenth century). The addition of
sizing made calcimine more durable than whitewash.

CARTRIDGE PAPER   A thick,
stiff wallpaper generally produced in a single color although
occasionally in patterns.

CEILING MEDALLION   A ro-
sette or disk, which might be
made of various materials (plaster, wood, papier mâché, or
metal), used to decorate the
center of a ceiling, generally
above a hanging light fixture (also
called a "center").

CHAIR RAIL   A plain or molded
strip of wood fixed to a wall to
protect it from being rubbed by
the backs of chairs.

COOL COLOR   Values of blue
and violet or gray, and white
tinted with those hues.

CORNICE   Molding placed at
junction of the wall and ceiling.

COVE   A simple concave molding placed at the junction of the
wall and ceiling.

DADO   A decorative border or
paneling covering the lower
portion of the wall and topped
by a piece of trim called a dado
rail. See Wainscoting.

DIAPER PATTERN   In woven
goods, a reversed twill that results in an overall diamond pattern; sometimes used to describe
designs composed of such repeating patterns.

DIAPHANIE   Transparent designs used on windows to simulate stained glass.

DISTEMPER  A term used principally in England for paint containing water, tempera colors, and sizing (*see* Calcimine).

DRAWING ROOM  A parlor or principal room in which to entertain guests.

DRUGGET  A durable, inexpensive fabric woven in England and popularly used under dining tables to protect better floor covering. The term came to mean any material used in that manner (sometimes called a "crumbcloth").

ENCAUSTIC TILE  A thick, durable ceramic tile first manufactured in England in the 1830s and in America by the 1870s. In England, the term refers specifically to patterned tiles produced by impressing a design into the soft tile and filling it with liquid clay of a different color before firing (*see* Geometric tile).

ENTRY HALL  The foyer or area between the front door or vestibule and the rest of the house.

FIELD  A term used during the 1870s and 1880s to describe the area of the wall between the wainscoting or dado and the frieze.

FILLING  A term used at the end of the nineteenth century to identify carpeting woven in a single solid color.

FLOORCLOTH  A term used through the first half of the nineteenth century to identify a linen, cotton, or jute cloth painted with oil-based paints and commonly used in entry halls and dining rooms, where it sometimes protected better carpeting.

FRESCO PAPER  Plain or patterned wallpaper used during the middle of the nineteenth century to create the illusion of panels.

FRIEZE  The area at the upper portion of the wall between the picture rail and the cornice.

GEOMETRIC TILE  Floor tiles without pattern produced in a limited number of colors and polygonal shapes. In America, these plain tiles, as well as the patterned ones, were marketed as "encaustic" tiles.

GRASS MATTING  A product woven in the Orient of various grasses and used as a summer floor covering or as the base for smaller carpets at other times of the year.

GROUND  Background color of wallpaper or carpeting.

HUE  A term that designates a color, such as red, yellow, or blue.

IMPERIAL  Another name for three-ply ingrain carpeting developed in Scotland c. 1824.

INGRAIN  An American term for a flat-pile, reversible carpet resembling a coverlet, in which the colors of the design on one side are reversed on the other.

INGRAIN PAPER  A thick, textured wallpaper permeated with color because the pulp is dyed before the paper is made. Ingrain paper was sold in plain and patterned varieties.

INTENSITY  The purity or saturation of a particular hue.

KIDDERMINSTER  Another term for ingrain carpeting denoting the weaving center near Birmingham, England, where ingrain was first made in the early eighteenth century.

LAMBREQUIN  A stiffened, unpleated fabric suspended from a cornice above a window and often embellished with cords, fringes, and an ornamentally cut hem.

LENO  A weave in which the warp and weft threads are interlocked, producing a loosely woven fabric suitable for use at windows.

LINCRUSTA-WALTON  An embossed, linoleumlike wall covering made of linseed oil, developed in 1877 in England by Frederick Walton.

LINOLEUM  A floor covering made primarily of linseed oil and flax, invented in 1864 in England by Frederick Walton.

LIST CARPETING  A woven, flat-pile floor covering using strips of selvage as weft.

MOQUETTE  A term used in America toward the end of the nineteenth century to describe cut-pile carpets virtually identical to machine-made Axminsters.

OILCLOTH  A term used during the second half of the nineteenth century to describe floorcloths.

PARLOR The room reserved for guests, which consequently contained the best furnishings. Also called "drawing room."

PARQUET A floor covering composed of thick hardwood blocks laid in geometric patterns and blind-nailed to the subflooring.

PICTURE RAIL A molding on the upper part of the wall below the cornice or the frieze that has a rounded top to hold picture hooks.

PIPED VALANCE *See* Valance.

PIVOT BLINDS Window shutters with movable louvers instead of fixed louvers or solid panels.

PORTIERE A curtain hung at a doorway as a substitute for a door or as decoration.

PRIMARY COLORS The three hues—red, yellow, blue—from which all other hues are derived.

RAG CARPET A floor covering using strips of fabric as weft in a woven carpet or, if braided, as the entire carpet.

RAINBOW PAPER A wallpaper (generally French) in which the ground or pattern was composed of blended colors. The technique was also known as *ombré* or *irisé*.

ROLLER BLIND A nineteenth-century term for window shades.

SCENIC PAPERS A term used today in America to describe wallpaper sets first manufactured in France depicting landscapes.

SCOTCH CARPETING Another name for ingrain carpeting derived from the early center of production for flat-pile carpeting.

SECONDARY COLORS Those hues produced by mixing two primary colors, e.g., red and yellow to form orange.

SHADE The darkened value of a particular hue obtained by mixing it with black.

SHORT BLINDS Lightweight curtains, often muslin, that covered the bottom sash of a double-hung window; called "half sash" or "Morris" curtains by the end of the nineteenth century.

SHUTTER BLINDS Window coverings consisting of wooden frames containing solid panels or louvers that were hung outside or inside of the house. If hung inside, the shutters often folded into recesses or slid into pockets alongside the windows.

SITTING ROOM The room in the house where the family gathered in the evenings and which often doubled as the dining room until the end of the nineteenth century.

SIZING Glue or casein added to water-base paints such as distemper or calcimine to give durability.

STENCIL A thin sheet of metal or heavy paper cut to reproduce a pattern when color is rubbed over it.

SWAG Fabric looped or draped in horizontal folds and suspended from a pole or cornice above a window; called a "French shawl" at the end of the nineteenth century.

TAPESTRY BRUSSELS Looped-pile carpeting developed in Scotland c. 1832 in which the face yarns were preprinted to form a pattern when woven.

TERTIARY COLORS Colors formed by mixing a primary and a secondary color; e.g., citron is obtained by mixing yellow and green.

THREE-PLY A technique developed in 1824 for weaving a flat-pile carpet composed of three layers of interwoven fabric (also called an "Imperial").

TINT The lighter values of a particular hue obtained by mixing the hue with white.

TONGUE-AND-GROOVE Method of joining the edges of boards where the tongue (tenon) of one board fits into the groove of the next.

TRIPARTITE WALL A decorative scheme popular during the 1870s and 1880s that divided the wall into three parts—the dado, the field, and the frieze.

TWO-PLY A method of weaving a flat-pile carpet resulting in two layers of interwoven fabric; commonly called an "ingrain."

VALANCE  Fabric arranged in vertical folds suspended from a pole or cornice above a window; sometimes identified in the nineteenth century as a "piped valance."

VALUE  The lightness (tint) or darkness (shade) of a particular hue.

VELVET  A term used to describe cut-pile carpeting first manufactured in 1832 in which the face yarns were preprinted to form a pattern when woven (sometimes called "tapestry Wilton").

VENETIAN BLIND  A window covering made of horizontal slats connected by cords that open or close the slats.

VENETIAN CARPETING  A reversible, flat-pile carpet usually woven of wool and jute and commonly striped along the warp.

VESTIBULE  An antechamber or small room located between the outside door and the inside one, usually opening into a hall.

VITROMANIA  A method of decorating window panes to imitate stained glass.

WAINSCOTING  Woodwork, often paneled, that covers the lower portion of the walls of a room. *See* Dado.

WARM COLORS  All the values of the red and orange hues, or grays and whites tinted with those hues.

WHITEWASH  A water-based paint containing finely ground chalk, salt, and lime. It could be tinted various hues. It takes its name from the chalk ("whiting"), which was a basic ingredient.

WILTON  A cut-pile carpet in which the various colored yarns are woven into the body of the carpet when not part of the face pile.

WIRE BLINDS  Window screens composed of wire mesh held in wooden frames.

WOOD CARPETING  An inexpensive substitute for parquet employing thin pieces of wood glued to a paper or fabric backing and nailed to the subfloor.

# NOTES

## CHAPTER 1

1. U.S. Bureau of the Census, *Statistical Abstract of the United States*, 77th ed. (Washington, D.C., 1956), Section 1.

2. Susan Previant Lee and Peter Passell, *A New Economic View of American History* (New York: W. W. Norton & Co., 1979), pp. 72–73, regarding the canal system; Thomas C. Cochran and William Miller, *The Age of Enterprise: A Social History of Industrial America* (New York: Harper & Row, 1942), p. 56, as to the speed of communication.

3. William Gibbons Papers, Drew University Archives, Madison, New Jersey.

4. Constance M. Greiff, *John Notman, Architect* (Philadelphia: The Athenaeum of Philadelphia, 1979), pp. 155–56; Frederick Law Olmsted, *A Journey in the Back Country* (New York, 1860), p. 17.

5. Carl H. Scheele, *A Short History of the Mail Service* (Washington, D.C.: Smithsonian Institution Press, 1970), pp. 73–83.

6. Alden Hatch, *American Express: A Century of Service* (New York: Doubleday & Co., 1950), pp. 17–19.

7. Harriet Bridgeman and Elizabeth Drury, eds., *The Encyclopedia of Victoriana* (New York: Macmillan Publishing Co., 1975), p. 67, regarding Loudon; G. H. Carvill & Co., New York City, bill of November 3, 1836, for Loudon's text for $17 from William Gibbons Papers at Drew University, Madison, New Jersey.

8. Andrew Jackson Downing, *The Architecture of Country Houses* (1850; reprint, New York: Dover Publications, 1969), p. 397.

9. John Claudius Loudon, *An Encyclopedia of Cottage, Farm, and Villa Architecture and Furniture* (London, 1833; new ed. London, 1846; reprint, New York, 1869), pp. 1014–16; also Downing, *Country Houses*, pp. 403–04.

10. Downing, *Country Houses*, pp. 403–05; Thomas Webster and Mrs. W. Parkes, *An Encyclopedia of Domestic Economy* (London, 1844; reprint, New York, 1849), pp. 75–77.

11. Loudon, *Encyclopedia*, pp. 1014–16; Downing, *Country Houses*, p. 404.

12. [A Lady], *The Workwoman's Guide* (London, 1838), p. 192.

13. Downing, *Country Houses*, pp. 368–69, 399–400.

14. Abraham G. Werner, *Nomenclature of Colours, Arranged so As to Render It Highly Useful to the Arts and Sciences* (Edinburgh, 1814), cited in Marjorie Ward Selden, *The Interior Paint of the Campbell-Whittlesey House, 1835–1836* (Rochester, N.Y.: The Landmark Society of Western New York, 1949), p. 15; Hezekiah Reynolds, *Directions for House and Ship Painting* (New Haven, 1812), reprinted in Richard M. Candee, "Preparing and Mixing Colors in 1812," *Antiques*, vol. 113 (April 1978), pp. 849–53.

15. Webster and Parkes, *Domestic Economy*, pp. 79–80; Downing, *Country Houses*, p. 369.

16. Andrew Ure, *A Dictionary of Arts, Manufactures, and Mines* (London, 1839), p. 923, cited in Catherine Lynn, *Wallpaper in America from the Seventeenth Century to World War I* (New York: W. W. Norton & Company, 1980), pp. 485–86.

17. Hellmut Lehmann-Haupt, *The Book in America* (New York: R. R. Bowker Co., 1951), pp. 86–87, regarding papermaking; Brenda Greysmith, *Wallpaper* (New York: Macmillan Publishing Co., 1976), p. 108, as to the speed of production; Lynn, *Wallpaper in America*, pp. 308–12, regarding the transformation from craft to industry; Downing, *Country Houses*, p. 398.

18. Downing, *Country Houses*, p. 398; Pugin as cited in Loudon, *Encyclopedia*, p. 1274.

19. Lynn, *Wallpaper in America*, p. 231, cites the Richmond, Virginia, merchant; Downing, *Country Houses*, pp. 398, 336.

20. Harriet Martineau, *Retrospective of Western Travel* (London, 1838), vol. 1, pp. 83–84, cited in Lynn, *Wallpaper in America*, p. 226; Lynn, *Wallpaper in America*, pp. 215–22; information regarding the California house, courtesy of Hank Dunlop.

21. Lynn, *Wallpaper in America*, pp. 182, 225.

22. Samuel J. Dornsife, in Bridgeman and Drury, eds., *Encyclopedia of Victoriana*, p. 305, and Greysmith, *Wallpaper*, p. 93, claim "The War of Independence" was issued in 1838, while Lynn, *Wallpaper in America*, p. 192, dates it 1852. For a survey of scenic papers see Eric A. Entwisle, *French Scenic Wallpapers 1800–1860* (Leigh-on-Sea, England: F. Lewis, 1972).

23. Lynn, *Wallpaper in America*, p. 181.

24. Odile Nouvel, *Wallpapers of France 1800–1850* (New York: Rizzoli International Publications, 1981), pp. 19, 124–30, regarding the early statuary papers; Lynn, *Wallpaper in America*, illustrates Washington on p. 243; *Godey's Lady's Book*, vol. 55 (November 1857), p. 473.

25. Lynn, *Wallpaper in America*, pp. 240, 288–89.

26. Lynn, *Wallpaper in America*, p. 274.

27. Loudon, *Encyclopedia*, p. 1274; Downing, *Country Houses*, p. 398; Webster and Parkes, *Domestic Economy*, describe the manufacturing technique on p. 80.

28. "Wallpaper" by Dornsife in Bridgeman and Drury, eds., *The Encyclopedia of Victoriana*, p. 301.

29. Webster and Parkes, *Domestic Economy*, p. 69

30. Loudon, *Encyclopedia*, pp. 272–74; Downing, *Country Houses*, pp. 370–71.

31. Loudon, *Encyclopedia*, pp. 274–77

32. Downing, *Country Houses*, pp. 184–85, 367.

33. Downing, *Country Houses*, p. 367, describes the cost as "trifling"; Webster and Parkes, *Domestic Economy*, p. 76, recommend graining to hide soil; Loudon, *Encyclopedia*, p. 277, suggests graining should only imitate the real thing.

34. Journals of Ruth Henshaw Bascom, American Antiquarian Society Collection, cited in Nina Fletcher Little, *Floor Coverings in New England before 1850* (Sturbridge, Mass.: Old Sturbridge Inc., 1967), p. 28.

35. Buie Harwood, *Decorative Painting in Texas 1840–1940: A Survey of the European Influence* (Texas A & M Press, forthcoming), includes many examples of decorative floor painting; Rufus Porter, *A Select Collection of Valuable and Curious Arts and Interesting Experiments* (Concord, N.H., 1825), pp. 29–30, cited in Little, *Floor Coverings in New England before 1850*, pp. 25–26; Downing, *Country Houses*, p. 371.

36. Little, *Floor Coverings in New England before 1850*, p. 19, recounts Barrell's order; Reynolds, *Directions for House and Ship Painting*; all other data from Anthony Landreau, *America Underfoot, A History of Floor Coverings from Colonial Times to the Present* (Washington, D.C.: Smithsonian Institution Press, 1976), pp. 7–8.

37. Little states in *Floor Coverings in New England before 1850*, p. 17, that large seamless floorcloths were available by 1754.

38. Webster and Parkes, *Domestic Economy*, p. 257.

39. Webster and Parkes, *Domestic Economy*, p. 257, regarding the two-year aging process and pricing variables; Miss [Eliza] Leslie, *The Lady's House Book*, 19th ed. (Philadelphia, 1854), p. 183.

40. *Autobiography of Lyman Beecher*, vol. 1, cited in Little, *Floor Coverings in New England before 1850*, p. 22; reminiscences (c. 1828) of Mary A. Walkley Beach of Southington, Connecticut, cited in Little, *Floor Coverings in New England before 1850*, p. 23; *Godey's Lady's Book*, vol. 73 (October 1866), p. 352.

41. Reynolds, in *Antiques*, vol. 113 (April 1978),

p. 853; Webster and Parkes, *Domestic Economy*, pp. 257–58.

42. Cited in Robert Bishop and Patricia Coblentz, *The World of Antiques, Art and Architecture in Victorian America* (New York: E. P. Dutton, 1979), p. 69.

43. Loudon, *Encyclopedia*, pp. 345–46.

44. Loudon, *Encyclopedia*, p. 280; Downing, *Country Houses*, p. 403.

45. Webster and Parkes, *Domestic Economy*, pp. 255–57 (Loudon includes similar information in *Encyclopedia*, pp. 346–47); Lydia Maria Child, *The American Frugal Housewife* (1835; 33rd ed., New York, 1855), p. 13.

46. Helene Von Rosenstiel, *American Rugs and Carpets, from the Seventeenth Century to Modern Times* (New York: William Morrow and Company, 1978), pp. 19–20.

47. The prices are cited in Von Rosenstiel, *American Rugs and Carpets*, p. 23, and Little, *Floor Coverings in New England before 1850*, p. 31.

48. *The Workwoman's Guide*, p. 202; Loudon, *Encyclopedia*, pp. 346–47.

49. Leslie, *The Lady's House Book*, p. 185; problems with soiling cited in Von Rosenstiel, *American Rugs and Carpets*, p. 19; Child, *The American Frugal Housewife*, p. 21.

50. Leslie, *The Lady's House Book*, pp. 176–77.

51. *The Workwoman's Guide*, p. 202.

52. *The Workwoman's Guide*, p. 202; Loudon, *Encyclopedia*, p. 345.

53. Webster and Parkes, *Domestic Economy*, p. 256.

54. Downing, *Country Houses*, p. 371.

55. Data taken from *The New England Farmer* cited in Little, *Floor Coverings in New England before 1850*, p. 30; Von Rosenstiel, *American Rugs and Carpets*, p. 30, states "broad looms" were used for home weaving.

56. Webster and Parkes, *Domestic Economy*, p. 55, state the origin of the term "Venetian" is unknown; data on American production of this carpeting from Von Rosenstiel, *American Rugs and Carpets*, p. 103.

57. Webster and Parkes, *Domestic Economy*, p. 255; *The Workwoman's Guide*, p. 202, includes the suggestion of laying carpet with rods secured to the floor.

58. Von Rosenstiel, *American Rugs and Carpets*, pp. 76, 93–94; Florence M. Montgomery, *Textiles in America 1650–1870* (New York: W. W. Norton & Company, 1984), p. 265,

dates the development of three-ply ingrain to 1822; *Godey's Lady's Book*, vol. 54 (March 1857), p. 233, attributes the development of three-ply to Morton but gives no date.

59. Loudon, *Encyclopedia*, p. 344; *The Workwoman's Guide*, p. 201; Ure, *A Dictionary of Arts*, pp. 263–64; Webster and Parkes, *Domestic Economy*, p. 255.

60. Von Rosenstiel, *American Rugs and Carpets*, p. 90; Montgomery, *Textiles in America*, p. 269, identifies "about 1801" as the year Jacquard invented the attachment, while Von Rosenstiel, *American Rugs and Carpets*, p. 92, claims he "perfected" the attachment in 1804. Von Rosenstiel puts the attachment in Philadelphia by 1825 (p. 118) and describes its role in increasing production (p. 96).

61. Samuel Dornsife, "Timetable of Carpet Technology," *Nineteenth Century*, vol. 7 (Autumn 1981), p. 40, states that by 1841 Bigelow's improved loom could produce twenty-five to twenty-seven yards a day; for details on Bigelow's work see Von Rosenstiel, *American Rugs and Carpets*, p. 99.

62. Alice B. Neal, "Furnishing; or, Two Ways of Commencing Life," *Godey's Lady's Book*, vol. 41 (November 1850), p. 303.

63. Loudon, *Encyclopedia*, pp. 344–45.

64. Loudon, *Encyclopedia*, pp. 344, 346. Loudon recommends carpeting two rooms identically in order to patch them as they become worn (p. 344) and Webster and Parkes, *Domestic Economy*, p. 256, make essentially the same point.

65. *The Workwoman's Guide*, p. 202; Child, *The American Frugal Housewife*, p. 11.

66. Child, *The American Frugal Housewife*, p. 90.

67. Downing, *Country Houses*, p. 373.

68. Loudon, *Encyclopedia*, pp. 269–71, 1075; Downing, *Country Houses*, pp. 305–06, 373–74.

69. See Loudon, *Encyclopedia*, pp. 341–42, and Webster and Parkes, *Domestic Economy*, pp. 80, 253, for a general discussion. For color, see Loudon (pp. 269–71) and Webster and Parkes (p. 253).

70. Loudon, *Encyclopedia*, pp. 269–71; *Godey's Lady's Book*, vol. 2, p. 254.

71. Loudon, *Encyclopedia*, p. 271; Webster and Parkes, *Domestic Economy*, p. 254, mention ornamenting these blinds but give no examples.

72. Webster and Parkes, *Domestic Economy*, p. 254;

*The Workwoman's Guide*, p. 204; Loudon, *Encyclopedia*, p. 342, all mention short blinds. For specific fabrics see Loudon, *Encyclopedia*, p. 342; Webster and Parkes, *Domestic Economy*, p. 254; *The Workwoman's Guide*, p. 205. Timothy Shay Arthur, "Country Boarding," *Godey's Lady's Book*, vol. 41 (August 1850), p. 109.

73. Loudon, *Encyclopedia*, pp. 341–42; Webster and Parkes, *Domestic Economy*, p. 254; for the American production of spring rollers see Ruth Lee, *Shades of History* (Chicago: Joanna Western Mills Co., 1969), p. 10 (which acknowledges the research of William J. Jedlick for his M.A. Thesis, "Landscape Window Shades of the Nineteenth Century in New York and New England"); *The Workwoman's Guide*, p. 206; *Godey's Lady's Book*, vol. 38 (June 1849), p. 432.

74. Loudon, *Encyclopedia*, p. 342; Webster and Parkes, *Domestic Economy*, p. 254; for illustrations of American window shades from the 1830s and 1840s see Lee, *Shades of History*, p. 10; Downing, *Country Houses*, pp. 375–76.

75. *Godey's Lady's Book*, vol. 39 (December 1849), p. 470.

76. Loudon, *Encyclopedia*, pp. 1272–73, 337–38; Webster and Parkes, *Domestic Economy*, p. 250.

77. Loudon, *Encyclopedia*, pp. 337–38.

78. Loudon, *Encyclopedia*, pp. 338–41, 1075. Webster and Parkes, *Domestic Economy*, p. 251, give essentially the same information, as does Downing, *Country Houses*, pp. 374–75.

79. These figures are based on Hazel E. Cummin, "What Was Dimity in 1790?" *Antiques*, vol. 38 (July 1940), pp. 23–25; Cyril G. E. Bunt and Ernest A. Rose, *Two Centuries of English Chintz 1750–1950, as Exemplified by the Productions of Stead, McAlpin & Co.* (Leigh-on-Sea, England: F. Lewis, 1957); Florence M. Montgomery, *Printed Textiles: English and American Cottons and Linens 1700–1850* (New York: Viking Press, 1970), pp. 28–29; and examples measured by Patricia O'Donnell, Director, in the collection of the Goldie Paley Design Center, Philadelphia College of Textiles and Science, Philadelphia, Pennsylvania.

80. *The Workwoman's Guide*, p. 203.

81. Loudon, *Encyclopedia*, illustration on p. 338, discusses rods pp. 338–41; Webster and Parkes, *Domestic Economy*, describe brass rods p. 250;

*The Workwoman's Guide* illustrates a double rod in figure 23 and describes it p. 204.

82. Pugin cited in Loudon, *Encyclopedia*, p. 1274.

83. Pugin cited in Loudon, *Encyclopedia*, pp. 1274–75.

84. Webster and Parkes, *Domestic Economy*, p. 251.

85. *The Workwoman's Guide* labels valances "straight" or "plain"; [Thomas King?], *The Upholsterer's Accelerator* (London, c. 1833) employs the term "geometric"; Loudon, *Encyclopedia*, and Webster and Parkes, *Domestic Economy*, illustrate them but label them merely as "valances"; *The Oxford English Dictionary* identifies the term "lambrequin" as American and not British.

86. For a list of fabrics see Loudon, *Encyclopedia*, pp. 341, 1074–76; Webster and Parkes, *Domestic Economy*, p. 251; Downing, *Country Houses*, p. 374; *The Workwoman's Guide*, pp. 205–06; and pertinent dictionary entries in Montgomery, *Textiles in America*.

87. Loudon, *Encyclopedia*, p. 1074 regarding "bullion" fringe and p. 1275 for the placement of fringe, quoting Pugin; Webster and Parkes, *Domestic Economy*, p. 251, and Downing, *Country Houses*, p. 374 for fabrics and colors suitable for cottages.

88. Loudon, *Encyclopedia*, p. 1074; Webster and Parkes, *Domestic Economy*, p. 251; Downing, *Country Houses*, p. 374.

89. *The Workwoman's Guide*, p. 203; Loudon, *Encyclopedia*, pp. 337, 1079–80.

90. *The Workwoman's Guide*, p. 193.

91. For the yardage needed see Montgomery, *Textiles in America*, p. 136, and Cummin, "What Was Dimity in 1790?" p. 25. Regarding valances, see Loudon, *Encyclopedia*, pp. 1079–80; Webster and Parkes, *Domestic Economy*, p. 291; *The Workwoman's Guide*, pp. 193–94.

## CHAPTER 2

1. Fredrika Bremer, *The Homes of the New World; Impressions of America* (New York, 1853), vol. 2, p. 603.

2. Bremer, *Homes of the New World*, vol. 2, p. 628.

3. Henry Dinwoodey Reminiscense, 1887, manuscript in the collection of the Dinwoodey Furniture Company, Salt Lake City, Utah; the

authors are indebted to Nancy Richards Clark for bringing this source to their attention.

4. Edgar W. Martin, *The Standard of Living in 1860* (Chicago: The University of Chicago Press, 1942), pp. 111–12 for New York City data; Catharine Beecher and Harriet Beecher Stowe, *The American Woman's Home* (1869; reprint, Hartford, Conn.: Stowe-Day Foundation, 1975), p. 38. Stowe is best known for *Uncle Tom's Cabin*, first published in serialized form in 1851–1852.

5. Bremer, *Homes of the New World*, vol. 1, p. 46.

6. David Potter, *People of Plenty, Economic Abundance and the American Character* (Chicago: University of Chicago Press, 1954), p. 179, regarding the growth of advertising; Martin, *The Standard of Living in 1860*, pp. 399, 409–11, 394 fn., includes salary figures at midcentury; Bellows as quoted in John F. Kasson, *Civilizing the Machine: Technology and Republican Values in America, 1776–1900* (New York: Penguin Books, 1976), p. 40.

7. Calvert Vaux, *Villas and Cottages* (1857; reprint, New York: Da Capo Press, 1968), pp. 236–37.

8. William H. Ranlett, *The Architect: A Series of Original Designs for Domestic and Ornamental Cottages* (New York, 1849), vol. 2, designs 63, 51, 52, 28.

9. Gervase Wheeler, *Homes for the People* (New York, 1855), pp. 37–38, 417; *Godey's Lady's Book*, vol. 54 (April 1857), p. 367. For biographical information on Gervase Wheeler, see Sandra L. Tatman and Roger W. Moss, *Biographical Dictionary of Philadelphia Architects: 1700–1930* (Boston: G. K. Hall & Co., 1985).

10. John W. Masury, *House-painting: Plain and Decorative* (New York, 1868), pp. 166–67.

11. Hay's work is cited in the following sources: John Claudius Loudon, *An Encyclopedia of Cottage, Farm, and Villa Architecture and Furniture* (London, 1833; new ed., London, 1846; reprint, New York, 1869), p. 1274; Andrew Jackson Downing, *The Architecture of Country Houses* (1850; reprint, New York: Dover Publications, 1969, pp. 400–02; "Art in Common Things," *Godey's Lady's Book*, vol. 79 (August 1869), pp. 131–32; and Masury, *House-painting*, pp. 170–72.

12. John Bullock, *The American Cottage Builder* (New York, 1854), pp. 231–33; Samuel Sloan,

*Homestead Architecture* (Philadelphia, 1861), pp. 266–68 (for further information on Sloan, see Tatman and Moss, *Biographical Dictionary of Philadelphia Architects: 1700–1930); and Godey's Lady's Book*, vol. 65 (December 1862), p. 574. Hay's theories were also employed to paint the structure housing the New York Exhibition of 1853–1854, according to Benjamin Silliman, Jr., and Charles Rush Goodrich, *The World of Science, Art, and Industry Illustrated from Examples in the New-York Exhibition, 1853–54* (New York, 1854), p. 85.

13. Masury, *House-painting*, includes a full range of color schemes, pp. 178–87.

14. Wheeler, *Homes for the People*, pp. 167–68; for decorative borders in corners of rooms and the library color schemes see Gervase Wheeler, *Rural Homes; or Sketches of Houses Suited to American Country Life* (New York, 1851), pp. 196–97.

15. Catherine Lynn, *Wallpaper in America* (New York: W. W. Norton & Company, 1980), pp. 254, 317, 303.

16. Hellmut Lehmann-Haupt, *The Book in America* (New York: R. R. Bowker Co., 1951), pp. 88–89, and Lynn, *Wallpaper in America*, pp. 302–03, both discuss the development of wood-pulp papers.

17. Masury, *House-painting*, pp. 25–28; *Godey's Lady's Book*, vol. 61 (August 1860), p. 174.

18. *Godey's Lady's Book*, vol. 55 (November 1857), p. 473; a statuary paper of George Washington is illustrated in Lynn, *Wallpaper in America*, p. 243.

19. Billhead of Josiah F. Bumstead of Boston (1859), The Athenaeum of Philadelphia collection.

20. Bullock, *The American Cottage Builder*, p. 24.

21. *Godey's Lady's Book*, vol. 45 (September 1852), pp. 300–01.

22. *Godey's Lady's Book*, vol. 65 (December 1862), p. 575.

23. *Godey's Lady's Book*, vol. 72 (May 1866), p. 457.

24. *Godey's Lady's Book*, vol. 65 (December 1862), p. 575.

25. Wheeler, *Rural Homes*, pp. 195–96.

26. Vaux, *Villas and Cottages*, pp. 81–86; Wheeler, *Homes for the People*, p. 75; Charles P. Dwyer, *The Economic Cottage Builder* (Buffalo, 1856),

p. 114; *Godey's Lady's Book*, vol. 72 (May 1866), p. 457.

27. Wheeler, *Rural Homes*, p. 106; the entry halls employing wainscoting and the formula for oiling wood are in Wheeler, *Homes for the People*, pp. 238, 418–19.

28. Dwyer, *The Economic Cottage Builder*, p. 110.

29. Vaux, *Villas and Cottages*, p. 244; Beecher and Stowe, *The American Woman's Home*, p. 41.

30. Sloan, *Homestead Architecture*, pp. 259–61.

31. Lewis F. Allen, *Rural Architecture* (New York, 1852), p. 96.

32. Buie Harwood, *Decorative Painting in Texas 1840–1940: A Survey of the European Influence* (Texas A & M Press, forthcoming).

33. "The Unexpected Visitor," *Godey's Lady's Book*, vol. 58 (January 1859), p. 14.

34. *Official Description and Illustrated Catalogue of the Great Exhibition 1851,* 3 vols. (London, 1851), vol. 1, pp. 1441, 1449; comparison of English and American oilcloths in *Godey's Lady's Book*, vol. 50 (March 1855), p. 285; Auction catalogue of M. Thomas & Sons, 1856, The Athenaeum of Philadelphia collection; and directions for making an oilcloth in *Godey's Lady's Book*, vol. 57 (September 1858), p. 286.

35. Miss Leslie, *The Lady's House Book*, 19th ed. (Philadelphia, 1854), pp. 183–84.

36. Beecher and Stowe, *The American Woman's Home*, p. 371.

37. *Godey's Lady's Book*, vol. 58 (May 1859), p. 416, and Leslie, *The Lady's House Book*, p. 185, warn against waxing oilcloths or using them on stairs; Catalogue from Cunningham's Emporium, Providence, Rhode Island (1850s), Dornsife Collection of the Victorian Society in America at The Athenaeum of Philadelphia; Leslie, *The Lady's House Book*, p. 179, suggests nailing strips of oilcloth to each tread.

38. Bullock, *The American Cottage Builder*, p. 27; Wheeler, *Homes for the People*, p. 37; Constance M. Greiff, *John Notman, Architect* (Philadelphia: The Athenaeum of Philadelphia, 1979), pp. 187–89; information regarding The Willows and the McDonnell-Pierce House from visits by the authors.

39. Sloan, *Homestead Architecture*, pp. 261–63, 61–62.

40. Leslie, *The Lady's House Book*, pp. 184–85.

41. Sloan, *Homestead Architecture*, p. 262.

42. Catalogue of M. Thomas & Sons.

43. Beecher and Stowe, *The American Woman's Home*, pp. 86, 93.

44. Leslie, *The Lady's House Book*, pp. 175–79.

45. Peale's home is illustrated in William Seale, *The Tasteful Interlude: American Interiors through the Camera's Eye, 1860–1917*, 2d ed., rev. and enl. (Nashville: American Association for State and Local History, 1981), p. 36; Inventory of James S. Smith of Philadelphia, 1857, authors' collection.

46. Douglass C. North, *The Economic Growth of the United States, 1790–1860* (New York: W. W. Norton & Company, 1966), p. 165, mentions the increase in American carpet production; Martin, *The Standard of Living in 1860*, p. 101, states the average value was fifty-nine cents a yard.

47. Dwyer, *The Economic Cottage Builder*, p. 50; Leslie, *The Lady's House Book*, p. 173.

48. Martin, *The Standard of Living in 1860*, p. 101.

49. Von Rosenstiel, *American Rugs and Carpets*, pp. 79–80.

50. Von Rosenstiel, *American Rugs and Carpets*, pp. 112, 80–82.

51. Samuel Dornsife, "Timetable of Carpet Technology," *Nineteenth Century*, vol. 7 (Autumn 1981), p. 40, states the technique was introduced to America in 1843, while Von Rosenstiel, *American Rugs and Carpets*, p. 119, dates it to 1846. Pearson's purchase of tapestry Brussels is in Greiff, *John Notman, Architect*, p. 157.

52. Dornsife, "Timetable of Carpet Technology," p. 41, and Von Rosenstiel, *American Rugs and Carpets*, p. 119, both discuss Bigelow's power-loom Brussels; Von Rosenstiel cites the jury's findings.

53. Catalogue of M. Thomas & Sons.

54. Inventory of James S. Smith.

55. Inventory of William Hunter, Jr., 1867, in the Collection of the Maxwell Mansion, Germantown (Philadelphia), Pennsylvania.

56. Two articles appeared in *Godey's Lady's Book*, vol. 50, on the topic of carpeting—one in March 1855, pp. 285–86, and the other in June 1855, p. 572. The June article specifically recommends ingrains for bedrooms.

57. *Godey's Lady's Book*, vol. 58 (April 1859), p. 380.

58. Beecher and Stowe, *The American Woman's Home*, pp. 85–86.

59. Alice B. Neal, "The Tapestry Carpet; or, Mr. Pinkney's Shopping," *Godey's Lady's Book*, vol. 52 (January 1856), pp. 15–19.

60. Alice B. Haven, "The Story of a Carpet," *Godey's Lady's Book*, vol. 58 (June 1859), pp. 531–37.

61. *Godey's Lady's Book*, vol. 51 (August 1855), p. 182.

62. Wheeler, *Rural Homes*, pp. 156, 194–95.

63. Silliman and Goodrich, *The World of Art and Industry*, p. 167.

64. Leslie, *The Lady's House Book*, pp. 174–75.

65. *Godey's Lady's Book*, vol. 58 (April 1859), p. 380.

66. *Godey's Lady's Book*, vol. 79 (August 1869), p. 131.

67. Bremer, *Homes of the New World*, vol. 1, pp. 35, 470.

68. Sloan, *Homestead Architecture*, pp. 244–45.

69. Allen, *Rural Architecture*, p. 75.

70. Sloan, *Homestead Architecture*, pp. 244–45, calls them "pivot blinds" and describes the locking mechanism, while Ranlett identifies them as "Venetian rolling blinds" in *The Architect*, vol. 2, design 31; Leslie, *The Lady's House Book*, p. 190.

71. Bremer, *Homes of the New World*, vol. 1, p. 72.

72. Wheeler, *Rural Homes*, p. 133; Bremer, *Homes of the New World*, vol. 1, pp. 280–81.

73. Mary W. Jarven, "Hyacinth Cottage," *Godey's Lady's Book*, vol. 67 (July 1863), p. 76.

74. Leslie, *The Lady's House Book*, pp. 191–92.

75. *Godey's Lady's Book*, vol. 60 (June 1860), p. 508; Beecher and Stowe, *The American Woman's Home*, p. 377.

76. Leslie, *The Lady's House Book*, pp. 190–91; *Godey's Lady's Book*, vol. 50 (April 1855), p. 381, gives suggestions for the use of fabric shades in the hall, dining room, library, parlor, and best chamber.

77. *Godey's Lady's Book*, vol. 60 (June 1860), p. 508.

78. *Godey's Lady's Book*, vol. 60 (June 1860), p. 508.

79. "The Unexpected Visitor," *Godey's Lady's Book*, vol. 58 (January 1859), p. 14.

80. *Godey's Lady's Book*, vol. 47 (August 1853), p. 176; *Godey's Lady's Book*, vol. 57 (August 1858), p. 171; shade colors were listed in *Godey's Lady's Book*, vol. 58 (June 1859), p. 554.

81. Carryl's products are described in *Godey's Lady's Book*, vol. 49 (August 1854), p. 171; a plea for undecorated shades appears in *Godey's Lady's Book*, vol. 43 (December 1851), p. 369; Billhead of Josiah Bumstead.

82. *Godey's Lady's Book*, vol. 43 (October 1851), p. 243; practical reasons for curtains appear in *Godey's Lady's Book*, vol. 60 (February 1860), p. 185.

83. The description of the widespread use of curtains appears in *Godey's Lady's Book*, vol. 51 (October 1855), p. 361; the curtains in the capitols of Pennsylvania and Texas described in *Godey's Lady's Book*, vol. 48 (February 1854), p. 166; the success of ordering curtains by mail from Carryl's appears in *Godey's Lady's Book*, vol. 48 (May 1854), p. 468.

84. *Godey's Lady's Book*, vol. 43 (October 1851), p. 243.

85. Carryl's cornices cited in *Godey's Lady's Book*, vol. 49 (August 1854), p. 171; a definition of "lambrequin" in *Godey's Lady's Book*, vol. 43 (October 1851), p. 244. Also see Florence M. Montgomery, *Textiles in America, 1650–1870* (New York: W. W. Norton & Company, 1984), pp. 73–78, regarding the evolution of lambrequins. *Godey's Lady's Book*, vol. 43 (August 1851), p. 127.

86. *Godey's Lady's Book*, vol. 43 (October 1851), p. 244.

87. *Godey's Lady's Book*, vol. 45 (August 1852), p. 191.

88. *Godey's Lady's Book*, vol. 60 (April 1860), p. 327.

89. *Godey's Lady's Book*, vol. 60 (April 1860), pp. 325–26.

90. A variety of methods to loop up curtains suggested in *Godey's Lady's Book*, vol. 60 (June 1860), pp. 507–08; Bohemian glass pins described in *Godey's Lady's Book*, vol. 47 (August 1853), p. 176.

91. Fabric types in *Godey's Lady's Book*, vol. 60 (April 1860), p. 326; costs of fabrics in *Godey's Lady's Book*, vol. 47 (August 1853), p. 176; the best fabrics used in parlors, dining rooms, and libraries according to *Godey's Lady's Book*, vol. 58 (June 1859), p. 554.

92. Fabrics in *Godey's Lady's Book*, vol. 49 (Au-

gust 1854), p. 171; costs mentioned in *Godey's Lady's Book*, vol. 58 (June 1859), p. 554.

93. *Godey's Lady's Book*, vol. 43 (October 1851), p. 244, for "union damask"; *Godey's Lady's Book*, vol. 57 (August 1858), p. 171, for "cotton damask."

94. Thomas Webster and Mrs. W. Parkes, *An Encyclopedia of Domestic Economy* (London, 1844; New York, 1849), p. 960, and "Draperies, Curtains, and Blinds" in *Godey's Lady's Book*, vol. 60 (April 1860), p. 325, for other fabrics recommended at the time.

95. *Godey's Lady's Book*, vol. 57 (August 1858), p. 171.

96. Sloan, *Homestead Architecture*, p. 323; Masury, *House-painting*, pp. 175–76.

97. "Showy" versus "quiet" curtains in *Godey's Lady's Book*, vol. 60 (February 1860), p. 185; a "question of taste" in *Godey's Lady's Book*, vol. 60 (March 1860), p. 282.

98. *Godey's Lady's Book*, vol. 49 (August 1854), p. 171.

99. *Godey's Lady's Book*, vol. 60 (April 1860), p. 326.

## CHAPTER 3

1. Maria Dewing, *Beauty in the Household* (New York, 1882), pp. 26–27.

2. Harriet Prescott Spofford, *Art Decoration Applied to Furniture* (New York, 1878), p. 147.

3. Donald C. Pierce, "Mitchell and Rammelsberg, Cincinnati Furniture Manufacturers 1847–1881," in *Winterthur Portfolio 13* (Chicago: University of Chicago Press, 1979), pp. 222, 229.

4. Charles L. Eastlake, *Hints on Household Taste in Furniture, Upholstery & Other Details* (London, 1868; Boston, 1872; first U.S. ed., from rev. London ed.), pp. 121, 124.

5. C[hristopher] Dresser, *The Art of Decorative Design* (1862; reprint, Watkins Glen, N.Y.: American Life Foundation, 1977), p. 102. Also see R. W. Shoppell, *Modern Houses, Beautiful Homes* (New York, 1887), p. 313; Fred Miller, *Interior Decoration: A Practical Treatise on Surface Decoration* (London, 1885), p. 93, for additional information regarding wainscoting.

6. H[enry] Hudson Holly, *Modern Dwellings in Town and Country Adapted to American Wants and Climate* (New York, 1878), p. 160. Clarence Cook, *What Shall We Do With Our Walls?* (New York, 1881), pp. 22–23, says approximately the same thing.

7. Ella Rodman Church, *How to Furnish a Home* (New York, 1882), p. 13; Cook, *What Shall We Do With Our Walls?* pp. 28–30.

8. Shoppell, *Modern Houses*, p. 17. See Eastlake, *Hints* (1872), pp. 189–92, Church, *How to Furnish a Home*, p. 67, and Clarence Cook, *The House Beautiful* (New York, 1881), pp. 143–45, regarding hanging pictures.

9. Catalogue of the John W. Boughton Company, Philadelphia, c. 1885, The Athenaeum of Philadelphia collection; Catalogue of the S. C. Johnson Company, Racine, Wisc., 1890, The Athenaeum of Philadelphia collection.

10. Henry T. Williams and Mrs. C. S. Jones, *Beautiful Homes; or, Hints in House Furnishing* (New York, 1878), pp. 43–44; *House Painting and Decorating*, vol. 1 (May 1886), p. 266, warns that touching up patches is nearly impossible; "Sanitary Decoration in the Home," *House Painting and Decorating*, vol. 1 (January 1886), p. 118.

11. Holly, *Modern Dwellings*, pp. 165, 168, 182, with illustrations pp. 152, 153, 156.

12. Catalogue of Fr[ederick] Beck and Company, New York, c. 1884, The Athenaeum of Philadelphia collection; *House Painting and Decorating*, vol. 1 (November 1885), p. 59; for information regarding the history, use, and repair of Lincrusta-Walton, see Bruce Bradbury, "Lincrusta-Walton: Can the Democratic Wallcovering be Revived?" *The Old-House Journal*, vol. 10 (October 1982), pp. 203–07.

13. See Miller, *Interior Decoration*, p. 137, regarding Tynecastle tapestry; Catherine Lynn, *Wallpaper in America* (New York: W. W. Norton & Company, 1980), pp. 441–42, for Japanese leather paper; and Bruce Bradbury, "Anaglypta & Other Embossed Wallcoverings: Their History & Their Use Today," *The Old-House Journal*, vol. 10 (November 1982), p. 231.

14. Miller, *Interior Decoration*, p. 128, labels ceilings "crude and harsh," and Church, *How to Furnish a Home*, pp. 48–49, finds them appropriate only if the rest of the room is very light. Clarence Cook, *What Shall We Do With Our Walls?* pp. 30–31; Almon C. Varney, *Our*

*Homes and Their Adornments* (Chicago, 1885), p. 221.

15. Williams and Jones, *Beautiful Homes*, pp. 42–44.

16. Catalogue of Samuel H. French & Co., Philadelphia, 1888, The Athenaeum of Philadelphia collection; Catalogue of Bakewell & Mullins, Salem, Ohio, c. 1885, The Athenaeum of Philadelphia collection.

17. Cook, *What Shall We Do With Our Walls?* pp. 30–31; Miller, *Interior Decoration*, pp. 122–23. Also see Shoppell, *Modern Houses*, pp. 326–27, for correct patterns.

18. Arnold W. Brunner and Thomas Tryon, *Interior Decoration* (New York, 1887), pp. 38–39.

19. Church, *How to Furnish a Home*, pp. 49, 99; *House Painting and Decorating*, vol. 1 (March 1886), pp. 185–86.

20. Cook, *What Shall We Do With Our Walls?* p. 5, observes the change in preferred colors; Constance Cary Harrison, *Woman's Handiwork in Modern Homes* (New York, 1882), p. 179; Miller, *Interior Decoration*, pp. 115–16; Holly, *Modern Dwellings*, pp. 160–61; Catalogue of the Sherwin-Williams Company, Cleveland, Ohio, 1884, The Athenaeum of Philadelphia collection.

21. Harrison, *Woman's Handiwork*, pp. 178–81; the list of recommended designs from Church, *How to Furnish a Home*, pp. 99–102, and Miller, *Interior Decoration*, p. 36; Brunner and Tryon, *Interior Decoration*, p. 36.

22. *House Painting and Decorating*, vol. 1 (November 1885), p. 46.

23. *House Painting and Decorating*, vol. 1 (November 1885), p. 41.

24. For details see M[ichel] E[ugène] Chevreul, *The Principles of Harmony and Contrast of Colors and Their Applications to the Arts* (1854; reprint, New York: Van Nostrand Reinhold Company, 1967, based on the first English ed., 1854, as trans. from the first French ed., 1839).

25. Chevreul, *Principles*, p. 90.

26. Charles L. Eastlake, *Hints on Household Taste in Furniture, Upholstery & Other Details* (New York: Dover Publications, 1969, from the 1878 ed.), p. 120; Church, *How to Furnish a Home*, p. 51; Miller, *Interior Decoration*, p.

27. Miller, *Interior Decoration*, pp. 13–14.

28. Eastlake, *Hints* (1872), pp. 53–55; Williams and Jones, *Beautiful Homes*, pp. 25–26; Church, *How to Furnish a Home*, pp. 13–14.

29. The first two schemes are from *House Painting and Decorating*, vol. 1 (June 1886), pp. 299–301, and the third from *House Painting and Decorating*, vol. 1 (September 1886), p. 409.

30. Shoppell, *Modern Houses*, pp. 312–13.

31. Brunner and Tryon, *Interior Decoration*, pp. 10, 15–16.

32. Williams and Jones, *Beautiful Homes*, p. 110; Cook, *The House Beautiful*, p. 45.

33. Spofford, *Art Decoration*, pp. 198–99, 215–17.

34. Williams and Jones, *Beautiful Homes*, pp. 14, 111.

35. Cook, *What Shall We Do With Our Walls?* p. 27; Harrison, *Woman's Handiwork*, p. 137.

36. Suggestions as to where to hang prints, watercolors, or oil paintings are found in Shoppell, *Modern Houses*, p. 317, and Eastlake, *Hints* (1872), pp. 189–92. Church, *How to Furnish a Home*, pp. 47–49.

37. The first two schemes are in *House Painting and Decorating*, vol. 1 (June 1886), pp. 300–01, while that for a "sunny cottage sitting-room" appears in *House Painting and Decorating*, vol. 1 (August 1886), p. 363.

38. For "a parlor on the south side of the house" see *House Painting and Decorating*, vol. 1 (June 1886), p. 300; suggestions for the house in Georgia appear in *House Painting and Decorating*, vol. 1 (March 1886), p. 176.

39. Shoppell, *Modern Houses*, p. 316. Shoppell's list is identical to one in H. J. Cooper, *The Art of Furnishing* (London, 1876; New York, 1881), p. 13.

40. Miller, *Interior Decoration*, p. 15; Spofford, *Art Decoration*, p. 191; Brunner and Tryon, *Interior Decoration*, p. 43; Church, *How to Furnish a Home*, p. 44; Eastlake, *Hints* (1872), p. 189.

41. Spofford, *Art Decoration*, pp. 191–94.

42. Cook, *The House Beautiful*, pp. 214–15, 229.

43. Church, *How to Furnish a Home*, pp. 25–27. For the source of this idea see Gervase Wheeler, *Rural Homes; or, Sketches of Houses Suited to American Country Life* (New York, 1851), pp. 196–97.

44. For the yellow or India-red dining rooms see *House Painting and Decorating*, vol. 1 (June

1886), p. 300; the olive-green room is described in *House Painting and Decorating*, vol. 1 (August 1886), p. 363.

45. Shoppell, *Modern Houses*, pp. 313, 316.

46. Holly, *Modern Dwellings*, p. 109.

47. Spofford, *Art Decoration*, pp. 210–11, 143–46.

48. Williams and Jones, *Beautiful Homes*, pp. 13–14.

49. *House Painting and Decorating*, vol. 1 (September 1886), p. 410.

50. Brunner and Tryon, *Interior Decoration*, p. 28.

51. Spofford, *Art Decoration*, p. 204; Church, *How to Furnish a Home*, p. 81. For north- and south-facing bedrooms see *House Painting and Decorating*, vol. 1 (September 1886), p. 409, and for east-facing bedrooms *House Painting and Decorating*, vol. 1 (May 1886), p. 265. Brunner and Tryon, *Interior Decoration*, p. 61.

52. Williams and Jones, *Beautiful Homes*, p. 80; Shoppell, *Modern Houses*, p. 320; *House Painting and Decorating*, vol. 1 (August 1886), p. 363.

53. Lynn, *Wallpaper in America*, pp. 395–96.

54. Dallas Finn, "Japan at the Centennial," *Nineteenth Century*, vol. 2 (Autumn 1976), pp. 33–36.

55. Eastlake, *Hints* (1872), p. 116; Dresser, *The Art of Decorative Design*, p. 142.

56. Cook, *What Shall We Do With Our Walls?* pp. 15–16.

57. Eastlake, *Hints* (1872), p. 122. Eastlake's advice was repeated by many critics, including Dresser, *The Art of Decorative Design*, pp. 181–83; Shoppell, *Modern Houses*, p. 325; Holly, *Modern Dwellings*, pp. 163–65; Brunner and Tryon, *Interior Decoration*, p. 46; Williams and Jones, *Beautiful Homes*, pp. 35–36; and *House Painting and Decorating*, vol. 1 (November 1885), p. 60.

58. Eastlake, *Hints* (1872), p. 126; data regarding the number of designs by Morris are from Brenda Greysmith, *Wallpaper* (New York: Macmillan Publishing Co., 1976), pp. 136–40; data on Bumstead and American imitators of Morris are found in Lynn, *Wallpaper in America*, pp. 383–84.

59. Lynn, *Wallpaper in America*, p. 398.

60. Williams and Jones, *Beautiful Homes*, pp. 35–36; Shoppell, *Modern Houses*, p. 317; *House Painting and Decorating*, vol. 1 (January 1886), p. 119.

61. Harrison, *Woman's Handiwork*, pp. 136–37.

62. Williams and Jones, *Beautiful Homes*, pp. 34–35, 45; Eastlake, *Hints* (1872), pp. 119–20; Shoppell, *Modern Houses*, p. 317.

63. Miller, *Interior Decoration*, p. 134.

64. *House Painting and Decorating*, vol. 1 (December 1885), p. 85. Prices are taken from the catalogue of C. H. Bacon's Furniture & Coffin Rooms, Danielsonville, Connecticut, 1884, The Athenaeum of Philadelphia collection, and Williams and Jones, *Beautiful Homes*, pp. 35–36.

65. Eastlake, *Hints* (1872), pp. 107–10.

66. Cook, *The House Beautiful*, p. 56; *House Painting and Decorating*, vol. 1 (January 1886), p. 118; carpets from "the lands of the Orient" in Williams and Jones, *Beautiful Homes*, p. 47.

67. Eastlake, *Hints* (1872), pp. 109–10. Critics agreeing with Eastlake include Shoppell, *Modern Houses*, p. 315; Spofford, *Art Decoration*, pp. 187–88, 193–94; Brunner and Tryon, *Interior Decoration*, p. 12.

68. Catalogue of the John W. Boughton Company; Church, *How to Furnish a Home*, pp. 12, 19–20.

69. Catalogue of the John W. Boughton Company. Both A. J. Bicknell, *Cottage and Villa Architecture* (New York, 1878), and Palliser's *New Cottage Homes* (New York, 1887), continue to specify softwood floors. Williams and Jones, *Beautiful Homes*, p. 20, suggest staining floors while Cook, *The House Beautiful*, pp. 55–56, recommends painting them. Spofford, *Art Decoration*, p. 203; catalogue of the Glidden Varnish Company, Cleveland, Ohio, c. 1890, The Athenaeum of Philadelphia collection; Catalogue of H. W. Johns M'f'g Co., Boston, New York, Philadelphia, 1894, The Athenaeum of Philadelphia collection.

70. See Andrew Jackson Downing, *The Architecture of Country Houses* (1850; reprint, New York: Dover Publications, 1969), p. 403; Gervase Wheeler, *Homes for the People* (New York, 1855), p. 75; Calvert Vaux, *Villas and Cottages* (New York, 1857), p. 214; and Samuel Sloan, *Homestead Architecture* (Philadelphia, 1861), pp. 261–63, for early references to encaustic tiles. Eastlake, *Hints* (1872), pp. 50–51; Williams and Jones, *Beautiful Homes*, p. 21.

71. Dianne H. Pilgrim, "The American Renaissance: Decorative Arts and Interior Design from 1876 to 1917," *Art and Antiques*, vol. 3 (January/February 1980), p. 50. The catalogue of Samuel H. French & Co., Philadelphia, 1888, The Athenaeum of Philadelphia collection, recommends their use in those locations. Shoppell, *Modern Houses*, p. 312.

72. Eastlake, *Hints* (1872), pp. 51–52.

73. For critics suggesting oilcloth for vestibules and stair halls see Church, *How to Furnish a Home*, p. 12; Williams and Jones, *Beautiful Homes*, p. 19; Shoppell, *Modern Houses*, p. 312; and Cook, *The House Beautiful*, p. 29.

74. Church, *How to Furnish a Home*, pp. 12, 19–20; catalogue of E. F. Denning & Co., New York, c. 1890, The Athenaeum of Philadelphia collection; catalogue of the Glidden Varnish Company, Cleveland, Ohio, c. 1890; a recommendation for a dining-room oilcloth with a parquet design is from Shoppell, *Modern Houses*, p. 316.

75. Helene Von Rosenstiel, *American Rugs and Carpets from the Seventeenth Century to Modern Times* (New York: William Morrow and Company, 1978), p. 63, describes kamptulicon, and [Frederick Thomas Hodgson], *The Practical Upholsterer* (New York, 1891), p. 88, gives instructions for installing it; Shoppell, *Modern Houses*, p. 322; Spofford, *Art Decoration*, p. 173; Williams and Jones, *Beautiful Homes*, p. 19.

76. Catalogue of E. F. Denning & Co.

77. Brunner and Tryon, *Interior Decoration*, p. 58, warn readers that the dyes do not penetrate far enough; Church, *How to Furnish a Home*, pp. 80–81.

78. Williams and Jones, *Beautiful Homes*, pp. 19–20; Church, *How to Furnish a Home*, p. 12; Shoppell, *Modern Houses*, p. 312, warns matting is too fragile for vestibules.

79. Shoppell, *Modern Houses*, p. 319.

80. Spofford, *Art Decoration*, p. 173, suggests flannel stamped with a pattern and on p. 193 recommends hooks to fasten them to the floor; Church, *How to Furnish a Home*, p. 27, suggests painted burlap as a drugget.

81. Church, *How to Furnish a Home*, p. 53.

82. Spofford, *Art Decoration*, p. 173, suggests using borders with wall-to-wall carpets; Williams and Jones, *Beautiful Homes*, p. 49.

83. Cook, *The House Beautiful*, pp. 50–52, regarding the correct size for carpets; Spofford, *Art Decoration*, p. 173, recommends a border with wall-to-wall carpeting.

84. Eastlake, *Hints* (1872), pp. 111–13; Cook, *The House Beautiful*, p. 52.

85. Samuel Dornsife, "Timetable of Carpet Technology," *Nineteenth Century*, vol. 7 (Autumn 1981), p. 41, regarding the machine production of Axminsters; prices as cited in Williams and Jones, *Beautiful Homes*, pp. 47–48, and the catalogue of E. F. Denning & Co., New York (c. 1890).

86. Prices for body and tapestry Brussels cited in the catalogues of E. F. Denning & Co.; B. B. Fowler, Glens Falls, N.Y., 1887; and Hamilton & Co., New Haven, Connecticut, c. 1880, all in The Athenaeum of Philadelphia collection. Spofford, *Art Decoration*, p. 174. Price comparisons between Wiltons and Brussels cited in the catalogue of E. F. Denning & Co. and in Williams and Jones, *Beautiful Homes*, pp. 47–48. For a description of moquette production, see Von Rosenstiel, *American Rugs and Carpets*, p. 135. Prices for moquette carpets cited in the catalogues of Hamilton & Co. and E. F. Denning & Co.

87. Spofford, *Art Decoration*, p. 174; prices in the catalogue of Hamilton & Co., and the catalogue of B. B. Fowler; Williams and Jones, *Beautiful Homes*, pp. 47–48; Church, *How to Furnish a Home*, pp. 96–98.

88. Spofford, *Art Decoration*, p. 174; Church, *How to Furnish a Home*, p. 96.

89. Eastlake, *Hints* (1872), pp. 47, 113–14, 162.

90. Church, *How to Furnish a Home*, p. 6, is critical of carpet patterns of "dazzling surfaces of flowers"; Williams and Jones, *Beautiful Homes*, p. 47.

91. Eastlake, *Hints* (1872), pp. 111–13, and Shoppell, *Modern Houses*, p. 338, both make these points regarding carpet patterns.

92. Spofford, *Art Decoration*, p. 171, suggests the carpet should set the main tint of the room. Suggestions for carpet colors are found in Williams and Jones, *Beautiful Homes*, pp. 45–46; Shoppell, *Modern Houses*, p. 319; Eastlake, *Hints* (1872), pp. 111–13; and *House Painting and Decorating*, vol. 1 (April 1886), pp. 232–33.

93. See Hodgson, *The Practical Upholsterer*, p. 116, and Church, *How to Furnish a Home*, p.

12, regarding correct stair carpeting and installation.

94. Cook, *The House Beautiful*, p. 331; Church, *How to Furnish a Home*, p. 47, warns against using a "pronounced carpet."

95. Williams and Jones, *Beautiful Homes*, pp. 156–57.

96. *House Painting and Decorating*, vol. 1 (January 1886), p. 118; Brunner and Tryon, *Interior Decoration*, p. 58, condemn "a few oases of mats"; Church, *How to Furnish a Home*, p. 82.

97. Isaac H. Hobbs and Son, *Hobbs's Architecture: Containing Designs and Ground Plans for Villas, Cottages, and Other Edifices, Both Suburban and Rural* (Philadelphia, 1873), p. 84; Bicknell, *Cottage and Villa Architecture*, and Palliser's *New Cottage Homes* all specify interior shutters.

98. Marion Harland, "Mrs. Prime's House," *Godey's Lady's Book*, vol. 85 (August 1872), p. 126.

99. Wheeler, *Rural Homes*, p. 133; Williams and Jones, *Beautiful Homes*, pp. 75–76, 171–73. (Church, *How to Furnish a Home*, pp. 104–05, also describes how to make blinds but gives no reason to use them.)

100. Catalogue of John W. Boughton; Shoppell, *Modern Houses*, p. 320.

101. Harland, "Mrs. Prime's House," p. 126; Catalogue of the William Cabble Excelsior Wire Manufacturing Co., New York, 1892, The Athenaeum of Philadelphia collection.

102. Elizabeth B. Custer, *Boots and Saddles* (New York, 1885), pp. 184–85.

103. Williams and Jones, *Beautiful Homes*, pp. 50–51.

104. Stern Bro's Fashion Catalogue, New York, 1885, The Athenaeum of Philadelphia collection; Harrison, *Woman's Handiwork*, p. 189; *Godey's Lady's Book*, vol. 90 (March 1875), p. 220; Williams and Jones, *Beautiful Homes*, p. 50, recommend uniform use of color and material across the front of the house.

105. Williams and Jones, *Beautiful Homes*, p. 50; Eastlake, *Hints* (1872), p. 194.

106. Williams and Jones, *Beautiful Homes*, p. 51.

107. Williams and Jones, *Beautiful Homes*, p. 160, list appropriate subjects for dining-room windows. For simpler windows, see Church, *How to Furnish a Home*, pp. 42–43, and Shoppell, *Modern Houses*, pp. 327–29.

108. Williams and Jones, *Beautiful Homes*, pp. 17–18, suggest the "epiphanie"; Church, *How to Furnish a Home*, p. 105, and Varney, *Our Homes*, recommend the putty bag; Williams and Jones, *Beautiful Homes*, pp. 17–18, and Church, *How to Furnish a Home*, pp. 42–43, suggest applying lace to glass.

109. Eastlake, *Hints* (1872), pp. 94–95.

110. Eastlake, *Hints* (1872), pp. 95–96.

111. Varney, *Our Homes*, p. 265; Shoppell, *Modern Houses*, p. 316, condemns tin grapes as pole ends and explains (p. 333) that the weight of the curtain would cause it to fall into natural folds; Cook, *The House Beautiful*, pp. 129–36, also recommends simple, yet sturdy-looking, curtain poles; simple curtain poles and encrusted cornices are found in Stern Bro's Fashion Catalogue, 1885, and the catalogue of B. B. Fowler.

112. Harrison, *Woman's Handiwork*, pp. 161–62.

113. Spofford, *Art Decoration*, pp. 178–79; *House Painting and Decorating*, vol. 1 (April 1886), p. 233, regarding the "unbroken line" of frieze or cornice.

114. Eastlake, *Hints* (1872), p. 95; Williams and Jones, *Beautiful Homes*, pp. 60, 74, 78, 79, for examples of designs copied from *Godey's Lady's Book*.

115. Eastlake, *Hints* (1872), pp. 96–97, regarding the origin of fringe; Williams and Jones, *Beautiful Homes*, pp. 13–14, recommend that the color of the curtain trim match that of the upholstery; Shoppell, *Modern Houses*, p. 319, admits some trimming might "look exceedingly well."

116. Eastlake, *Hints* (1872), pp. 99–104; Spofford, *Art Decoration*, pp. 84–85, 177–78, suggests velvets or woolens fancifully embroidered; and Cook, *The House Beautiful*, pp. 137–43, praises Japanese designs.

117. Shoppell, *Modern Houses*, p. 334, contains a description and illustration. Church, *How to Furnish a Home*, pp. 43–44, suggests placing five-inch-wide bands every eighteen inches on the entire panel.

118. Shoppell, *Modern Houses*, p. 333.

119. Eastlake, *Hints* (1872), pp. 99–104. Prices are taken from the catalogue of R. H. White & Co., Boston, 1883, The Athenaeum of Philadelphia collection; the catalogue of B. B. Fowler; and Stern Bro's Fashion Catalogue.

Harrison, *Woman's Handiwork*, p. 187, writes disparagingly of designs of "former days"; catalogue of R. H. White & Co., Boston 1883, derides the ornately patterned curtains popular earlier and recommends plain cheesecloth in their place; Spofford, *Art Decoration*, p. 176, suggests muslin with lace insets or lace borders.

120. Spofford, *Art Decoration*, pp. 179–80.
121. Spofford, *Art Decoration*, pp. 83–84; Harrison, *Woman's Handiwork*, pp. 160, 163–65. Also see Williams and Jones, *Beautiful Homes*, p. 54, and Brunner and Tryon, *Interior Decoration*, p. 40.
122. Church, *How to Furnish a Home*, pp. 102–03, prefers portieres to any door, and Williams and Jones, *Beautiful Homes*, pp. 67–71, recommend disposing of them to the lumber room or a lover of doors; Harrison, *Woman's Handiwork*, pp. 163–65, advises that portieres and curtains in a room should not match. For fabrics recommended to make up portieres see Varney, *Our Homes*; Church, *How to Furnish a Home*, pp. 102–03; and Harrison, *Woman's Handiwork*, pp. 163–65, 200.
123. Harrison, *Woman's Handiwork*, pp. 161, 167.
124. Eastlake, *Hints* (1872), p. 137, lists accessories for the mantel; Church, *How to Furnish a Home*, p. 57, labels marble mantels as "cold" and "unsuggestive"; Harrison, *Woman's Handiwork*, pp. 171–72, 175, and Cook, *The House Beautiful*, p. 126, both recommend a lambrequin or drapery hanging from the mantel shelf.
125. Church, *How to Furnish a Home*, p. 67; Harrison, *Woman's Handiwork*, pp. 176–77, gives suggestions for draping pianos.
126. Eastlake, *Hints* (1872), p. 120, states the colors should "correspond"; Cook, *The House Beautiful*, p. 136, cautions to use accent colors in small amounts only; Shoppell, *Modern Houses*, p. 333, recommends that curtains, portieres, and walls should all "gently contrast" in color.
127. Cook, *The House Beautiful*, p. 265.
128. Eastlake, *Hints* (1872), pp. 215–16; Williams and Jones, *Beautiful Homes*, pp. 90–92, give the yardage necessary.
129. Stern Bro's Fashion Catalogue.
130. Eastlake, *Hints* (1872), pp. 217–18; Williams and Jones, *Beautiful Homes*, pp. 95–103; Spofford, *Art Decoration*, p. 208.
131. Eastlake, *Hints* (1872), pp. 213–16.

132. Elizabeth Wood Kane, *Twelve Mormon Homes Visited in Succession on a Journey through Utah to Arizona* (Salt Lake City: University of Utah Library, 1974), pp. 55–56 (the authors are indebted to Nancy Richards Clark for bringing this source to their attention).

## CHAPTER 4

1. Harold T. Williamson, "Mass Production for Mass Consumption," in *Technology in Western Civilization*, ed. Melvin Kranzberg and Carroll W. Pursell, Jr. (New York: Oxford University Press, 1976), vol. 1, pp. 686–87, discusses the bicycle; John B. Rae, "The Internal-Combustion Engine on Wheels," in *Technology in Western Civilization*, ed. Kranzberg and Pursell, vol. 2, pp. 133–34, includes the demands by the League of American Wheelmen and the automobile companies for better roads.
2. Thomas M. Smith, "Late Nineteenth-century Communications: Techniques and Machines," in *Technology in Western Civilization*, ed. Kranzberg and Pursell, vol. 1, pp. 644–45, regarding the telephone system; Carl H. Scheele, *A Short History of the Mail Service* (Washington, D.C.: Smithsonian Institution Press, 1970), pp. 105–06, 91–92.
3. Scheele, *A Short History of the Mail Service*, pp. 115–17.
4. *House Painting and Decorating*, vol. 8 (September 1893), p. 1100.
5. Rodris Roth, "The New England, or 'Olde Tyme,' Kitchen Exhibit at Nineteenth-Century Fairs," in *The Colonial Revival in America*, ed. Alan Axelrod (New York: W. W. Norton & Company, 1985), p. 175.
6. Clarence Cook, *The House Beautiful* (New York, 1881), p. 187; George T. B. Davis, "A Talk about Colonial Furniture," *House Beautiful*, vol. 6 (June 1899), p. 19; *House and Garden*, vol. 2 (February 1902), p. 106; Edith Wharton and Ogden Codman, Jr., *The Decoration of Houses* (New York, 1897), p. 17. Wharton was also a well-known novelist, author of *The House of Mirth* (1905), *Ethan Frome* (1911), and *The Age of Innocence* (1920) for which she won a Pulitzer prize.
7. Wharton and Codman, *The Decoration of Houses*, pp. xxi–xxii.

8. *House Painting and Decorating*, vol. 8 (March 1893), p. 618.

9. John Valentine, "The Furniture of the Empire," *House Beautiful*, vol. 2 (June 1897), p. 20.

10. *House Beautiful*, vol. 3 (March 1898), pp. 137–38; Wharton and Codman, *The Decoration of Houses*, p. 62.

11. *House Beautiful*, vol. 3 (January 1898), p. 61, favors the Craftsman style for its simplicity and social benefit, while Donald Warren, author of "New Furniture," *House Beautiful*, vol. 5 (January 1899), p. 51, sees it as a protest against false construction.

12. *House Painting and Decorating*, vol. 8 (June 1893), p. 833.

13. *House Painting and Decorating*, vol. 1 (June 1886), p. 300, calls attention to the disappearance of the dado; Wharton and Codman, *The Decoration of Houses*, p. 37.

14. *House Painting and Decorating*, vol. 8 (July 1893), pp. 911–21.

15. "At the Paper-hanger's," by John Crane, *House Beautiful*, vol. 5 (December 1898), pp. 26–30, and *House Painting and Decorating*, vol. 8 (April 1893), p. 702, both describe papers popular for traditional interiors. The lists are nearly identical.

16. Kayser and Allman frieze papers as cited in *House Painting and Decorating*, vol. 8 (April 1893), p. 702; for frieze-paper sizes and changes in design see *House Painting and Decorating*, vol. 8 (April 1893), p. 703; *House Painting and Decorating*, vol. 8 (December 1892), p. 233, and *House Painting and Decorating*, vol. 8 (February 1893), p. 429, both discuss various types of frieze papers including those with an *irisé* ground; William Martin Johnson, *Inside of One Hundred Homes* (Philadelphia, 1891), p. 12, illustrates a room in which the wall and frieze papers are reversed colorways of the same pattern.

17. The paper of H. Bartholomae & Company is described in *House Painting and Decorating*, vol. 8 (April 1893), p. 703; Lillie Hamilton French, *Homes and Their Decoration* (New York, 1903), attributes the end of frieze papers to the growing popularity of cove molding.

18. The patterns of English firms who exhibited at the fair are illustrated in *House Painting and Decorating*, vol. 8 (May 1893), pp. 774–87; *House Beautiful*, vol. 2 (September 1897), pp. 105–06.

19. *House Painting and Decorating*, vol. 8 (April 1893), p. 729.

20. Arthur Seymour Jennings, *Wallpapers and Wall Coverings* (New York, 1903), p. 131, mentions burlaps and canvas, while *House Beautiful*, vol. 3 (April 1898), pp. 149–153, includes denims and grass cloths.

21. The "East India Room" is in *House Painting and Decorating*, vol. 8 (October 1892), p. 19; the "Japanese Room" in *Household News*, vol. 3 (February 1895), p. 87; and the "artistic rooms" with festoons of Manila rope or moss in *House Painting and Decorating*, vol. 8 (December 1892), p. 235.

22. The trade catalogue of Kayser & Allman, Philadelphia, 1896, The Athenaeum of Philadelphia collection, suggests matching borders on the ceiling; Jennings, *Wallpapers and Wall Coverings*, p. 118; Paul N. Hasluck, ed., *House Decoration* (London, 1894), pp. 110–13, 154; *House Painting and Decorating*, vol. 8 (December 1892), pp. 223–25.

23. *Household News*, vol. 2 (January 1894), p. 288; *Household News*, vol. 3 (March 1895), p. 119; Wharton and Codman, *The Decoration of Houses*, pp. 96–99.

24. Jennings, *Wallpapers and Wall Coverings*, p. 125, recommends using the same paper for ceiling and frieze; *House Beautiful*, vol. 3 (April 1898), pp. 149–53, 178, suggests painting the ceiling.

25. *House Painting and Decorating*, vol. 1 (June 1886), p. 300, recommends white woodwork for all but the dining room and entry hall; *House Painting and Decorating*, vol. 8 (December 1892), p. 236, notes that even the wealthy now painted their woodwork.

26. Wharton and Codman, *The Decoration of Houses*, p. 46, oppose cords or pictures that tilt away from the wall; *House Beautiful*, vol. 4 (June 1898), p. 35, suggests cords only for large pictures to "indicate the means of support."

27. *House Painting and Decorating*, vol. 8 (November 1892), p. 171; Walter Pearce, *Painting and Decorating* (London, 1898), color plate 4; Wharton and Codman, *The Decoration of Houses*, p. 28.

28. *House Painting and Decorating*, vol. 8 (November 1892), p. 171, advises against using

pure chroma in contrasting color schemes; Oliver Coleman, "Concerning the Drawing Room," *House Beautiful*, vol. 2 (November 1897), p. 149.

29. *House Beautiful*, vol. 5 (December 1898), p. 26, and Jennings, *Wallpapers and Wall Coverings*, p. 22, both comment on the open plan; *House Beautiful*, vol. 3 (February 1898), pp. 97–98.

30. Pearce, *Painting and Decorating*, pp. 7–10, 236–37.

31. *Household News*, vol. 3 (March 1895), pp. 118–19.

32. *Household News*, vol. 2 (June 1894), p. 517.

33. Catalogue of the Wood-Mosaic Co., Rochester, New York, 1898, The Athenaeum of Philadelphia collection.

34. *Household News*, vol. 2 (September 1894), p. 663; *House Painting and Decorating*, vol. 8 (April 1893), p. 727.

35. Catalogue of the Heath & Milligan M'f'g Co., Chicago, c. 1900, The Athenaeum of Philadelphia collection.

36. Catalogue of R. H. & B. C. Reeve Company, Camden, N.J., c. 1890, The Athenaeum of Philadelphia collection; Wharton and Codman, *The Decoration of Houses*, p. 104; Catalogue of Sears, Roebuck and Company, Chicago, reprint of 1897 ed.

37. Catalogue of John H. Pray & Sons, Boston, 1906, The Athenaeum of Philadelphia collection.

38. Catalogue of Boch Frères, Maubeuge, France, 1884, The Athenaeum of Philadelphia collection.

39. The differences between Chinese and Japanese mattings are described in Helene Von Rosenstiel, *American Rugs and Carpets from the Seventeenth Century to Modern Times* (New York: William Morrow and Company, 1978), p. 24; *Household News*, vol. 2 (February 1894), p. 331; Wharton and Codman, *The Decoration of Houses*, pp. 132–33; French, *Homes and Their Decoration*, p. 143, suggests denim.

40. *House Painting and Decorating*, vol. 8 (April 1893), pp. 682–83.

41. *Household News*, vol. 2 (November 1894), p. 747.

42. Von Rosenstiel, *American Rugs and Carpets*, p. 99, states that ingrain continued in production until the 1930s; *Household News*, vol. 2 (November 1894), p. 747, lists the prices, and *Household News*, vol. 2 (March 1894), pp. 370–71, the areas of use.

43. Wharton and Codman, *The Decoration of Houses*, pp. 100–01.

44. French, *Homes and Their Decoration*, and Wharton and Codman, *The Decoration of Houses*, p. 102, all recommend carpets with simple patterns in two values of the same hue; an early mention of "filling" is in *Household News*, vol. 2 (November 1894), pp. 744–47; French claims in *Homes and Their Decoration* (p. 309) that the popularity of solid-colored carpets led to broadlooms.

45. *House Painting and Decorating*, vol. 8 (July 1893), p. 912, labels Bartholomae & Company as unique and earlier, in vol. 8 (February 1893), p. 444, hypothesizes it will advance interior decoration.

46. *Household News*, vol. 2 (November 1894), p. 747, describes the "sportive moth" and earlier, in vol. 2 (February 1894), p. 329, stresses hygiene in the bedchamber.

47. *House Beautiful*, vol. 3 (April 1898), pp. 153–56; *Household News*, vol. 2 (March 1894), pp. 370–71; Henry T. Williams and Mrs. C. S. Jones, *Beautiful Homes; or, Hints in House Furnishing* (New York, 1878), p. 306.

48. Wharton and Codman, *The Decoration of Houses*, pp. 28–29.

49. Wharton and Codman, *The Decoration of Houses*, pp. 70–73.

50. N. W. Jacobs, *Practical Handbook on Cutting Draperies* (Minneapolis, 1890), p. 37. F. A. Moreland makes the same point in *Practical Decorative Upholstery* (Boston, 1890), reprinted as *The Curtain-Maker's Handbook*, ed. Martha Gandy Fales (New York: E. P. Dutton, 1979), p. 19.

51. Catalogue of the Willer Manufacturing Co., Milwaukee, Wisconsin, c. 1895, The Athenaeum of Philadelphia collection; *Household News*, vol. 3 (July 1895), pp. 296–97.

52. [Frederick Thomas Hodgson], *The Practical Upholsterer* (New York, 1891), p. 90, recommends placing the pattern toward the glass; French, *Homes and Their Decoration*.

53. Jacobs, *Practical Handbook on Cutting Draperies*, pp. 10, 17; Moreland, *Practical Decorative Upholstery*, p. 12.

54. *House Painting and Decorating*, vol. 8 (No-

vember 1892), p. 164; Johnson, *Inside of One Hundred Homes*, p. 35, recommends placing the curtain hardware beyond the window moldings; Wharton and Codman, *The Decoration of Houses*, p. 70.

55. This plain window treatment is described in *House Beautiful*, vol. 4 (October 1898), p. 159; Hodgson, *The Practical Upholsterer*, pp. 90–91; French, *Homes and Their Decoration*; and Jacobs, *Practical Handbook on Cutting Draperies*, pp. 25–30. A list of fabric choices is found in Jacobs, *Practical Handbook on Cutting Draperies*, pp. 25–30, and French, *Homes and Their Decoration*. Also see Jacobs, *Practical Handbook on Cutting Draperies*, pp. 25–30, regarding various designs employing curtain panels. Both Hodgson, *The Practical Upholsterer*, pp. 90–91, and Moreland, *Practical Decorative Upholstery*, pp. 170–77, illustrate "Austrian shades."

56. Jacobs, *Practical Handbook on Cutting Draperies*, mentions the amount of material needed to curtain a window (p. 128) and the placement of hooks behind each pleat (p. 89). *House Beautiful*, vol. 4 (October 1898), p. 159, includes both curtain lengths.

57. Both Hodgson, *The Practical Upholsterer*, p. 69, and Jacobs, *Practical Handbook on Cutting Draperies*, p. 65, illustrate various patterns for valances, but "valance fringe" appears only in Jacobs, p. 20.

58. Jacobs, *Practical Handbook on Cutting Draperies*, pp. 40–41, 70–71.

59. Jacobs, *Practical Handbook on Cutting Draperies*, p. 126.

60. Lists of fabric choices appear in *Household News*, vol. 2 (January 1894), p. 288, vol. 2 (September 1894), p. 660, and vol. 2 (August 1894), pp. 611–13, and in Jacobs, *Practical Handbook on Cutting Draperies*, p. 14. Also see Jacobs, p. 128, for a description of the workroom technique of interlining curtains.

61. Wharton and Codman, *The Decoration of Houses*, pp. 59–60; *House Beautiful*, vol. 3 (March 1898), pp. 126–29, praises portieres.

62. These suggestions are found in Jacobs, *Practical Handbook on Cutting Draperies*, pp. 104–08, and *House Beautiful*, vol. 3 (March 1898), p. 127.

63. Jacobs, *Practical Handbook on Cutting Draperies*, pp. 106–08.

64. Jacobs, *Practical Handbook on Cutting Draperies*, pp. 114–16; catalogue of John H. Pray & Sons; *House Beautiful*, vol. 3 (March 1898), p. 120.

65. Jacobs, *Practical Handbook on Cutting Draperies*, p. 16, comments that cottons are used in bedrooms of all but the wealthiest houses. *House Beautiful*, vol. 3 (March 1898), pp. 126–27; *Household News*, vol. 2 (February 1894), p. 330.

# SELECT BIBLIOGRAPHY

The following bibliography is divided into four sections: Pictorial Sourcebooks, Wall Coverings, Floors and Floor Coverings, Window Coverings and Fabric Use. These sections are not intended to be comprehensive and they *do not* include all the sources mentioned in the text or footnotes. Although a few obscure primary sources have been included, in most cases we have selected items that are available from larger academic and public libraries across the country. Some of the books listed under one topic—say, wall coverings—will also contain material useful on another topic; works such as Ella Rodman Church's *How to Furnish a Home* are obviously not restricted to a discussion of window coverings and fabric use. Preceding these four sections are those primary sources that are so important that they must be mentioned separately rather than buried in the lists that follow.

John Claudius Loudon's *An Encyclopedia of Cottage, Farm, and Villa Architecture and Furniture*, first published in London in 1833, contains over eleven hundred pages and two thousand illustrations and was aimed at what can best be described as a middle-class audience in both England and America. Loudon had five thousand prospectuses distributed in America prior to the publication in England, and as late as 1869 editions were simultaneously published in New York and London. There was even a New York edition in 1883. Parts of Loudon's work were reprinted (without credit) by Louis Godey, who began publishing the *Lady's Book* in Philadelphia in 1830 and whose subscribers numbered 150,000 by 1860. And Andrew Jackson Downing, America's first widely read architectural critic, acknowledged Loudon's influence in *Cottage Residences* (1842) and *The Architecture of Country Houses* (1850), both seminal works republished throughout the 1840s and 1850s. Rivaling Loudon was Thomas Webster and Mrs. Parkes's *An Encyclopedia of Domestic Economy*, which was first published in London (1844) and appeared in an American edition in 1845 with subsequent New York or Boston editions in 1847, 1848, 1849, and 1852, and, in the guise of *The American Family Encyclopedia*, through at least six editions in the 1850s. Readers seeking a single primary source for insight into nearly all aspects of the mid-nineteenth-century middle-class home could hardly do better than Webster and Parkes's *Encyclopedia*.

The topical bibliographies and the footnotes mention many of the nineteenth-century critics, architects, and designers we have consulted. The works of Catharine Beecher and Charles L. Eastlake—like Downing's books, for example—could easily have appeared under all headings. Beecher's *Treatise on Domestic Economy* appeared in 1841 and with her sister, Harriet Beecher Stowe, *The American Women's Home* in 1869. Eastlake's influential *Hints on Household Taste* first appeared in London in 1868, but was not published in America until the Boston edition of 1872; thereafter it appeared regularly throughout the 1870s.

## PICTORIAL SOURCEBOOKS

Early in this century, several European scholars—particularly Germans and Austrians—published important pictorial works on nineteenth-century interiors that are little known today. Josef Folnesics's *Innerräume und Hausrat der Empire und Biedermeierzeit in Österreich-Ungarn* (Vienna, 1922), and Marianne Zweig's *Zweites Rokoko: Innerräume und Hausrat in Wien um 1830–1860* (Vienna, 1924) come particularly to mind. There was also the handsome portfolio of color plates and text volume of *Vor Hundert Jahren: Festräume und Wohnzimmer das Deutschen Klassizismus und Biedermeier* (Berlin, 1920) assembled by Hermann Schmitz. These works featured high-style European interiors commissioned by the aristocracy, many of which have since been greatly altered or destroyed.

A renewed interest in pictorial sourcebooks began with Mario Praz's *An Illustrated History of Furnishing* (London, 1964), which drew mainly from European sources but did contain a few American examples, such as the famous A. J. Davis "Interior of a New York House" from the New-York Historical Society collection. Praz concentrated on an overview of interior settings as captured in contemporary prints, oil paintings, watercolors, and photographs. "The flights of rooms and corridors," he wrote, "glimpsed through the doors, and the walls thick with paintings, the knick-knacks, the busts, the statuettes and porcelains, the flowers under glass bells, breathe an intimacy that you never find in the rooms which serve as backgrounds for the official portraits." Praz was followed in this country by Harold L. Peterson, whose pictorial sourcebook of American domestic interiors, *Americans at Home,* appeared in 1971. Peterson believed, "One cannot hope to understand American social history without at least a basic knowledge of the physical surroundings that comprised the American home." Indeed, it is this concern for the totality of the domestic environment that sets both Praz's and Peterson's books apart from earlier works by decorative-arts historians and presages the work of

William Seale and others in the United States and the United Kingdom. Both Praz and Peterson concentrated mainly on *prephotographic* sources, a tradition brilliantly continued by English historians such as John Cornforth in his *English Interiors, 1790–1848* (London: Barrie & Jenkins, 1978), Susan Lasdun in *Victorians at Home* (New York: Viking Press, 1981), and Peter Thornton in his comprehensive *Authentic Decor: The Domestic Interior, 1620–1920* (New York: Viking Penguin, 1984). Of its type, Thornton's is the most important and useful book yet to appear.

The strength and appeal of a photographic book such as Seale's *The Tasteful Interlude: American Interiors through the Camera's Eye, 1860–1917,* (2d ed., rev. and enl. Nashville: American Association for State and Local History, 1981), is that it begins where most books either end or trail off into passing references that reflect the author's waning interest or the publisher's caution. To architectural and decorative-arts historians trained since World War II, not to mention the thousands of old-house owners, Seale offers an unblinking look at a period heretofore largely ignored. Also, having proved to publishers in 1975 that the market for such compilations existed, Seale helped to open the floodgates. From England came Nicholas Cooper's *The Opulent Eye* (Whitney Library of Design, 1977) and from America a host of Dover publications such as Clay Lancaster's *New York Interiors at the Turn of the Century* (1976) and David Lowe's *Chicago Interiors* (1979). Finally, as a blending of both old and new approaches to the American interior, we have *A Documentary History of American Interiors: From the Colonial Era to 1915* (New York: Scribner's, 1980) by Edgar deN. Mayhew and Minor Myers, Jr., which leans heavily on contemporary visual sources of all types, tied together by a narrative in place of the explanatory captions used by Praz, Peterson, and Seale.

## WALL COVERINGS

Ackerman, Phyllis. *Wallpaper, Its History, Design and Use.* London, 1923.

Aslin, Elizabeth. *The Aesthetic Movement: Prelude to Art Nouveau.* New York: Praeger, 1969.

Fr[ederick] Beck and Company. *A Description of Lincrusta-Walton: Its Artistic and Sanitary Value in Interior Decoration.* New York, c. 1884. Trade catalogue in The Athenaeum of Philadelphia collection.

M. H. Birge and Sons. *A Series of Plates of Interiors and Ceilings.* Philadelphia, 1885. Trade catalogue in The Athenaeum of Philadelphia collection.

Bradbury, Bruce. "Anaglypta & Other Embossed Wallcoverings: Their History & Their Use Today." *The Old-House Journal,* vol. 10 (November 1982), pp. 231–34.

————."Lincrusta-Walton: Can the Democratic Wallcovering Be Revived?" *The Old-House Journal,* vol. 10 (October 1982), pp. 203–07.

Candee, Richard M. "Preparing and Mixing Colors in 1812." *Antiques,* vol. 113 (April 1978), pp. 849–53, within which is a reprint of Hezekiah Reynolds, *Directions for House and Ship Painting* (New Haven, Conn., 1812).

Carlisle, Lilian Baker. *Hat Boxes and Bandboxes at Shelburne Museum.* Shelburne, Vt.: Shelburne Museum, 1960.

*Colour Studies.* Manchester, England: The Decorative Art Journals Co. Limited, 1892.

Cook, Clarence. *What Shall We Do With Our Walls?* New York, 1881.

*Decorator and Furnisher.* New York, 1882–1898.

Dornsife, Samuel J. *Exterior Decoration: Victorian Colors for Victorian Houses.* Philadelphia: The Athenaeum of Philadelphia, 1975. This book contains an important bibliography of original paint sources.

————."Wallpaper." *The Encyclopedia of Victoriana.* New York: Macmillan Publishing Co., 1975, pp. 301–13.

Entwisle, Eric A. *The Book of Wallpaper.* London: Arthur Baker, 1954.

————. *French Scenic Wallpapers 1800–1860.* Leigh-on-Sea, England: F. Lewis, 1972.

————. *A Literary History of Wallpaper.* London: B. T. Batsford, 1960.

————. *Wallcoverings of the Victorian Era.* Leigh-on-Sea, England: F. Lewis, 1964.

Frangiamore, Catherine Lynn. *Wallpapers in Historic Preservation.* Washington, D.C.: National Park Service, 1977.

Gardner, Franklin B. *The Painter's Encyclopedia.* New York, 1906.

Greysmith, Brenda. *Wallpaper.* New York: Macmillan Publishing Co., 1976.

Hotchkiss, Horace. "Wallpapers Used in America, 1700–1850." In *The Concise Encyclopedia of American Antiques.* 2 vols. New York: Hawthorn Books, 1958, pp. 488ff.

*House Painting and Decorating (A Journal Devoted to the House Painter and the Decorator).* Philadelphia, 1885–1898.

*Household News.* Philadelphia, 1893–1896.

Jennings, Arthur Seymour. *Wallpapers and Wall Coverings.* New York, 1903.

Lynn, Catherine. *Wallpaper in America from the Seventeenth Century to World War I.* New York: W. W. Norton & Company, 1980.

Masury, John W. *House-painting: Plain and Decorative.* New York, 1868.

McClelland, Nancy V. *Historic Wall-papers from Their Inception to the Introduction of Machinery.* Philadelphia: Lippincott & Co., 1924.

Miller, Fred. *Interior Decoration: A Practical Treatise on Surface Decoration.* London, 1885.

Moss, Roger W. *Century of Color: Exterior Decoration for American Buildings 1820–1920.* Watkins Glen, N.Y.: American Life Foundation, 1981.

Nouvel, Odile. *Wallpapers of France 1800–1850.* New York: Rizzoli International Publications, 1981.

Nylander, Richard C. *Wallpapers for Historic Buildings.* Washington, D.C.: The Preservation Press, 1983.

Oman, Charles C., and Jean Hamilton. *Wallpapers: An International History and Illustrated Survey from the Victoria and Albert Museum.* New York: Harry N. Abrams, 1982.

Pearce, Walter. *Painting and Decorating.* London, 1898.

Penn, Theodore Zuk. "Decorative and Protective Finishes, 1750–1850: Materials, Process, and Craft." Thesis, University of Delaware, 1966.

Rossiter, E. K., and F. A. Wright. *Modern House Painting.* New York, 1882.

Teynac, Françoise, Pierre Nolot, and Jean-Denis Vivien. *Wallpaper, a History.* New York: Rizzoli International Publications, 1982.

Vaux, Calvert. *Villas and Cottages.* 1857. Reprint. New York: Da Capo Press, 1968.

Volz, John. "Paint Bibliography." *Newsletter of the Association for Preservation Technology,* February 1975.

## FLOORS AND FLOOR COVERINGS

Blackman, Leo, and Deborah Dietsch. "A New Look at Linoleum: Preservation's Rejected Floor Covering." *The Old-House Journal*, vol. 10, (January 1982), pp. 9–12.

Boch Frères [manufacturers of ceramic tiles]. Maubeuge, France, 1884. Trade catalogue in The Athenaeum of Philadelphia collection.

Bradbury, Fred. *Carpet Manufacture*. Belfast, Ireland, 1904.

Comstock, Helen. "Eighteenth Century Floor Cloths." *Antiques*, vol. 67 (January 1955), pp. 48–49.

Cook, Alexander N., ed. *A Century of Carpet and Rug Making in America*. New York: Bigelow-Hartford Carpet Co., 1925.

Decorative Wood Carpet Company. Warren, Ill., c. 1880. Trade catalogue in The Athenaeum of Philadelphia collection.

Dornsife, Samuel J. "Timetable of Carpet Technology." *Nineteenth Century*, vol. 7 (Autumn 1981), pp. 38–41.

Ewing, John S., and Nancy P. Norton. *Broadlooms and Businessmen: A History of the Bigelow-Sanford Carpet Company*. Cambridge: Harvard University Press, 1955.

Harwood, Buie. *Decorative Painting in Texas 1840–1940: A Survey of the European Influence*. Texas A & M Press, forthcoming.

Jacobs, Bertram. *Axminster Carpets, 1755–1957*. Leigh-on-Sea, England: F. Lewis, 1957.

Landreau, Anthony N. *America Underfoot: A History of Floor Coverings from Colonial Times to the Present*. Washington, D.C.: Smithsonian Institution Press, 1976.

Little, Nina Fletcher. *Floor Coverings in New England before 1850*. Sturbridge, Mass.: Old Sturbridge Inc., 1967.

John H. Pray & Sons. Boston, 1906. Trade catalogue in The Athenaeum of Philadelphia collection.

R. H. & B. C. Reeve Company. *Stock Patterns—Oil Cloths*. Camden, N.J., c. 1890. Trade catalogue in The Athenaeum of Philadelphia collection.

Von Rosenstiel, Helene. *American Rugs and Carpets from the Seventeenth Century to Modern Times*. New York: William Morrow and Company, 1978.

Weeks, Jeanne G., and Donald Treganowan. *Rugs and Carpets of Europe and the Western World*. New York: Weathervane Books, 1969.

## WINDOW COVERINGS AND FABRIC USE

Ackermann, Rudolph. *The Repository of Arts, Literature, Commerce, Manufactures, Fashions, and Politics*. London, 1809–1828. A selection of plates and descriptions from Ackermann's *Repository* has been published as *Ackermann's Regency Furniture & Interiors*, text by Pauline Agius with an introduction by Stephen Jones. Wiltshire, England: The Crowood Press, 1984.

Brunner, Arnold W., and Thomas Tryon. *Interior Decoration*. New York, 1887.

E. T. Burrowes Co. *Wire Window and Screen Doors*. Portland, Maine, Chicago, Philadelphia, 1892. Trade catalogue in the collection of The Athenaeum of Philadelphia.

William Cabble Excelsior Wire Manufacturing Co. New York, 1892. Trade catalogue in the collection of The Athenaeum of Philadelphia.

Church, Ella Rodman. *How to Furnish a Home*. New York, 1882.

Cook, Clarence. *The House Beautiful*. New York, 1881.

Cummin, Hazel E. "What Was Dimity in 1790?" *Antiques*, vol. 38 (July 1940).

Dornsife, Samuel J. "Design Sources for Nineteenth-century Window Hangings." In *Winterthur Portfolio 10*, pp. 69–99. Charlottesville: University of Virginia Press, 1975.

Gobelin Curtain Fixture Co. *The Gobelin Curtain Fixture*. Washington, D.C., c. 1900. Trade catalogue in the collection of The Athenaeum of Philadelphia.

*Godey's Lady's Book*. Philadelphia, 1830–1892; New York, 1892–1898.

Harrison, Constance Cary. *Woman's Handiwork in Modern Homes*. New York, 1882.

[Hodgson, Frederick Thomas]. *The Practical Upholsterer*. New York, 1891.

*House and Garden*. Philadelphia, 1901–1903.

*The House Beautiful*. Chicago, 1896–1901.

Jacobs, N. W. *Practical Handbook on Cutting Draperies*. Minneapolis, 1890.

Johnson, William Martin. *Inside of One Hundred Homes*. Philadelphia, 1898.

Kimball, J. Wayland. *Book of Designs: Furniture and Drapery*. Boston, 1876.

[King, Thomas?]. *The Upholsterer's Accelerator*. London, c. 1833.

Kirsch Company. *Window Treatments Through the Ages*. Sturgis, Michigan, 1976.

[Lady, A]. *The Workwoman's Guide*. London, 1838.

Lee, Ruth. *Shades of History*. Chicago: Joanna Western Mills Co., 1969.

*Le Garde-meuble, ancien et moderne*. Paris: G. Guilmard, n.d.

McMorris, Penny. *Crazy Quilts*. New York: E. P. Dutton, 1984.

Montgomery, Florence M. *Printed Textiles: English and American Cottons and Linens 1700–1850*. New York: Viking Press, 1970.

———. *Textiles in America, 1650–1870*. New York: W. W. Norton & Company, 1984.

Moreland, F. A. *Practical Decorative Upholstery*. Boston, 1890. Reprinted as *The Curtain-maker's Handbook*, edited by Martha Gandy Fales. New York: E. P. Dutton, 1979.

Nylander, Jane C. *Fabrics for Historic Buildings*. Washington, D.C.: The Preservation Press, 1983.

Schoelwer, Susan Prendergast. "Form, Function and Meaning in the Use of Fabric Furnishings: A Philadelphia Case Study, 1700–1775." *Winterthur Portfolio 14* (Spring 1979), pp. 25–40.

Seale, William. *Recreating the Historic House Interior*. 1979. 2d ed., rev. and enl. Nashville: American Association for State and Local History, 1981.

Smith, George. *The Cabinet-maker and Upholsterer's Guide*. London, 1826.

Spofford, Harriet Prescott. *Art Decoration Applied to Furniture*. New York, 1878.

Streitenfield, A. *The Decorator's Portfolio*. Berlin and New York, 1885.

Varney, Almon C. *Our Homes and Their Adornments*. Chicago, 1885.

Jay C. Wemple [shade] Company. New York and Chicago, c. 1895. Trade catalogue in the collection of The Athenaeum of Philadelphia.

Williams, Henry T., and Mrs. C. S. Jones. *Beautiful Homes; or, Hints in House Furnishing*. New York, 1878.

# INDEX